UNFORGIVEN

"Was the Holocaust Punishment for Sin?"

de la Lieux

Copyright © 2020 by Dr. Adalbert Lallier.

ISBN-978-1-6455-0974-5

All rights reserved. No part of this book may be reproduced or transmitted in any form or by any means, electronic or mechanical, including photocopying, recording, or by any information storage and retrieval system, without permission in writing from the copyright owner.

The views expressed in this work are solely those of the author and do not necessarily reflect the views of the publisher, and the publisher hereby disclaims any responsibility for them.

Matchstick Literary
1-888-306-8885
orders@matchliterary.com

To my beloved brother André, who even though member of the Hungarian community was forced by into the Waffen-SS by the Nazi-Germans in April 1942 and was murdered before the end of the war, one of the millions of innocent victims of Hitler's totalitarian Third Reich mania.

Contents

Chapter 1	The Author's Forced, Illegal Recruitment into Hitler's Waffen-SS	1
Chapter 2	Hitler's Occupation of the Balkans: The War (1941–1945)	20
Chapter 3	Waffen-SS 1Officer School and the Murder of Seven Jewish Prisoners	33
Chapter 4	The Murder Postmortem: Reflections on Nazi Motives and War Crimes	51
Chapter 5	The End of the War: Free at Last	60
Chapter 6	The United Nations Refugee Organization and the Holocaust Survivors	67
Chapter 7	Canada, My Destiny: Conscience and Redemption	75
Chapter 8	The "Eye for an Eye": Revenge versus Retribution	95
Chapter 9	The Trial of Julius Viel: Anticipation versus Reality	98
Chapter 10	Insights into Hitler's Nazism versus the Ethics of Natural Justice	106
Conclusion		
	Specific Experiences and Concerns	125

Bibliography 135

Appendix 1
  The Massive Postwar Amnesia of the Waffen- SS about the
  Holocaust: Did They Know? 137

Appendix 2
  Quo Vadis, the Jewish People of Israel and in the Diaspora? 145

Appendix 3
  Additional Postwar Data on Top-Level Nazis 147

Appendix 4
  Additional Personal Information: 149

Appendix 5
  Waffen-SS Officers in the S.D., RSiHA, HSSPF, Gestapo,
  Einsatzgruppen, VOMI, RFSS, Dirlewanger, Jagdverbände 157

Appendix 6
  Waffen-SS Officers Posted in Nazi Concentration Camps 199

Appendix 7
  Gisela Friedichsen's Neo-Nazi Inspired Misrepresentations
  and Lies 227

Concluding Statement 235

Chapter I
The Author's Forced, Illegal Recruitment into Hitler's Waffen-SS

Our family not having been a member of the German-speaking minority in the *Bánát* and the *Bácska* does not mean that my father was not actively watching the evolution of international power politics—Adolf Hitler's Nazi Germany pushing itself to the forefront. Uncertainty and fear were increasing after Hitler's troops invaded Austria and Czechoslovakia, with Hungary clearly the next victim. In April 1941 and without declaring war, Third Reich troops attacked the Kingdom of Yugoslavia, fought a two-week battle, and remained in the Balkans until April 1945. As an immediate consequence, Croatia created its own fascist nation. However, *Bácska* returned to Hungary. A few days into the battle, the Second Waffen-SS Division, *Das Reich* (one of whose regiments, *Der Führer*, was staffed entirely with Austrian Nazis), stormed from the east (Romania) into the *Bánát* and set itself up in *Nagy-Becskerek* (Hungarian name for its largest city), where we were then living. They renamed it German style, *Großbetscherek*, and proceeded within a few days to round up dozens of Serbs and to hang them on the lampposts on the city's main square, justifying their mass murders by calling them *Kommunisten und Bandenbekämpfung* (communists and bandits).

Witnessing—at the age of only sixteen—these atrocities, I saw my dreams going down the drain, even though the German occupation authorities had left the Hungarian minority alone after "cleansing" it of its Jewish members and of the few presumed communists. The *reichsdeutsch* occupiers, aided by their local *volksdeutsch* collaborators, then turned even more *en masse* upon the Serbs, hanging hundreds of them and making the Serbian Jews vanish without a trace. I remember hearing that most of them had been herded into the local brick factory, whence they were shipped through Hungary to the *KZ*s in occupied Poland.

How do we explain Nazi Germany's invasion of the Balkans and its eventual forced recruitment of the German minorities then living in Yugoslavia, Hungary, and Romania into the *Waffen-SS*?

As a former professor of international politics and political economy, my scientific, objective fact-finding attempts had left me with the following explanations:

- The direct consequences of the Treaty of Trianon.

- Adolf Hitler's rise to power and the creation of the Third Reich.

- Hitler's racial policy: the importance of the millions of Germans who were foreign citizens.

- The forced recruitment of almost three hundred thousand *Volksdeutschen* into the *Waffen-SS*.

- The military use of the recruited *volksdeutsch* men.

- Resulting in the wanton extermination of Yugoslavia's *volksdeutsch* community.

- *The Treaty of Trianon*, whose main concern—in its application of the Wilson Doctrine—was how to go about the dissolution of the dual empire of Austria-Hungary and how to apportion its non-Germanic parts to the newly emerging sovereign states in Central Europe. One of the main end results was the splitting off of more than 3 million Germans to Czechoslovakia (the *Sudetendeutschen*). The other was the splitting off of about 1.3 million *Volksdeutsche* into the newly created sovereign states of Hungary, Romania, and Yugoslavia. In this manner, as per the demands of the governments of Britain and France, the former *k.u.k.* (*kaiserlich* und *königlich*), i.e., imperial and royal citizens, suddenly found themselves as officially sanctioned *minorities* in these three new states, without any regard to already existing international treaties concerning their treatment by their new "masters."

- *Adolf Hitler's official power grab* in a Germany that had been economically ruined and rendered politically impotent by the demands of the Treaty of Versailles, especially its enormous reparation claims and the imposition of prohibitive tariffs on German exports. The kaiser's abdication that was followed by two unstable governments and resulted in the rising fear of a Soviet-style communist revolution were the main factors that induced the Germans to vote for Hitler's *NSDAP* and, only two years later, to witness Hitler's taking absolute power and submitting his population to Hitler's propagation of the creation of the Thousand-Year Reich.

- *Aligned with Hitler's worldwide ambitions* was *the Third Reich's increasing interest in the Auslandsdeutschen* (German-root citizens born in and living as citizens of other countries), be it for ideological (i.e., spreading of Nazism beyond the boundaries of the Third Reich), for political (i.e., arranging for the reascendance of Germany to nonpariah status), for economic (i.e., enabling the rapid resumption of exports as well as securing the importation of strategic ores and resources), or for military (i.e., securing, if necessary by war, the potential use as reserve of up to thirty million of German-origin citizens born and living abroad, not only as agents and saboteurs for, but also as soldiers of the Third Reich). Special consideration was given by the Nazis to the sizeable German-root minorities in Central Europe. In the region of the *Bánát* and the *Bácska* (formerly in Hungary and in Yugoslavia between the early 1920s and 1941, then back to Hungary during WWII), about one and a half million members of the German community were living there in 1940. They were descendants of German and Austrian immigrants in the eighteenth century who spoke their own German dialect and were engaged mainly in farming. A simple, God-fearing but politically naive people, the *Volksdeutschen* had their own social organization, the *Kulturbund* (Cultural Association). They were led by Dr. Kraft, who had been democratically elected with the mandate to secure in Belgrade equal minority rights especially in education.

Soon after Hitler's conquest of Yugoslavia (April 1941), four *volksdeutsch* men who had studied in Nazi Germany had been converted into ardent and keen supporters of Hitler's warmongering ideas. They were supported by the Third Reich military that had remained stationed in the Bánát. These men proceeded to displace Dr. Kraft and renamed its old title *Kulturbund* into *Deutsche Volksgruppe*, reflecting the political bent of the language of the *reichsdeutsch* Nazis. With the approval of their *reichsdeutsch* occupiers, they appointed themselves as its leaders: Dr. Sepp Janko as the *Volksgruppenführer* (political chief of the German minority); Josef-Sepp Lapp, responsible for policy; Dr. Jakob Awender, culture and liaison; Dr. Franz Reith, chief of the paramilitary and the police; and Dr. Georg

Spiller, chief of the secret police, with the special mandate to hunt down Serbian communists and to hang them. Very soon, rumors were spreading that the local Serbs and the very few opposing German speakers were referring to those four men as quislings who had sold out to Hitler and whose henchmen had converted their community to Nazism, not only using Hitler's slogan of *Ein Volk, ein Reich, ein Führer* (one people, one Reich, one leader), but also forcing upon them the official greeting of *Heil Hitler* and *Sieg Heil* (Hail victory). As member of the Hungarian community with very poor knowledge of their strange *volksdeutsch* accent, I was feeling amused—but was keeping very quiet—when hearing them talk and raising their right arm in the Hitler salute.

Who was responsible for the forced recruitment of the *Volksdeutschen* in WWII in Yugoslavia? The decision-making role of the highest authority in Berlin was the *SS-Führungshauptamt* (operational headquarters of the whole SS), especially its *Waffen-SS* headquarters. It was run by *Obergruppenführer* (General) Gottlob Berger, an early member of the *NSDAP* and closely linked to Heinrich Himmler. He was personally involved in and responsible for the recruitment— almost entirely under duress—of more than three hundred thousand *volksdeutsch* men from the above-specified three countries and for having sent them, after only minimal training as recruits, onto the Eastern Front and the Balkans, causing the death of at least two-third of them. While he did appear in a war crime court in 1947, his direct involvement with the forced recruitment of the *Volksdeutschen* was never mentioned. At first condemned to a prison term of twenty-five years, he eventually served only two years but was let go upon the personal recommendation by George G. McCloy, the American military governor of West Germany, as well as by Konrad Adenauer, West Germany's first postwar democratic chancellor. Regaining his freedom after only two years, Gottlob Berger's full rights as a citizen were also restored—yet another highest-ranking *Alt-Nazi* (early member of the *NSDAP*) who had remained singularly unpunished for his massive war crime of ordering the use of those politically naive and God-fearing *Volksdeutscher* as second-rate cannon fodder and for sending them to their certain deaths.

Increasingly secure in their trusting the *volksdeutsch* quadrumvirate, the *reichsdeutsch* authorities proceeded late in 1941 to incite young *volksdeutsch* males to volunteer for *Waffen-SS* service on the *Ostfront* (the eastern front), successfully raising several dozens of them: "You are Christian soldiers with God's mandate to defeat the godless communists." Then in early 1942, the *reichsdeutsch* Nazis launched a massive propaganda campaign promising the "volunteers" medals for heroism as well as Third Reich citizenship. Himmler himself had ordered the *SS-Obergruppenführer* (SS three-star general) Gottlob Berger to organize and conduct this campaign in the attempt to induce at least twenty thousand young *volksdeutsche* males to *volunteer* in creating a new *Waffen-SS* division, whose name had already been chosen: *Die freiwillige 7. Waffen-SS Gebirgsdivision Prinz Eugen* (the volunteer Seventh Waffen-SS division Prinz Eugen). The official attempt had to emphasize the term *freiwillig* (volunteer), since the Hague Convention of 1899 concerning the laws of war had forbidden the recruitment of foreign citizens into one's own country's national army and their engagement in a war against their former fellow citizens.

Too bad for the Hitler Germans, but a large proportion of the *volksdeutsch* men in the age group of eighteen to forty had failed to volunteer. In consequence, the *reichsdeutsch* military command, jointly with the *volksdeutsch* quadrumvirate, proceeded to make up a list of the "eligible" *volksdeutsch* men, thereby *forcing* them to "volunteer"—in total disregard for the then already existing international treaties. Yet in spite of their much more energetic attempts, the SS recruiters were still having great trouble securing even the very minimum of twenty thousand *Volksdeutscher* and were forced to add to the list a large number of men from the other minorities and even with non-German family names—Slavs, Hungarians, and even a few French names—singling out those whose fathers had served in the armies of Austria-Hungary during World War I. In my own case, not only did my French family name end in -er (which is typical of most German family names), but my father had also been an officer in the army of the kaiser—apparently enough justification to add me and my brother to the list regardless of the fact that my family had been during the past four generations fully ensconced in the local Hungarian community and that my brother had never been in a local German school and that he had graduated from a Hungarian secondary school.

I'll never forget the terrifying experience that had been brought totally unexpectedly into our home. Unannounced, the *Banater Staatswache* colonel Dr. Franz Reith (see above, p. 11), fully dressed in his Nazi-style uniform, appeared in my father's study, raised his arm in the *Heil Hitler!* salute, and revelling in his Swabian dialect, yelled at him: "*Lallier, Sie waren Leutnant Leutnant in der kuk Armee. Adolf Hitler, unser Führer, braucht mindestens 20,000 volksdeutsche Freiwillige um den Kommunismus zu bekämpfen. Ich muss Sie warnen ihre beiden Söhne nicht zu verstecken, denn wir werden sie finden und an die Wand stellen. Die Namen Ihrer Söhne sind schon in der Liste enthalten und sie beide werden sich noch vor Anfang Juni an ihrem bezeichneten Standort melden müssen.*" (Lallier, you were a lieutenant in armed forces of Austria-Hungary. Adolf Hitler, our leader, needs at least 20,000 *Volksdeutsche* volunteers in order to fight the communists. I must warn you not to hide your two sons since we will find them and put them up against the wall. The names of your two sons have already been entered in the recruitment list. Both of them will have to report early in June to their respective recruitment centers.)

My brother was forced to join against his will in April 1942. My turn, only seventeen years old, came on June 1, 1942, one week after my graduation ceremony. Somewhat later, I discovered that among the seventy *real volksdeutsch* recruits who were German high school graduates and were to serve in the signals unit, only five were real *volunteers*. My name, as well as that of my brother, Andràs, should never have been on that list since our mother was Hungarian and we had never been members of the *volksdeutsch* community.

The overall forced recruitment campaigns of *volksdeutsch* men went on from early 1942 to early 1945. The first recruitment effort was conducted mainly in the *Bánát* region. It required a massive forced drive in order to deliver the minimum number of soldiers for complete *Waffen-SS* division: twenty thousand. Of the somewhat higher final total, only several handful turned out to have been *true* volunteers (and looking as such: blond, blue eyes, 180 cm or taller). Rumor had it that several—blonds as well as not blonds—had been shot for refusing to be inducted. That the *Waffen-SS* top brass was viewing this first *volksdeutsch* contingent only as second-grade cannon fodder was attested to by the fact none of these men ever received their *Waffen-SS* numbers—as required for the true volunteers—and that none of them were offered the citizenship of the Third Reich, even though it had been promised by Adolf Hitler himself in mid-1943.

On a smaller scale, concerning the new recruits' levels of education, each and all the graduates of the two German-language high schools (*Gymnasien*) were drafted—a total of seventy graduates, most of whom only eighteen years old—into the *Nachrichtenabteilung* (signal corps) of the *Prinz Eugen*. Of these, as I was to learn after my own forced recruitment, only five admitted to have been real true volunteers. I should perhaps also note at this point that of these seventy graduates, only seven had survived the war—a horrendous and totally immoral waste of lives of promising young men caused by Adolf Hitler and his *SS* cohorts.

While the massive recruiting campaign was being prepared locally, the *reichsdeutsch* commanders proceeded with their *volksdeutsch* collaborators to organize their own security police, *die Banater Staatswache*, with the mandate to maintain law and order and to assist the *reichsdeutsch* occupying forces in their quest to hunt down and hang every presumed Serbian communist. Led by one of the four *volksdeutsch* quislings, Dr. Franz Reith, and the equally Nazi-oriented but devout Catholic Dr. Georg Spiller (the commandant of the secret service), its two battalions went on to commit continuous atrocities against the Serbs and the Gypsies, conducting continuous raids against them and torturing and hanging most of those who looked and acted like communists. In revenge, after "liberating" the *Bánát* and the *Bácska* from their Nazi occupiers in the fall of 1944, the Titoists went on to execute many hundreds of the captured German officers and soldiers, as well as each of those *volksdeutsch* men who were wearing Nazi uniforms. One of their first captives was Dr. Franz Reith, who was hanged after being declared guilty of having tortured to death several top-level communists. In my humble view, even though I had seen neither, he deserved what he got (after even siring five children as per Adolf Hitler's command in order to have his wife obtain the Motherhood Medal in gold).

The eventual military use of those who were forced into the *Waffen-SS* commenced mid-June 1942, after my own induction into the signal corps of the *Prinz Eugen*. We were transported to *Unna*, a small town in Westphalia, for training as wireless set operators in what was then officially referred to as the *Nachrichtenabteilung* (signal corps) of the Seventh Voluntary Waffen-SS mountain division *Prinz Eugen*. Evidently, infantry weaponry, infantry combat, and antitank warfare were embedded requisites in our training, lasting overall almost four months. Unlike in the *Wehrmacht* (the Third Reich's national army), much emphasis was placed on physical exercise and conditioning. During the first four weeks, I *was* having serious problems of understanding both the *reichsdeutsch* and the *volksdeutsch* accents of their spoken German. All the instructors and officers, as well as NCOs, were *Reichsdeutsche*. Officers specialized in ideology were lecturing with repeated emphasis upon the purity and racial superiority of the German nation. Even though their *volksdeutsch* recruits were viewed only as lower-class *Waffen-SS* cannon fodder, the NCOs were inculcating them with the ideology of Nazism. They propagated that the Soviets were godless Bolsheviks and, therefore, the archenemies of Western civilization that had to be destroyed. The Nazi ideology also maintained that the Slavs were *Untermenschen* (the subrace) and were therefore subservient to the German *Herrenmenschen* (master race). These propagations were soon accepted—some quietly, others enthusiastically—by quite a few of the blond, blue-eyed *volksdeutsch* recruits with high school matriculations, for all of a sudden, they had implicitly been raised to *Herrenmensch* status (I still recall Sepp Schütz, Nikolas Laub, *Uscha* Retz, *Uscha* Öl). However, most of the nonmatriculated recruits were darker-haired sons of peasants, sullen and pigheaded and unwilling to obey orders instantly—forms of behavior that induced quite a few of the *reichsdeutsch* NCOs of similar background to throw at their trainees disparaging epithets like *Balkaneser* (being from the Balkans, you are a lower, stupid, hopeless kind of a nonperson), *S*peckfressers (dumb peasants from feasting exclusively on raw bacon), *Lochköpfe* (hole heads, implying no brains and therefore no intelligence), *Vollidioten* (behaving like idiots), or *Schweinehunde* (pig dog–like, lowest-form human beings). In my own situation, with my weak comprehension of German and my non-Germanic looks, I was also often referred to as *Zigeuner* (Gipsy) and as *Magyarone* (a lower level of human whose ancestors had arrived from Central Asia).

Within four months, the minimal requisite for the first phase of military training in the *Waffen-SS*, the instructors did succeed in their quest to coerce into military discipline the somewhat more than twenty thousand *volksdeutsch* recruits, the young and the not-so-young-anymore men. Most of them were mainly peasants who believed in the Christian God, who had worked ungodly hours to keep their lands fertile, and who had had no choice but to accept the post-Trianon reality as minority citizens of a newly created country—the Kingdom of Serbia, Croatia, and Slovenia—to whom they did not owe any allegiance. In consequence, most of them had at first accepted as "liberation" the arrival of Hitler's armies, having no idea that most of them would be drafted against their will by their Nazi "liberators" as second-class cannon fodder into battling Tito's communist partisans and Stalin's Red Army. And yet here they were in September 1942, having been converted by their *reichsdeutsch* officers and NCOs into an *almost*-perfect fighting machine. Why (only) *almost* perfect? Because the notion of "perfect" had been reserved (by the SS leadership) exclusively for the native-born *reichsdeutsch Waffen-SS* members, the *real* Waffen-SS officers and men, the chosen pure blond and blue-eyed Aryans, the only ones that Hitler and Himmler had deemed to be able to demonstrate their highest level of fealty and obedienceand, consequently, the highest degree of effectiveness in war. Drafted against their will and looked down upon by their Nazi superiors, they were easy prey for the advancing Red Army. Hitler's strategy had paid off. With more than two hundred thousand of killed *Volksdeutschen*, the lives of an equal number of the real *reichsdeutsch* volunteers had been saved.

During the entire almost four months of military training, intelligence was frowned upon and replaced by emphasis upon what the instructors called *wahres Mannestum* (uncompromising, real manhood) as the highest aspired moral quality that was required from the *Waffen-SS* soldiers. In addition, *absolute obedience* to one's officers and NCOs was a fundamental requirement. Preached and practiced every day, these two attitudes had originated from the personal oath of all *Waffen-SS* personnel to Adolf Hitler, their *Führer*, the *Treueid* (Oath of Fealty). Often revealing the instructors' own racial prejudices against their non-*reichsdeutsch* recruits, these practices and orders from above were meant to enforce upon them both Hitler's absolute power and the superiority of the Nazi German *Herrenrasse*. Indoctrination had replaced inborn humanness with the practice of absolute brutal power over the life and death of their victims, whether they were opponents from within Germany or *Untermenschen* from Eastern Europe, in particular Jews, Slavs, and Gypsies. Hitler's own two *Führerbefehle* (orders directly from the *Führer*, which were therefore absolutely binding)—the instant execution of Red Army political commissars who were Jewish and the executions of one hundred local civilians who were deemed to be communist, in retaliation for the partisans' killing of even just one German soldier—were horrendous examples of the Hitler regime's disregard for human rights and human lives.

Taking (subjecting a soldier to?) the *Waffen-SS*'s Oath of Fealty to Adolf Hitler was obligatory, an organized, festive, public ceremony. For us in *Unna*, it took place after the completion of the training at the end of September 1942. The original number of recruits had been reduced by the dismissal of a handful who had failed to qualify. My oral German had improved enough to understand most of the *Befehle* (orders) as well as the wording of the oath. About 250 young men's yelling at the pitch of their voices enabled me to whisper, wishing not to be discovered that Hitler and his ideology had remained alien to my *Untermensch* status—in Hungarian, my own private oath of fealty to Hungary's then chief of state, Miklós Horthy.

Since we had not been granted Third Reich citizenship, no attempt was made by *reichsdeutsch* instructors during the two weeks before being shipped out to the front to induce us to apply for membership with the *NSDAP*. Unlike the real *reichsdeutsch* volunteers, we were not granted the *Waffen-SS* registration numbers, for we were neither citizens nor real volunteers. However, I still remember marching from the "field of honor," singing one of the favorite German war songs, "*Der Sommer geht zu Neige . . .*" (The summer is on the decline . . .)

My person, considered racially inappropriate even though physically quite acceptable, was trained as a wireless-set communicator, member of a group of seven with their special vehicle, a German-made medium-size Horch-17 truck, twelve of which—adjoined to the headquarters of the division—were required to make up a fully effective wireless communications company. Early in October 1942, the entire communications unit (*Abteilung*), a total of about one thousand men, was transported not to the eastern front but to the Balkans to join the already assembled main body of the *Prinz Eugen,* to wage war first against the pro-King Serbian četniks and, starting in November 1942, against the much more numerous and more active communist partisans of Josip Broz Tito. Arriving at the headquarters in *Kraljevo* (Serbia), we found ourselves only about a three-hour car drive from our home province but were immediately told that there would be no furlough until Tito's partisans once and for all had been beaten and eradicated. Totally contrary to the Hague Convention of 1899 that had forbidden the recruitment of foreign nationals and their military use in their native lands within a few days, our *reichsdeutsch* officers forced us to start marching against our former neighbors and even friends, the Serbs, in their homes in the *Bánát* and the *Bácska*, as well as in the Serbian and Bosnian mountains. Partisan warfare: no holds barred, no mercy given.

There were war crimes galore on both sides, under the banners of mighty Nazi Germany against the Red Flag of Tito's communist partisans, nationals of an undeveloped, poor country who were courageously and fearlessly displaying their Titoist citation, "*Smrt fašizmy, sloboda narodu!*" (Death to the fascists, freedom to our people.)

Before my forced induction and right through the war itself, I had been before the war what the Germans call a *Jungmann* (male virgin; in Hungarian, *újonc*) in the best tradition of the Calvinist moral commitment. I believed in the (three) God(s) of the Christians. I wished to abide by the Calvinist canons, yet I often went with my Catholic comrades to Holy Mass. Before the war, I had been hoping to find and hold on to, until the end of my life, my one and only love with whom I would procreate at least two children, caring for them in conditions of peace and security in my quest to contribute to world peace and the enhancement of human happiness. These two aspirations and dreams reflected my own need as a young man to feel free to make my own socially appropriate decisions concerning my future.

Thinking back to 1941–42, with the arrival of Hitler's troops and the imposition of their Nazi ideology, I was being pushed onto the opposite path—totalitarian tyranny. My allegiance to the Calvinist version of traditional Christianity was subjected to Hitler's Nazi *master race* ideology. Adolf Hitler's insistence upon total fealty and obedience to him was robbing me of the right to exercise my freedom of choice. Worst of all, the disparaging views against my person by my *Waffen-SS* superiors as described above were making me feel, as a non-*volksdeutsch* individual, dehumanized, a condition resembling acute slavery. Only a seventeen-year-old who had grown up in a very protected domestic environment, I was unable to understand— in spite of my high school graduation—why these awful things were being imposed upon my person (and that of my brother). Deep inside myself, hidden resentment was starting to grow about being called all those awful insults, being forced to serve as cannon fodder in Hitler's attempt to conquer all of Russia, being compelled to push to boundaries of the *Eintausendjähriges Reich* all the way to the Ural Mountains and to serve there as a soldier in the *Waffen-SS* uniform, with the imposed lifelong purpose to protect Western civilization against the attempts by the "hordes from Asia" to destroy it.[1] [2] [3] But without any

---

[1] **Heinz Höhne**, The Order of the Death-Head: The Story of Hitler's SS (London: Pan Books, 1969, 442-443): "Berger's method of press-ganging 'racial Germans' into the Waffen-SS were highly imaginative...volunteering was an elastic notion: where the siren-song of propaganda failed, strong-arm squads came to the assistance of the Nazi-majority leaders...those who did not volunteer will have their houses broken up."

[2] **Wolfgang Scheider,** ed., *Die Waffen-SS* (Berlin: Rowohlt, 1998, 187-1988): "Bis zum Jahre 1940, war die SS eine völlig freiwillige Organisation. Nach Errichtung der Waffen-SS im Jahre 1940 fand eine sich langsam steigernde von **Zwangseinziehungen** in die Waffen-SS statt. Es scheint, daß ungefähr ein Drittel der Gesamtzahl derjenigen, die in die Waffen-SS eintraten, zwangs - weise eingezogen wurde..." [Until the year 1940, the Waffen.-SS had been an entirely volunteer organization. After the creation of the Waffen-SS in the year 1940, **a slowly Increasing number of forced recruitment into the Waffen-SS was taking place.** It appears that about one-third of the total number of those who entered the Waffen-SS were drafted against their will].
Wikipedia: *Volksdeutsche,* December 29, 2016: *Volksdeutsche in the Waffen-SS:* "Das geschah vor allem bei den Volksdeutschen auf dem Balkan. So kame es u.e. zur Aufstellung der 7.SS - Frei-willigen Gebirgsdivision 'Prinz Eugen', wobei Angehörige der deutschen Minderheit zum Teil **zwangs-verpflichtet wurden"** ["Ethnic Germans in the Waffen-SS: That happened first of all with the ethnic Germans living in the Balkans, the setting up of the 7th Volunteer mountain division Prinz Eugen, by the forceful recruitment of a large part of the German minority".]
Wikipedia sources: Thomas Casagrande, *Die volksdeutsche Division "Prinz Eugen": Die Banater Schwaben und die national-sozialistischen Kriegsverbrechen (*Frankfurt: Campus-Verlag, New York, 2003). **Robert Herzog,** *Die Volksdeutschen in der Waffen-SS,* Band 5.

[3] Rolf Michaelis, *DieVolksdeutschen in the ... Waffen-SS.* (Atglen: Schiffer Military History, 2012), 74-75: 'The **disparaging treatment of volksdeutsch recruits** by their reichsdeutsch superiors was posing more and more serious problems with the rapidly increasing inflow of **the mostly forced 'volunteers'.** It involved not only the insulting terms as named above but also very dehumanizing tasks (like having to scrub toilet bowls with one's own toothbrush), all of these with the attempt to punish the recruits, individually or jointly, for their 'laziness, pretending not to understand German, and recalcitrant attitude." It reached a crescendo under the new division commander, Waffen-SS *Brigadeführer* von Oberkamp, in August 1943, after the ethnic German recruits had been repeatedly referred to as 'gypsies' and other insulting words, with the result that 173 members of their regiment refused to continue serving, and resulting in the commanding general's decision (*Obergruppenführer Phleps*) to dismiss Oberkamp. As described above, such mistreatments had commenced early during the first training phase and was conducted mainly by the enthusiastic Nazi NCOs, many of whom had been six-foot tall, blond, blue-eyed but uneducated and unemployed labourers before happily joining the Waffen-SS. Each of the original sources in this writ emphasized the mistreatment of the *Volksdeutschen* by their *Reichsdeutsh*-superiors.

answers and fearing for my life, I was keeping my mouth shut, hoping to survive the war. It was only after my arrival in Canada that I was able to actively proceed with my quest to find the answers through university education in the social sciences. It was a prolonged process of learning that would enable me to understand how Adolf Hitler had succeeded in just ten years to impose upon the German nation—a modern state with its remarkable achievements in philosophy, in the pure and social sciences, and in social welfare legislation—the totalitarian madness of his proposed *Eintausenjähriges Reich* (thousand-year empire) and thereby forcing his so-called *Herrenrassen-Volk* to descend to the nadir of absolute inhumanity.

Forced recruit as a 17-year old.

One year later.

My brother in uniform.

My Brother. Two months before his death.

Chapter II
Hitler's Occupation of the Balkans:
The War (1941–1945)

By mid-October 1942, the newly created Seventh Volunteer Mountaineer Waffen-SS Division *Prinz Eugen* was ready for battle. Its first action involved several smaller offensives against the rebelling population of the Nazi German–occupied former Yugoslavia, first against the still royalist *četnik* Serbs and their leader, General Draža Mihajlović, and then following Adolf Hitler's idiotic invasion of the Soviet Union against Tito's communist partisans made up mainly of Serbs, Bosnians, and Montenegrins.

During the late evening of the third day after our arrival in Serbia, I was ordered to do night duty in our wireless-set truck, specifically to be on the alert for Morse code–deciphered messages being received and with answers to be sent. After several hours, the field telephone rang. It was the commanding voice in the Prussian dialect of a *Waffen-SS* staff officer. I got so scared I was unable to understand his very urgent message. I asked timidly in my infantile German to repeat his message. Instead of helping, he threw the *Vollidiot* at me and hung up. For the remaining part of the night, I spent it in a state of terror, fearing terrible consequences. I was anxiously waiting for the morning, knowing that I was obliged to report the incident to my then company commander, *Obersturmführer* (First Lieutenant) Giermann. The call did come very early to report to the commander of the communications unit. I was given a stern lecture, was instantly demoted from my post as wireless-set operator, and was sent immediately to groom dozens of mules in their stables. Even though formerly a ranking graduate of secondary school, I became a pariah, an *Untermensch*. But I was still permitted to wear the uniform of the *Waffen-SS*, the *NSDAP*-linked elite military formation, with the assigned task to tend daily to the needs of dozens of mules in the attempt to save Western civilization from the onslaught of Stalin's T-34 and thus to defeat his godless communist empire. For almost an entire year, my mule—I promptly named him Diogenes—became my only true friend. It was pigheaded yet clearly with a soul, because he never called me any names! I fed him, curried him, talked to him, and hunted with him Tito's bandits by loading him up with the wireless set and holding on to his rein, making him climb up and descend the many mountains, and by keeping myself warm lying by his side during the very cold winter nights. Diogenes's endurance kept me going, inducing in me the wish to survive the Nazis and their war. However, very much my regret, the stables' commanding *Waffen-SS* NCO lacked the intelligence to recognize the existence of my spiritual togetherness of the *Lochkopf*-Magyarone, grooming an animal that was generally viewed as hopelessly pigheaded and therefore dumb. The increasing KIA of wireless-set operators forced my superiors to reconsider, tranfering me from the stables to training as wireless truck driver and auxiliary wireless-set operator. I bid Diogenes a hearty farewell and proceeded to have a first look at the vehicle, a four-ton monster with a motor that was strong enough to pull out of the mud even a *Panzer IV*. I named it Felix, soon viewing it as my second home for the duration of the war.

I was living through these experiences as soldier of the *Waffen-SS* while the *Prinz Eugen* had gotten involved in the first two major offensives against Tito's partisans after battling to royalist Serbs, commanded by their General Draža Mihajlović, to a standstill. As already stated above, partisan warfare was waged by both without understanding of and respect for the then already-existing international treaties concerning the laws of war. Repeated and forever more gruesome atrocities were being committed by each of the two enemies upon the *Waffen-SS* soldiers, as well as upon the Tito bandits, but primarily upon the unfortunate mainly Serb, Bosnian, and Montenegrin civilians. The Nazi Germans were hanging more and more frequently forever larger numbers of both Serbian partisans and civilians. On the opposing side, death by torture of captured German soldiers had become the norm for Tito's partisans. Wounded POW exchange was not undertaken until mid-1944.

My first sighting of German soldiers massacred by the partisans occurred in the spring of 1943, a lorry that had been waylaid by the Titoists and set on fire, with the massacred bodies of seven dead Germans lying close by, a terrible sight that induced in me massive vomiting and many sleepless nights. In retaliation, the German soldiers—by then a mix of *Wehrmacht* and *Waffen-SS*—burned down three adjacent villages, killing almost all the inhabitants.

The increasingly frequent sight of more and more German and Titoist dead bodies eventually invoked in me physical indifference. War is war, and dead bodies—often just in pieces—are its primary visible consequences. But at burial, some respect was paid to one's own (even though they had often been stripped of their boots by the partisans), while the bodies of the partisans were just left there to rot, also usually barefoot. Because of our indoctrination viewing the first German KIAs, we felt sorrow and pain. But viewing the bodies of the first dead partisans evoked only feelings of disgust of *Schadenfreude*, and even hatred. But such negative feelings dissipated during the year 1943 and were replaced by apathy, for too many had died and buried, with more and more frequent questions about the existence and purpose of God.

We should note here that the Hague Convention of 1899 had been signed exclusively by the imperialistic countries, authorizing them to exercise absolute power in the colonial territories that they had invaded and conquered. They had the right to mete out severe punishment upon the local population and even to take revenge by killing them. In their partisan-war strategy, the Nazi German occupiers were calling the Tito partisans bandits, accusing them of a behavior that ran contrary to the Hague conventions. In the Germans' view, they were legally entitled in their brutal and merciless treatment of the partisans and their local supporters. In this sense, the Nazi German occupiers of Yugoslavia may be presumed to have acted within the provisions of the agreement and that their referring to Tito's partisans as bandits was legally justified, implying that killing *en masse,* first the Serb royalists and then Tito's partisans, did not, in fact, constitute a war crime. At that time, I did not know anything about the Hague conventions.

After the third offensive (early fall 1943), the level of my rising indifference arrived at its dead end. It was a feeling of total spiritual emptiness, a walking corpse that wished to see nothing, to hear nothing, to feel nothing, and to think of nothing—the mind-and-conscience-destroying consequence of Hitler's delusional ideology concerning his attempt to create, at any price in human lives, his *Eintausenjähriges Reich* that was to be ruled by his world-domineering *Herrenrassen* Germans under his own war cry: *Macht ist Recht* (Might is right), a negation of human rights. Here I must aved that I had no idea that there was such a thing as "human rights."

By mid-1944, fearing for my own life, the increasing feelings of sorrow deep within myself concerning the numerous victims, both the low-ranking soldiers and the local civilians, remained carefully hidden. However, in spite of continuous indoctrination, not surprisingly more and more so, not for the *reichsdeutsch* fallen but for the dead *Volksdeutschen,* as well as the Serbs and even the very young among the partisans, I confirmed that the *Reichsdeutschen* were definitively not my people. The tragedy of the entire second group was really touching me, because before the war, they all had been decent, hardworking, and God-believing individuals and families, many of them really poverty-stricken.

Also by mid-1944, my command of the German language had improved significantly enough to perform more and more of my duties as wireless-set operator. Very much to my surprise—since once a *Magyarone*, always a *Magyarone*—I was even promoted, first to *Oberfunker* (private first class) and then to *Sturmann* (corporal); however, the new ranks meant nothing to me since my postwar plans, if I were to survive, had nothing to do with Hitler's Reich. Desperately hoping to survive the war, I had turned into, like millions of others in my situation, a *Mitläufer* (a postwar addition to the German language, involving mainly millions of Germans [and "forced Germans" like myself] who would eventually, in the postwar denazification process in 1947, claim to have "heard nothing," "seen nothing," and "thought nothing" in the hope that they would be cleared of the accusation of having aided and abetted the real Nazi war criminals). The three major offensives during the year 1944 contributed to the vastly increased hemorrhage of the *Prinz Eugen*. From the very small number at its incipient stage, Tito's partisan movement had become a Balkan-wide agglomeration of South Slavs, Bosnians, Albanians, a few Hungarians, and even a handful of *Volksdeutschen,* as well as several units of Mussolini-hating Italians (following the anti-Mussolini coup in 1943). By mid-1944, Tito had set up several well-organized divisions and was receiving massive military aid from the Western allies. In late summer 1944, aided by the massive breakthrough of more than one million strong Red Army Ukrainian Front into Romania, Bulgaria, and Eastern Serbia, the partisans were forcing the German occupiers of the Balkans into continuous battles for survival in order to secure the withdrawal of about 250,000 German troops from

Greece. This huge avalanche comprising mainly of Red Army communist forces was opposed by the despairing motley of four truncated German divisions, including the *Prinz Eugen*, which was left at most with only about ten thousand officers, NCOs, and soldiers.

I will never forget the two major events that occurred during the course of that year, events that reinforced my view that the *reichsdeutsch* officers and soldiers were not, and never could become, my people. The first event involved the death sentence upon a *volksdeutsch* soldier in the telephone-communication company of the signal corps of the *Prinz Eugen*. I do not recall his name or his rank, but I can still see the *Todesangst* (fear of death) in his eyes right after he had been condemned to execution by shooting. Just a week earlier, having heard of the Red Army's advance into the vicinity of the *Bánát*, he took off without bothering to ask for special furlough, determined to get back to his family and save his highly pregnant wife from suffering multiple rape at the hands of the Red Armists. Having placed her into the by then huge *volksdeutsch* refugee stream in the direction of Vienna, he quickly returned and made the mistake of reporting his presence to his *reichsdeutsch* company commander. Within minutes, two SS-*Feldgendarmerie* (military police) appeared, grabbed him, accused him of desertion, and locked him up. Within another few minutes, the commander of the signal corps contacted his superiors at division headquarters and was authorized to set up a *fliegendes Feldgericht* (traveling field court), selecting three *reichsdeutsch Waffen-SS* junior officers from the signal corps: *Untersturmführer* (Second Lieutenant) *de la Chaux* (a very ardent Nazi, even though descended from a very illustrious Huguenot family that had been able to escape the wrath of the French Catholics and find a new home in Prussia) as the principal defender; *Untersturmführer Kostmann*, also an ardent Nazi, as the military prosecutor; and another *Untersturmführer* whose name was unknown to me, as the assistant judge. A handful of lower ranks were also ordered to be present as witnesses, none of them presumably having any idea about proper legal *Waffen-SS* procedure in AWOL cases.

Overall, with my accumulated knowledge in my postwar studies of court proceedings in similar cases in Hitler's military, I soon recognized from the descriptions of what had conspired that the poor *volksdeutsch* conscript had been subjected to a kangaroo court treatment: he had not been allowed to explain his absence; had been branded a traitor and a *Schweinehund* (pig dog) even by *de la Chaux*, his legal defense counsel; and was within barely fifteen minutes condemned to death by shooting. Even before the beginning of the court proceedings, the remaining about two hundred of the lower-rank *Volksdeutschen* were ordered by the handful of *reichsdeutsche* officers and NCOs to form unarmed a quadrant in the adjacent field. We did, and the accused was dragged forward. The firing squad had already been formed exclusively of *reichsdeutsche* NCOs and soldiers who had volunteered, since not even one of the *volksdeutsch* conscripts had done so. The condemned soldier was pushed onto the site of the execution with the *Waffen-SS* judges already present and was instantly shot dead. The final command sounded *Einscharren!* (bury him!) right there into the meadow and without any markers except for the ashes of his *Soldbuch*, as if the poor sod had never existed. Only later did we learn that even though surrounded by partisans, the order to appear unarmed at the shooting had been issued to prevent the other *Volksdeutschen* from causing any problems and that the order to impose the death sentence and to carry it out immediately had been passed down just before the proceedings, with the aim to demonstrate to the *volksdeutsch* conscripts what would happen to them if they decided to go AWOL.

Many times during the course of my long life, my mind has kept going back to that particularly dehumanizing scene and what I can only refer to as a wanton murder of that innocent farming *volksdeutsch* man from the

Bánát. Recalling the 1936 Olympics in Berlin, as a non-German, I am still asking myself, How do we explain that most of the German citizens who had opted *en masse* for Adolf Hitler in 1932 were still viewed even through to mid-1938 by the English and the French as belonging to the "civilized" world, with remarkable achievements in the sciences, in philosophy, and even in the arts? With the opening of the *KZ* Dachau in 1933 and the murder of Ernst Röhm in mid-1935 as proofs that Hitler had no qualms to order such horrendous act of violence even against his own cocitizens? Was it a naturally embedded tendency in the top-level Nazi leadership? Or was it the consequence, the end result of the violence that had persisted in World War I, a war that had lasted far too long, long enough to crack and to destroy what had turned out to have been only the thin veneer of a presumed civilization? How was it possible that the traditional German elite from Bismarck right through WWI and the Great Depression had been able more or less to maintain its historical privileged status, only to see itself fall—apparently with such ease in such a voluntary manner and in such large numbers—under the spell of Adolf Hitler, a *Lumpenproletarier* (riff-raff proletarian) from Austria-Hungary, and the steel-studded *Knobelbecher* (marching boots) of Hitler's *Wehrmacht* and *Waffen-SS*? What explains that the "traditional German elite" did nothing when Hitler decreed the two Nuremberg Laws in September 1935, still very early after being appointed the chancellor?

During the Viel trial, I asked myself several times about Julius Viel's motivation to kill those seven Jewish prisoners, because I was not in agreement with Judge Winkler's conclusion, "Viel had committed the war crime . . . out of lust for murder and basic motives." Before the war, Viel had spent almost two years in the Dachau concentration camp with a continuous inflow of German Jews *after* the Nazis had passed the Nuremberg Laws of 1935, literally authorizing every SS officer to become legally certified executioner. At the *Waffen-SS* officers' schools both in Nuremberg and in Leitmeritz since 1943, the January 20, 1942, Wannsee Conference decisions concerning the Final Solution must have been a discussion topic among the *Waffen-SS* staff officers, most likely having a murdering influence upon some of the younger officers of their teaching staff. After all, how long would it have taken for the young officers' hatred of Stalin and his Jewish commissars to overspill into acute hatred for all Jews living in Germany? Didn't the Oath of Fealty to Adolf Hitler imply that since *Der Führer* had ordered the killing of Jews, he was expecting all members of the *NSDAP* and all *Waffen-SS* officers to get busy and do it?

The second major, even more tragic event occurred mid-October 1944, in *Niš*, Serbia: the almost total destruction of the divisional headquarters of the *Prinz Eugen*—more than two thousand officers and soldiers, as well as one thousand vehicles, tanks, etc.—in two days of battle involving the Red Army, two Bulgarian divisions that had overnight switched sides to the Red Army, and two Tito partisan divisions. They had encircled the German troops while the latter were preparing, under their then commander, *Waffen-SS* brigadier Otto Kumm (wearer of the Knight's Cross for "exceptional heroism" on the *Ostfront*), to break out, not knowing about the turncoat Bulgarians and their plan to destroy the one and only escape route, the bridge across the river *Morava*. While each and all the captured German officers and soldiers were instantly executed by the Bulgarians and the partisans, the commander himself, with a couple of handful *reichsdeutsch* staff officers, somehow managed to get away by swimming across the river and, about a week later, to arrive safely behind the new German defense line.

At this point, it might be interesting at this time to make a special mention of the then Brigadier Otto Kumm. On the *Ostfront*, he was quickly promoted to staff officer ranks in the first-tier *Waffen-SS* divisions because he had twice managed to break, albeit at terrible cost in lives, through the encirclement of several Red Army guard and tank divisions, each time having arrived with only a couple of dozen surviving officers and soldiers behind the new front line. His promotion to commandant of the *Prinz Eugen*, a second-tier *Waffen-SS* division that had been set up by mainly second-rate soldiers, the *Volksdeutschen*, confirmed Hitler's expectation that Kumm was the staff officer who would most likely secure the orderly withdrawal during the second half of 1944 back to Germany of up to 250,000 German troops that had gotten stuck in Greece, most of the withdrawing Germans having to make through areas that were heavily infested by Tito partisans, a distance of about one thousand kilometers from Greece to Croatia. Having succeeded, he was then awarded by Hitler himself the swords to the oak leaves to the Knight's Cross (Hitler Germany's second-highest award for valor).

Kumm did survive the war, but his postwar critics singled out his double breakouts on the eastern front and the encirclement at *Niš* as "saving his skin by running away, a cowardly act that left his soldiers to their certain deaths." After the war, Brigadier Kumm had been kept in an American prison for trial as a war criminal, but he managed to escape by "jumping across the wall," supposedly with American help, because of his expertise on the *Ostfront*, as well as in partisan warfare. He remained hidden until the creation of the Adenauer government in 1955. His successor as commander of the remnants of the *Prinz Eugen*, *Standartenführer* (Colonel) Schmidhuber, also an avid Nazi, was taken prisoner by the Titoists, was tried for multiple war crimes, and was hanged in Belgrade in 1946. My personal involvement with Otto Kumm occurred in 1997, when, wondering how he would react, I wrote to him about the murder by Julius Viel of the seven Jews at the *KZ Theresienstadt*. Having broken two times through Red Army encirclements, how would he feel, fifty-three years after the end of the war, about war crimes? Very much to my surprise, he sent me the following answer: "*Waffen-SS Kameradschaft endet, wo Kriegsverbrechen begangen werden.*" (*Waffen-SS* comradeship ends when war crimes begin.) He died in 2003, still respected by some of the veterans but loathed by others.

Mid-October 1944, my life and those of my other six comrades serving as wireless-set operators in my *Horch-17* lorry were saved by being ordered three days earlier to drive up toward the Danube river and to join the headquarters of a *Kampfgruppe* (large battle group) comprising various *Wehrmacht* units and commanded by General Fischer. After our arrival, we remained for several days without any communication with the headquarters of the *Prinz Eugen*, having absolutely no idea as to what might have happened to them. Finally, the message of that vast catastrophe was relayed to us. Most of our signal corps *Kameraden* had been captured and shot on the spot, and all nine of the remaining wireless-set lorries had been captured by the Titoists, leaving my own as the only one for the decimated headquarters of the *Prinz Eugen*. Retreating before the onslaught by almost one million Red Armists of the Ukrainian front, the battle group Fischer got bogged down in a vast marsh by the river Plana, with only a two-lane road leading through it and toward a rickety bridge across the river with a Z-form curve right before it. The Titoists had captured one of the Germans' PAKs (German antitank gun) and had zeroed it in onto that curve, shooting at and hitting almost every second vehicle, several of them remaining burning on the road, while others had slid into the swamp. Queuing up my *Horch-17*, I discovered that I would be the second car to go into what appeared as certain death for all seven of us. Driving slowly across the bridge, we were certain to be hit, while driving fast would likely make us slide into the swamp. At the last moment, entering that S-curve before the bridge, I decided to step upon the gas pedal all the way down while keeping the steering wheel firmly in my hands to keep the vehicle on the road. The sudden acceleration did result in some loss of traction in the curve, but I managed to pull it out by pumping the gas pedal. We had made it. The sudden acceleration saved our lives because it had not been anticipated by the Titoist PAK-rocket crew. Their missile had passed my lorry just a couple of meters behind the tail pipe, falling into the swamp. After crossing the bridge, I continued straight into the upcoming village, where I hid the *Horch-17* right behind the church, totally out of sight of the Red Armists. But we lost Hans Lissy, one of the seven, on the following day after he had carelessly wandered onto the church square and right into a barrage of Soviet grenades.

A couple of days later, the remnants of the Fischer battle group managed to break through toward the west and were quickly absorbed into the new defensive position. The remaining five of us and I were ordered to give up our *Horch-17* and to join on foot the then really pitiful remnants of the *Prinz Eugen*, withdrawing toward the north to the river *Sava*.

Marching, stopping, fighting, and marching again, we were joined by only one additional former graduate of the *volksdeutsch* high schools, leaving only seven alive of the original seventy plus myself from the Hungarian high school. For another agonizing several weeks, we were continually retreating, stopping, fighting, and literally running backward, pursued by huge numbers—including their thousands of T-34s—of the Ukrainian front as well as the Titoists, right up to the small Bosnian town of *Brčko* at the confluence of the river *Drina* (historically, the river had become famous as the dividing line of the Western Roman Empire from the Eastern Roman Empire) with the river *Sava*.

I had just turned nineteen and feeling very old while watching the newly arriving replacements. Most of them were barely seventeen-year-old German-speaking raw recruits wearing previously used *Waffen-SS* uniforms, with smaller numbers of non-German volunteers: Albanians, Croatians, Romanians, and even several Hungarians, as well as a whole bunch of Ukrainians (the latter coming from the remnants of the only recently created Ukrainian *Waffen-SS* division, Ukrainian nationalists who hated the Red Army more than the *Wehrmacht*). Having been for three long years an ostracized outsider among the thousands of *reichsdeutsch* officers and NCOs and *volksdeutsch* recruits, I was suddenly feeling much more comfortable surrounded by those teenagers because they looked totally un-German like me.

Chapter III
Waffen-SS 1Officer School and the Murder of Seven Jewish Prisoners

As already mentioned above, it was in *Brčko* that I met my brother for the last time. During the third week of December, the seven surviving *Voksdeutsche* high school graduates and I were ordered to appear appropriately dressed—steel helmet and belt but no rifle—to the tent of the company commander, *Hauptsturmführer* (Captain) Giermann. Even though each of us was undernourished and clearly tired looking, he kept on staring at us for quite a long time as if appraising our military bearing and our survival capacity. Finally, with his face turning very formal, he informed us that we were being sent to the *Waffen-SS* signal officers—school in Nürnberg (Nuremberg). Gone were the times when *Waffen-SS* officer cadets had to be blond, blue-eyed, at least 180 cm tall, with athletic bodies and haughty bearings—as had been appropriate for the ideological requisites of the *Herrenrasse*. Only two of us resembled the complete image of the pure Aryan *Herrenmenschen* while the next three had the looks but not the height. The sixth had red hair and green eyes. The seventh had light brown hair and light brown eyes. And the eighth, Adalbert Lallier, could, with his dark hair and deep-brown eyes, be easily mistaken for an *Untermensch* from the Balkans. Evidently, the *Waffen-SS* had run out of the picture-perfect pure Aryan type and was now forced to search at the bottom of the Nazi racial barrel for subrace individuals like myself, with the grudging hope that they might make it as officer candidates with qualities other than just the appropriate racial looks.

Glancing furtively at the other seven, I quietly suspected that each of them would, during their follow-up interviews, say anything that would guarantee their final approval as officer candidates, since being sent back for at least six months to Germany would literally guarantee their survival. While the other seven had already been confirmed as *reinrassig* (racially pure), I was treated differently: "Lallier, you would first have to face within a few days three doctors from the *Waffen-SS Rassenamt* [the SS office for the purity of the Germanic race] for final approval." I was surprised (evidently without revealing it) that at this final and apparently losing phase of the war, the *Waffen-SS* was, for reasons of ideology, still withholding from the eastern front many able-bodied officers whose presence on the front might have made a winning difference. After all, by this time (early 1945), almost one hundred thousand of racially less-than-perfect recruits had already been mustered even from totally un-Germanic nations (Bosnians, Albanians, Ukrainians, even Indians and Vlasov's Russian army). The original "official look" of the *Waffen-SS* as pure, elite Germanic soldiers had, by the end of December 1944, changed into a horde of almost one million of several races and even religious backgrounds, officially for a total of thirty *Waffen-SS Divisionen* but with vastly diminished fighting qualities. But none of this mattered to me, since I too wished to be saved from getting killed. At the end of the meeting, we raised in unison our right arm in the Hitler salute and expressed our gratitude and commitment with a loud "*Jawohl, Hauptsturmführer!*" (Yes, sir, Captain!)

Two days later, I was ordered to present myself to the three-officer delegation (one of whom a *Waffen-SS* medical staff officer). I was told to undress completely for the *Frischfleischbeschau* (fresh flesh examination), German military slang for situations in which the soldiers had to present themselves in the nude for various tests and examinations, including venereal disease. A *Waffen-SS Sturmbannführer* (major) examined me with a running commentary, "Muscular strength somewhat weak but promising. Needs more nourishment. Cranium well developed with a remarkable protruding occiput well above the norm. Lallier, you seem very intelligent. Propagation apparatus, very impressive. Color of skin, hair, eyes, totally against the racial requirements for reichsdeutsch Waffen-SS officers. I'm sorry, but I can recommend you only for training as an officer for our Albanian or Bosnian divisions."

A lively discourse then ensued between the *Sturmbannführer* and our *Hauptsturmführer*. The captain emphasized the most urgent need for junior officers, both in the elite and the second-order *Waffen-SS* divisions, the KIA rate of junior officers getting killed within the first three months after returning to the eastern front having surpassed 60 percent. After some more argumentation, the medical *Sturmbannführer* turned to me and declared that I would be allowed to join the other seven cadets, but with the following condition: "Lallier, after we win the war [dear reader, please recall that this statement was made at the end of December 1945, by which time, the war had already been lost], once a Waffen-SS officer, you will get married to a light-blond, blue-eyed reichsdeutsch girl so as to improve the racial looks of your family. You will sire four children. As per our racial theory, two of the four will turn out blonds with blue eyes, as required. The third will have light-brown hair and light-brown eyes and will then have to marry a blond and blue-eyed girl. Unfortunately, as predicted by our racial profiling, your fourth child will resemble you—dark-skinned, dark-haired, and dark-eyed—a dismal situation that can only be corrected if he or she marries another light-blond and blue-eyed Reichsdeutsch girl."

Desperately wishing to survive the war—but being extremely careful not to show it—I recalled uttering, "*Vielen Dank, Sturmbannführer*" (Thank you,

Major), while resenting deep inside myself for being even ordered what kind of girl I would have to marry and how many children I would have to sire, feelings that I kept but which attested to the fact that even after more than three years of brainwashing, deep inside my being, I had remained immune to complete Nazi indoctrination.

Early in January 1945, our group took a military train (they were still running even though the partisans kept on destroying the tracks) from *Bosanski Brod* to *Zagreb* (then already for three years the capital of the Croatian fascist regime) and then by express train through *Vienna* to our planned final destination, *Nürnberg*. However, upon arrival, we discovered that the city had been destroyed two days earlier by hundreds of British bombers, which dropped upon the city phosphor bombs and high-pressure air mines, killing an estimated thirty-five thousand German civilians. Our planned sojourn at the officers' school had to be transferred to another site because several air mines had also destroyed all its buildings, the mines tearing apart more than four hundred cadets and officers while they were having lunch—the incomprehensible tragedy of yet another terrible example of how two supposed "civilized" nation states would go about to destroy each other, apparently with great pleasure. We spent two weeks looking for and burying the dead, most of whom had burned to death, charcoal black but with their facial features still recognizable.

During the course of the final week in January 1945, by now our group of cadets totaling about 250 were embarked into *SS* trucks to be driven to *Leitmeritz* (today *Litoměřice* in the Czech Republic) as the alternative site for our training, into a building that had been as high school for girls before the war. About ten kilometers before our arrival, we were ordered to turn our faces to the left for about fifteen minutes, at the threat of severe punishment if we did not. We obeyed instantly. Exposed for several years to intensive totalitarian brainwashing by our superiors, our inborn capacity to reason and to rationalize about such strange orders had well nigh disappeared. Instantly, all of us, including myself, turned our faces to the left. It was only several days later that rumors were being circulated concerning the reasons for that strange order—*Konzentrationslager für Juden* (concentration camp for Jews), a *KZ!* This particular one had been named *Theresienstadt.* In the past, whether on or off the front, most of us had already heard that acronym but had no idea about what might be going on in it. Some of us believed that they were sites that provided housing for civilians who had been bombed out. But to some others, including myself, it sounded ominous, despairing, frightening. I couldn't help recalling that I had never found out why and how my brother's Jewish fiancée had so suddenly disappeared and where to.

Those of us who had passed the first set of examinations in mid-February discovered only in mid-March the real reason for the existence of concentration camps in the Third Reich—the mass killing of Jews, of many Soviet POWs, and scores of other "racially undesirables.".Five of the cadets who had become close friends and who did not look down upon me (two *Reichsdeutsche,* two *Volksdeutsche*, and myself—Barocka, Obst, Birg, Illiewich, and myself) were very disturbed but remained in total silence after realizing that we had been misled by Hitler into losing our final remnants of innocence but also agonizing about being unable to do anything out of fear for our own lives.

On postwar hindsight, my four friends and I, even though in officers' school, had become like millions of Germans—*Mitläufer* (quiet supporters of Hitlers Nazi ideology and its murder of millions of innocent victims). However disillusioned, we kept our mouths shut, not wishing to be sent back to the *Ostfront*, and really working hard in order to pass the next set of examinations. As you, the readers, would notice below, our disappointment intensified even more in mid-March 1945, when we witnessed *Untersturmführer Julius*

Viel, our own commanding officer, murder seven Jewish prisoners in the antitank ditch just off the *KZ Theresienstadt* and when we also heard that a large number of the cadets did not seem inclined to criticize Julius Viel for his murdering those seven *Saujuden* (swinish Jews). At night, all alone, deep inside myself, my non-Germanic conscience woke up asking why the God of the Christians would permit—order?—Hitler's Third Reich's Nazis to engage in this massive killing, and why the G-d of the Jewish people would allow it to happen. For the first time in my life, I began to doubt that we, the humans, were really God's own children.

After yet another set of examinations early in March 1945, an additional number of cadets were dismissed and sent back to the *Ostfront* (by then only about eighty kilometers away).

Those who had passed were promoted to the rank of *Junker* and were officially recognized as officer candidates. My understanding of the German language in that *hochdeutsch* setting had much improved, even though my oral expression still viewed as completely alien with its strange-sounding and uninviting Hungarian accent.

In the afternoon of March 17, 1945, the school commandant, *Standartenführer* (Colonel) Ernst Kemper (yet another wearer of the *Ritterkreuz*), received an order from the *SS-Hauptamt* in Prague to organize a group of about one hundred well-armed *Junkers* and to have them brought on the following day to the entrance of the concentration camp's prison, a fortified site named *Kleine Festung* (small fortress), where the *Junkers* would replace the concentration camp guards and march the mostly Jewish prisoners to the middle of a vast plain between the concentration camp and *Leitmeritz*. The purpose was to supervise the prisoners' digging of a four-kilometer-long antitank ditch that was supposed to put a halt to the advancing hundreds of Soviet T-34 tanks. An identical order had also been transmitted to the *Kommandeur* of the *KZ Theresienstadt*.

Once again our small group of just promoted officer candidates was very disturbed about this order, one that compelled *Waffen-SS* officer candidates to supervise *KZ* prisoners. This order not only contradicted what we had been taught in our course on the laws of war, but also defeated the premise that the officers of the *Waffen-SS* were just like the officers in all other armed forces, viewed as "gentlemen" with the same ethos and the same respect for their NCOs and recruits, albeit also with a very special personal fealty to Adolf Hitler as their *Führer.* Subject to provisions of the Hague conventions, as officers, they were also obliged to transmit to their own subordinates the orders from higher-up and to see to their implementation. Nowhere in our lectures on rules of war had we been taught that the officer candidates had to act as concentration camp guards. Yet even though surprised and even shocked, once again we said and did nothing for fear of being sent back to the eastern front.

However, we heard rumors about disagreement among our senior officers that resulted in the school commander asking the *Waffen-SS* supreme commander in Prague for an urgent explanation and a written confirmation. The confirmation must have been transmitted early in the morning because we were assembled to proceed with the selection of the required numbers for guard duty, most of whom coming from the wireless-set *Inspektion*, with its leader, *Untersturmführer* (Second Lieutenant) Julius Viel.

March 18, 1945, began unusually early for the Nazis and the Jewish prisoners. The various *Wehrmacht* units had reveille at 0400 hours and were put on march toward the *KZ Theresienstadt* by 0430 hours. The *Waffen-SS* officer candidates at the *Nachrichtenschule Leitmeritz* were loaded into their lorries at 0600 hours and trucked for their seven-kilometer ride right up to the gates of the *Kleine Festung,* where about 1,500 male Jewish prisoners were already waiting, supervised by their regular *Allgemeine-SS* concentration camp guards. The prisoners had not had any breakfast. The skies were still dark under the forming heavy clouds as the long desolate-looking columns of the many hundreds of Jewish prisoners were lined up and ordered to march in the direction of *Leitmeritz*.

On this occasion, the permanent *KZ* guards, none of whom were wearing any medals or looking battle-hardened, were armed with MP38s or carbines from different manufacturers. However, just about one kilometer off the *Kleine Festung*, as the long column of half-starved, rag-covered bodies were about to enter what looked like a vast plain, it was met by our orderly assembly of soldiers wearing the insignia of the *Waffen*-SS and looking like *Frontsoldaten* (battle-hardened veterans) and wearing a whole assortment of medals for valor. The prisoners could not possibly have known that this group of about one hundred soldiers were in fact officer candidates from the nearby *Waffen-SS Nachrichtenschule*. But they could not help observing the different bearing of these Germans, a large number of whom were armed with what looked like brand-new assault rifles, the *Sturmgewehre*, a weapon that had recently been brought into the *KZ*. Rumor had it that these weapons were produced right there in the *Protektorat Böhmen und Mähren*, in the Škoda factory. To the prisoners, the eyes of these very young-looking German soldiers appeared as if devoid of any feeling.

Surrounded by their new guards, the column continued moving on with a slower and slower pace toward the center of the plain, observed by two slow-moving *Volkswagen-Schwimmwagen* (amphibious jeep-like vehicles), each manned by a couple of *Waffen-SS* NCOs and armed with what looked like a mounted MG42, Nazi Germany's feared machine gun. Among their marching guards, several were also carrying a pipelike weapon with a visor at one end and a rocket-like projectile up front, a *Panzerfaust*.

Pushed and driven, the prisoners shuffled on until suddenly, one of them, looking up at the sky, sang out, quickly joined by another and then by many, a melody of pain, despair, and death in words that sounded like Slavic. Surprised, some of the German guards, apparently frightened, quickly reached for their weapons. Ever since that moment, all my remaining life, I have been unable to forget its sadness and the look of despair in the eyes of the prisoners. The *laah-laah-laah-lahlahlahlaah* went on higher and lower for several minutes until a shot rang out, followed by the guards pushing and shoving even more, with their weapons ready to shoot. Finally, the prisoners arrived at the center of the plain, still surrounded by their *Wehrmacht* and *Waffen-SS* guards, and were ordered to line up in front of several *Wehrmacht* and *SS* trucks to grab spades, shovels, and picks and to start digging a deep trench across the entire plains, the length of about four kilometers.

This massive effort continued all day amid a lot of yelling, screaming, and distant rifle shots that had become more frequent late in the afternoon. I had been standing all day very close to the edge of the ditch with the Czech-made ten-shot carbine hanging on my right shoulder, about twenty meters from a small group of our officers. Even the *Kommandeur* had appeared, standing around for a little while but looking indifferent.

By the evening, the following report was filed: "More than two kilometers were dug to about one-half of the required depth, and twenty-eight of the Jewish prisoners were liquidated for not being willing to continue working."

Back in the *Kleine Festung*, the returning Jewish prisoners barely had enough strength left to make it through the gate and to their barracks. They were served lukewarm, watery fish soup with bits of fish and a small slice of rye bread that was rumored to contain more sawdust than rye. Literally falling over, most of them did not even bother to wash, terrified that the morrow would be their last day alive. Back at the officers' school, a new reality had, by the end of the day, hit our little group: witnessing the terrible doings at the antitank ditch, Hitler's war seemed much more involved than only holding Stalin and his Red Army off Western Europe. We, the young ones, had never been told that it would also involve the killing of Jews. However, none of us dared to speak up. After a supper of thin slices of pork, boiled potatoes, and red beet salad, the *Kommandeur* announced that the exercise would be repeated the following day, with the same *Mannschaft* (unit) and the same order of the day.

March 19, 1945, followed the pattern of the previous day with an early reveille of the officer candidates, their arrival at the gates of the *Kleine Festung*, and the forced conduit of the prisoners to the site of the digging. On this day, there was no singing. The Germans were again armed with the new assault rifles. I was once again posted at the edge of almost at the same spot, looking down into the ditch, at a depth of about five feet, one-half of what was required to stop the advance of Soviet T-34s. I noticed a group of seven prisoners working somewhat detached from the others, and it occurred to me that just like my little group, even concentration camp prisoners—Jews or non-Jewish—were likely to form little groups of their own, perhaps hoping that it might help them survive or, if not, that they would die together less frightened. Occasionally, I was also glancing at the group of my officers, recognizing the highly decorated *Kommandeur*, his adjutant with his Iron Cross First Class, the officer responsible for *Weltanschauung* (meaning Hitler's ideology) but without any medals, and the leader of my *Inspektion, Waffen-SS Untersturmführer Julius Viel*, with his Iron Cross Second Class as well as with his *Verwundetenabzeichen* in silver (the equivalent of the US Purple Heart), implying that he had been seriously wounded at least twice.

Throughout the morning, there was no singing but a lot of digging noise, yelling, and infrequent rifle shots. Once again, except for Julius Viel, the eyes of the other officers showed cold indifference. But on this day, Viel's whole face and behavior seemed agitated, his eyes filled—both before and after our fifteen-minute luncheon break—with what I thought was physical pain, as well as revulsion and even hatred. I kept on looking furtively several times at Viel and then glancing back to that little group of prisoners who were shovellng at the bottom of the ditch. By that time, only their heads and upper chests were visible. Then I saw Viel staring for quite a while at that little group of seven prisoners, quickly detaching himself from the officers and grabbing one of the carbines from the tripod. Appearing extremely agitated, he paused for a moment, adjusted the weapon for a single-shot sequence, loaded the first bullet into the chamber, raised the rifle to his shoulder, and looked through its telescopic sight while I was watching the whole scene from about only fifty-foot distance, not knowing what to make of it but suddenly feeling very frightened. Then I looked more closely into the ditch, discovering that each of the seven Jewish prisoners looked different, even though clothed in identical bits of the striped clothing that they were wearing. I could clearly distinguish a giant of a man with a deep red-colored beard; a frail, almost-bald-headed younger blond prisoner; and a tall, lanky, skin-and-bones, darker-skinned prisoner. The fourth one had had a pallid face with almost sunken dark eyes looking extremely frightened. The fifth had high cheekbones and strands of dirty blond hair. The remaining two were bent over with their shovels. Then I glanced back at Viel and saw him pull the trigger.

The first shot rang out, hitting the forehead of the very frail young blond Jew, who was working on the left side of the giant prisoner with the dark-red beard. Forehead shots causing instant death, the first victim of the murderer took one step ahead and collapsed into the mud. Within seconds, deep in my subconscious, the friendly, caring face of my Jewish step-grandfather (the second husband of my paternal grandmother) appeared, looking at me, then a five-year-old kid who had just lost his mother, sitting on his lap and happily listening to his stories about the Exodus, the kings David and Solomon, and the many blissful moments from his family's history. How dared Julius Viel took a rifle and killed those Jewish prisoners, most likely grandfathers, fathers, and sons? Then the image vanished, leaving me very, very frightened.

Up at the sites of the German officers, absolutely nothing was happening. The *Wehrmacht* officers were too far to see anything, even though they must have heard the shooting. The several *Waffen-SS* officers turned their heads toward the ditch, but even though standing about only five meters from their murdering *Kriegskamerad*, not even one of them moved to try to stop the killing. A few moments later, Julius Viel took aim at the Jew with the pallid face, pulled the trigger, and scored a direct hit, which, upon hitting the prisoner's chest, sounded like a hollow thud, inducing the officers to pay more attention while I was just standing at the edge of the ditch, frightened, shocked, and unable to move, staring at the sight of the rapidly spreading patch of blood at the bottom of the ditch.

Without pausing, Julius Viel continued his bloody work, the giant Jew being the next victim. He had seen the killing, had dropped his pick, and asked the remaining four other Jews to put down their tools. Then they stood up as erect as their emaciated bodies would allow, stared directly at the killer, and intoned the previous day's death song. But by then, the *Waffen-SS Untersturmführer* Julius Viel seemed totally taken in by the urge to kill, manifesting in his maniacal ideological state of hatred against Jews that he had become one of Hitler's *Herrenrassen* executioners, a killing machine and master over the lives and deaths of all *Untermenschen*. Having sworn his *Treueid* to Adolf Hitler, he was responsible to no other, knowing that his *Führer* would approve. To him, the murdered victims were just yet another bunch of the Jewish *Untermenschen* who had to be disposed of in order keep the German Aryans pure. It was also his revenge for the Jews having murdered Jesus Christ, a deed that both the Christian gods Father and Holy Ghost and the Holy Father in the Vatican would also approve.

Apparently convinced that he was doing the morally right thing, Julius Viel continued with his killing, untouched by the sight of the half-starved and totally defenseless Jewish prisoners. He took aim at the giant with the dark-red beard, hitting him in the chest and seeing him fall over. But the Jew managed to extricate himself from the mud to stand up and even to raise his right fist at the *Waffen-SS* officer. The fourth shot rang out, hitting the giant in the belly. He fell with his face in the mud, struggled to get up and eventually did, standing there, wobbling but unable to raise his arms. Within seconds, he was hit with the third bullet right into his heart. He fell down into the mud with his face down and remained still. Then the pace of the shooting picked up. Loading, aiming, and pulling the trigger were accomplished within a few seconds, undisturbed by his superior *Waffen-SS* officers.

While the *Untersturmführer* appeared ice-cold, deep in me, turmoil was raging and rapidly swelling into horror—disgusted, benumbed, ashamed, and paralyzed. Having been ordered to guard that section of the ditch, I was not allowed to move unless permitted. Then five more shots rang out, hitting four more defenseless human targets, and four more Jewish prisoners fell dead into the mud of the *Panzergraben*.

Seconds after the first shot was fired and seeing Viel's first victim falling facedown into the mud at the bottom of the ditch, my conscience suddenly woke up from its three-year slumber and told me that what Julius Viel had done was *wrong*, the ultimate *evil*. Apparently, my classical Hungarian upbringing had prevailed over the Nazi-inspired attempts at indoctrination since June 1942. The *Waffen-SS Untersturmführer* Julius Viel had committed a monstrous crime right in front of my eyes. But what was I to do? My conscience heated up and demanded that I should run over to Viel and grab the rifle from the murderer's hands. But I was totally unable to move physically while my reason was attempting to force me to do nothing, for attacking one's own commanding officer would result in immediate incarceration, court-martial, and execution: *Wehrzersetzung*.

In Hitler's Germany, *Wehrzersetzung* (impairing the will to fight) constituted the worst form of military misdemeanor, and therefore, the preferred form of punishment being instant hanging or fusillade. I must add here that during the last four months of the war, rumors were circulating that following Hitler's personal orders, more than ten thousand German officers and soldiers accused of cowardice or for going AWOL especially on the eastern front were instantly shot or hanged.

The *Waffen-SS Untersturmführer* Julius Viel had apparently undertaken at his own discretion to comply with Hitler's highest level order for the *Drittes Reich* (the Third Reich) concerning *totaler Krieg* (total war): the *Führerbefehl* (Hitler's own personal order), "that for each German killed by the enemy during the course of the war, one hundred of the enemy shall be shot or hanged," implying that each (pure German) Aryan's life was worth at the very least one hundred of non-Aryan—Jewish or non-Jewish—lives. During the postwar, war crimes trials of several major shootings involving hundreds of civilians were documented as reprisal killings in several places, including Italy after the fall of Mussolini in August 1943. In all these cases of massive war crimes, Viel's particular case seems just a minute detail, even though those he was about to murder were half-starved and totally defenseless in the mud of the ditch and using the last bit of their physical capacity to prevent the invading hordes of the Red Army from breaking even deeper into the remnants of Hitler's *Grossdeutschland* and raping *en masse* thousands of German women. Critics of Viel have, understandably, pointed out that Julius Viel's unauthorized act should have resulted in an immediate court-martial because it diminished, by his killing those seven Jewish prisoners, the German's capacity to stop the advance of the Red Army.

Having terminated his killing spree, the *Waffen-SS Untersturmführer* Julius Viel returned the rifle to the pyramid, took a few steps toward his *Kommandeur*, and standing rigidly at attention, raised his arm in the Hitler salute and reported, "*Obersturmbannführer, ich melde sieben tote Juden. Diese Untermenschen hatten es nicht verdient, weiter zu leben.*" (Lieutenant Colonel, may I report seven dead Jews. These subhumans did not deserve to continue living.) Not even one of the other officers had tried to stop the killing. Instead, the *Kommandeur* listened to the report, returned the Hitler salute, took a few steps toward the antitank ditch, and looked at the dead Jews. The other officers, including Julius Viel, followed. Down below, the digging was resumed as if nothing whatsoever had happened.

The Nazi-German anti-tank ditch in which the seven Jewish KZ-prisoners were murdered

A few minutes later, a standard-issue, two-wheel cart was brought by three emaciated Jewish prisoners to the edge of the by that time much deeper trench. While the *Waffen-SS* officers were watching with renewed interest, the three prisoners slid down into the ditch, got hold of the first dead body, swung it a few times and threw it up squarely upon the platform of the cart, with one of his arms hanging down. Two more followed with equal swings, piled upon the first one and with more arms hanging over the side of the cart. The corpse of the giant Jew needed three more inmates from the bottom of the ditch to lift him up seven feet and throw him, with several additional swings, on top of the three others. After lifting even more efficiently the remaining three, with more arms and even legs hanging over the sides of the cart, two of the prisoners grabbed the rudder pole and, aided by the third one who was pushing from the rear, parted toward the little fortress. Soon everything went back to normal—yelling, shouting, manifold metallic sounds of the tools, the occasional rifle shot—as if nothing unusual had happened. At sundown, the remaining prisoners were herded back to the Small Fortress, the *Wehrmacht* unit was marched off, and the *Waffen-SS* officer candidates were back on their trucks, direction *Leitmeritz.*

Twenty-one more Jewish prisoners were reported killed on the same day, several of whom had simply fallen over dead while the others had been shot dead or beaten to death.

The next day at the school, lectures and exercises were also resumed without any discussion of the murder, as if nothing at all had happened. However, at noon, four candidates from our group of seven, their average age just about twenty-one years, decided after lunch to approach their *Kommandeur* and to ask for permission to submit a petition with the assurance that none of them would be prosecuted. The request was for an explanation of the murder and its possible consequences. Permission was instantly granted. The inquiry would be arranged, and the official announcement of the decision would be made and posted within two or three days. Also there would be no court-martial for attempts at subordination.

Toward the evening of the following day, the news was spreading that the *Kommandeur* had ordered *Untersturmführer* Julius Viel to report dressed in formal uniform with *Stahlhelm* and *Koppel* (steel helmet and belt) but unarmed. The day after, rumors had it that Viel had received a severe reprimand, but he had been permitted to resume his teaching and his post as the commanding officer of the wireless-communication *Inspektion.* In my little group, many speculations had been silently exchanged about Viel's presence in the *Kommandeur*'s office. Rumors had been circulating that the highest *Waffen-SS* command in Prague had ordered that its officer candidates should be sent as guards in a *KZ* in order to test their allegiance to the Oath of Fealty to Adolf Hitler. If the rumors were true, could the *Untersturmführer*, known as an avid Nazi, have been ordered to kill several Jews as a test of the reaction? In our very quiet and noiseless discussion at night, we agreed that given the vertical order of ranking from the very top down, Viel could not possibly have acted on his own, since the task of digging the antitank ditch was very urgent. It would have made no sense to kill even one of the Jewish prisoners. At the same time, we also recalled that Viel, in his lectures, had often expressed his hatred of the Jews in the Soviet Bolshevik politburo and that he had incurred his two severe wounds on the eastern front in support of the Third Reich's quest to "clean the world of Aryans, from the increasing threat of Jewish contamination." He had also complained of continuing severe pain in the chest caused by splinters from his wounds and the need to keep on swallowing many painkillers. We concluded that if Julius Viel had really acted totally on his own, he would have been accused of *Wehrzersetzung* and would therefore have been most severely punished. However, our conclusion caused us even more disillusionment as we were in a bind between the claim that "like all officers in the armies of nation states, the *Waffen-SS* officers, too, were gentlemen" and the acute possibility that it had been the *Waffen-SS*'s highest command's order to use us, the officer candidates, as guinea pigs in testing our "allegiance" to the *Führer*, in which attempt, Julius Viel must have been ordered to become the trigger.

As promised, the *Kommandeur*'s verdict was announced, without any explanation, and posted on the third day on the school's bulletin board:

What happened two days ago, can no longer be called back or rectified. In a total war many more and much greater problems need to be solved. Winning this war will absolve us of any responsibility, for anything. Should we lose this war, presumably we all will be dead. There will be no official inquiry into this event; neither will the named officer be prosecuted. I order therefore, that all of us should forget that this thing ever happened. According to your Oath of Fealty to our Führer, Adolf Hitler, all of us of the Waffen-SS, each enlisted man, each non-commissioned officer, and each fully commissioned officer shall henceforth be obliged to remain silent, unto their death.

Special note 1. The *Kommandeur* did not know that the murder of the seven Jews was recorded in a little black book the very same evening by one of the concentration camp clerks.

Special note 2. Fifty-five years later, 1999–2002, during the war crimes trial of Julius Viel, only two of the nine former officer candidates who were still living and present as witnesses testified that Julius Viel had been the killer—Manfred Obst and I. The other seven were still committed to the oath to keep the silence until their deaths. Two of the seven had been with my small group of five. The third one (Sepp Schütz) had already died.

Chapter IV
The Murder Postmortem: Reflections on Nazi Motives and War Crimes

Caught between the urge to save the lives of the Jewish prisoners and the fear for my own life, I went through long, painful moments of impotence while watching the murder of the remaining four poor Jews. Before the end of the war, during many sleepless nights, my conscience kept on pestering my reason about its decision to do nothing while the images of the killings kept on reappearing and causing me endless hours of feelings of intense shame and disgust with my own person—ultimately culminating in an almost unbearable feeling of guilt. It had remained anchored in my subconscious throughout my long life, eventually inducing me after more than fifty years to do a search for the murderer and to bring him to trial. It was also the main reason for writing this personalized Holocaust account.

During almost six decades, I have been devoting much time to fact-finding, research, seeking answers and explanations concerning the tragedy in the *Panzergraben*. Here's my summary view as it has emerged up to the present (December 2016):

Mid-March 1945, I wasn't even twenty years old but had been coerced to serve for almost three years in Hitler's *Waffen-SS*. During those fateful thirty-three months as mule caretaker, truck driver, and wireless-set operator—all at the division headquarters—I had neither shot at nor murdered anyone, civilian or wearing the uniform of Tito's partisans. But

I had been witness to the wanton killings by both the *Wehrmacht* and the *Waffen-SS* of hundreds of human beings— mainly Serbs, Bosnians, and Montenegrins dressed as civilians or wearing a partisan uniform—as well as the burning down of scores of villages inhabited by humans leaving at the margins of subsistence. I had also lost most of the forcefully recruited *volksdeutsch* soldiers in the *Nachrichtenabteilung*, several of whom died while I was holding on to them, hoping for the miracle of their survival. In addition, on March 19, 1945, I experienced my personally most touching agony when witnessing totally helpless the horrendous sight of seven Jewish KZ inmates being shot to death one at a time and without any cause or justification. Having been raised a Christian, I looked up to heaven after the first Jewish prisoner was murdered and asked our three-in-one God, how could the three of them permit such slaughter to happen? Not having received any answer, I lowered my expectation concerning divine revelation and turned my attention to the study of economics, international politics, and law, disciplines known for their fact-based research that might enable me to discover the real-life causes and to provide rational and objective answers. See explanations below.

Reflecting upon Julius Viel's war crime and analyzing the presumed causes that might have induced him to shoot and kill, I wish to submit the following explanations:

- Viel was known to have been an early member of both the *NSDAP* and the *SS*.

- He was also known to have been posted for several years at the first Nazi concentration camp, in *Dachau*, from which he was transferred to the Second *Waffen Division Das Reich* in 1941, fighting first on the eastern front and, in 1944, against the allied forces in France, where he was heavily wounded. After partially recovering, he was sent—not yet fully recovered—to the signal officers' school in *Nuremberg* and then to the alternate site in *Leitmeritz* to take command of the second *Inspektion*, the training of wireless-communications officer candidates.

- He had received only three medals: Iron Cross Second Class, 1941 Winter War campaign on the *Ostfront*, and the medal for wounds in silver. He was also known to be suffering almost intolerable pain from his stomach wound, necessitating heavy doses of painkillers.

- During his lectures, he often emphasized the importance of the Oath of Fealty to the *Führer* and the commitment as Christian to destroy godless communists, demonstrating ideology-induced aversion bordering on hatred against the *Untermenschen*, both the Slavs and the Jews. On hindsight, in my eyes, it was a sad example of a young German's mind having been totally successfully brainwashed by Hitler's Nazi ideology and the promise of the creation of a world empire ruled by the German master race.

- By mid-April 1945, an air of pessimism bordering on hopelessness had spread at the officers' school, even though no one dared to discuss it in public. Two weeks later, with the news that Hitler had died as a hero, and with the beloved *Führer* gone and no adequate replacement visible, the Red Army menace—only eighty kilometers away—looked frightening in a setting in which everyone at the school was seeking ways to save his life. The perception that the "savior of the nation" was gone left most the officers and the cadets with the unspoken conclusion, "*Es gibt keinen Ausweg mehr.*" (There is no way out anymore.) A real-life perception that did eventually surface in the *Kommandeur*'s announcement was that Julius Viel would not be tried, one of the reasons being, "If we lose the war, we'll all be dead anyway and will therefore not be responsible."

- So adding up Julius Viel's conditions, physical as well as psychological, I might have a valid conclusion as to which factors might have triggered Julius Viel into pulling the trigger of the carbine ten times and killing those seven unfortunate Jewish prisoners: (a) the almost hopeless but unspoken setting that the war had been lost; (b) a perception that as officer, his Oath of Fealty to Adolf Hitler obliged him to fulfill any of his *Führer*'s commands, especially the command to kill as many Jews as possible; (c) the agony of physical pain from the wound and the perception it had been caused by the archenemy, the Jews (Viel had in fact been wounded by Americans, but that was irrelevant, because according to Nazi dogma, the Jews had taken command of both Moscow and Washington), a bunch of whom were only about twenty meters away, conveniently unarmed and already half dead; (d) Hitler had ordained that each Red Army Jewish commissar captured be shot on sight; and (e) taking revenge for having been seriously wounded, revenge for the death of *Der Führer* and for what appeared to have become a lost war.

- I have no idea if any of these "causes" could have been instrumental in inducing Julius Viel's mind to proceed with the murders. But I did see the expressions in his face and in his eyes, in their cold-blooded indifference, revealing absolutely nothing about what might have been going through before concluding that the killing would be "morally acceptable." Had he been ordered to kill, he would not have been permitted to waste time pondering about the moral implications.

- In my own case, I went through five decades of conscience turmoil, from the initial feelings of guilt and shame, then to the rising pressure to "confess" in private, followed by the intellectual urge to fact-find through research, and finally on to the decision to go public and to initiate court proceedings— culminating in the following reflections concerning Julius Viel's war crime:

- The fact that I let fear prevail over my conscience while watching the murder signals to me that at that moment, I had not yet attained the moral maturity that would have been required for me to understand the meaning of and the implications arising from Viel's war crime. Even if I had had, during the seconds of the killing, any notion about human rights, the fear for my own life would have stopped me from doing anything to prevent the killing. Instead, I remained totally numbed.

- Without having experienced feelings of guilt, we are unable to understand the meaning of the idea of justice. Even in a democratic setting, a person who has been brought up with respect for the law and ready to take on individual responsibility as the moral foundations of his/her society, fear will prevent such an individual from making an effective contribution to putting a stop to such crimes while they are being committed. Whereas in a totalitarian system, the formation of the individualistic meaning and significance of justice is prevented, thereby rendering impossible the creation of the personal feeling of accountability and responsibility. In this sense, Julius Viel's war crime, even though committed by an individual, also becomes the war crime of his entire, totalitarian, system, justifying the war crimes trials of its leaders (and their hanging). But it does also raise the question of legal fairness: When a totally brainwashed person in a totalitarian system proceeds to commit a crime (whether or not ordered to do so), is it fair to condemn him to death by hanging while letting his totalitarian leaders go free?

- Unless we have gone through the soul-agonizing process starting with the feeling of shame, then on to the feeling of guilt, then on to the feeling of accountability and responsibility, and finally, all the way up to the invocation of justice as the intellectually required eschatological steps that must be taken, we will remain unable to understand both mentally and spiritually the meaning and significance of the process of natural justice.

- If, as witnesses to a war crime, we are to participate effectively in the pursuit of the course of natural justice, we must first accept the risk of engaging in a public confession. Individuals in a free society, who are guided by its moral principles, are expected to arrange without conditions for their public confession, which means without first having undertaken an assessment of possible post-confession antagonistic views of and repercussions upon the confessing person.

- Respect for human rights involves the highest moral judgment of a society and its individual citizens. As the expression of its highest ethical standards, it surpasses absolutely and uncompromisingly the material meaning of debit and credit.

- In my own case, my personal participation in the process of natural justice resulted in creating feeling of positive life-embracing pulsation, a satisfying sequel to having gone public without any prior material conditions. My several appearances as witness before the war crimes court in Ravensburg in the setting of the presently Western-style democratic *Bundesrepublik Deutschland* enabled me to portray to the public my own decade-long feelings of shame and guilt in the hope that they, the democratic Germans, had become also deeply committed to the process of natural justice, preferably even still feeling guilty when recalling the terror and the killing fields that had been perpetrated by their Nazi fathers and grandfathers. I had high hopes that this anticipation would enable me to make it much easier for me to share the tragedy of my experience with them and to result in a feeling of release, of purification that Catholics are said to experience after making their confession (except that in their case, they must then also proceed to communion if they are to be truly forgiven). However, very much to my regret, my high hopes concerning the feeling of release and of purification never materialized in full, diminished by the presence of and viciously unfair comments by quite a few German media persons, some of whom even naming me in public as a "traitor."

- The phenomenon of "massive" forgetting (the oblivion effect): My fundamental perception that human conscience is equally innate in all women and all men and will therefore always result in responsible and honest forms of behavior was seriously contradicted during my presence at the court in Ravensburg. I observed that the entire group of witnesses who were present in defense of Julius Viel, except for only *one*, Manfred Obst, were claiming not to have seen, not to have heard, or not even to have been present while Julius Viel was committing his war crime. Each and all those present at the trial had been soldiers of and officer candidates in the *Waffen*-SS, had been present at the antitank ditch, and knew that Viel had committed the murders. But they had not only sworn at their festive induction several years earlier the Oath of Fealty to their *Führer*, Adolf Hitler, but had also been ordered by the *Kommandeur* of the officers' school to keep secret for the rest of their lives Julius Viel's war crime. Early in May 1945, they had also been told that Adolf Hitler had died, a fact that immediately relieved them from the commitment to the Oath of Fealty. In addition, each of them had also survived the war and was given a lifelong opportunity to enjoy the democratic lifestyle and its guarantee of human rights. All in all, I had expected them to *remember* and to *confess* in court. However, very much to my surprise and regret, they did not, except for Manfred Obst. So I was left with the question what might have induced them to lie, even though they had been sworn in to "speak the truth and nothing but the truth." Was it as simple as their still sticking with the Oath of Fealty to Adolf Hitler, a lifetime commitment, whether Hitler was still alive or already dead? Or was it a more complex reaction, like remnants of Hitler's ideological influence, aversion to being labeled a traitor, or fear of being accused as accessories to murder and jailed?

This unexpected discovery had left me in a personal intellectual quandary concerning my presumption, *viz* that "conscience is inborn in humans." The witnesses who had lied before the war crimes court were providing a living proof that Hitler's totalitarian system had succeeded by applying years of Nazi indoctrination into the brains and beings of his adherents, with the result of destroying their inborn human propensity for conscience and their natural inclination for justice.

Concluding the description of the tragedy in the *Panzergraben* just off the *KZ Theresienstadt*, we are now ready to ask the question whether during the war crimes trial of the murderer Julius Viel the process of natural justice did result in what may be termed a *just* verdict. Will the verdict reflect the ancient Davidian-Solomonian legal system of "an eye for an eye"? Or will it express acceptance of and adherence to the modern system of jurisprudence, *restitution*, as had been agreed upon in the United Nations and applied to the agreement between the new state of Israel and West Germany—that was still occupied mainly by American troops—and its democratic chancellor Dr. Konrad Adenauer? For the answer, please see chapter 10.

Chapter V

The End of the War: Free at Last

A few days after the massacre of the seven Jews, life in the *Nachrichtenschule* returned to its normal pulse until orders came through that smaller groups of officer candidates should be sent toward the *Ostfront* as urgent reinforcement. In mid-April 1945, the Red Army broke into the northern part of what is today the Czech Republic. Early in May, the news about Adolf Hitler's "heroic" death after a prolonged hand-to-hand battle with the Red Army was announced, inducing many of the officers to break out crying while also preparing the entire school for its own final battle against the Soviets. By the end of April 1945, with the attrition having drained about one-half of the candidates and their superior officers, the *Kommandeur* ordered the cessation of instruction and put the remaining *Junkers* and staff on full alert.

Early in the morning of May 7, 1945 (which happened to be my twentieth birthday but also turned out to be the last day before the official surrender of the Third Reich), a general alarm was sounded. The *Kommandeur* proceeded to divide the remaining *Junkers* into twelve squads of ten, each commanded by an officer from the school. The first one was led by the *Inspektionsführer Untersturmführer* Julius Viel; the second one, by *Waffen-SS Hauptsturmführer* (Captain) Frauendiener. I got assigned to the second one jointly with the *Junkers* Kuno Barocka, Manfred Obst, and Sepp Schütz. We were fully armed with brand-new 'koda-type assault rifles, hand grenades, and *Panzerfäuste*. By noon, the whole school had been moved out, leaving the city of *Leitmeritz* open for conquest by the Red Army and its liberation of the thousands of Jewish prisoners in the *KZ Theresienstadt* and in the *Kleine Festung*. Embarked on *Waffen-SS* trucks, we drove north-northeast toward yet another one of the Soviets' breakthrough spots. These twelve squads of *Junkers* with their officers, a total of about 140 signal corps officer candidates, were supposed to halt the advance of several Red Army guard divisions and tank brigades.

We were unloaded in the dense *Böhmerwald* forest and were stealthily advancing on one of its trails until we became aware of the crushing noise that was typical of the feared Soviet T-34 tanks storming from the east. Our squad leader, *Hauptsturmführer* Frauendienst, ordered us to disperse in the woods even though the tanks seemed to have stopped, with the turret of the first one already clearly visible. A flawless high-German's command voice arose in front of the lead tank, "Give yourselves up. You are surrounded. This is the advance unit of the Seidlitz army [German POWs who had been captured by the Soviets and had volunteered to serve under the captured General von Seidlitz, the former chief operating officer for Field Marshall Paulus at Stalingrad]. You will not be harmed after you put down your weapons." With the voice slowly coming closer and closer, we saw a soldier who wore a Red Army captain's uniform with the badge of the Seidlitz army. He stopped and waited, as did the tank. After a few seconds of hesitation, Frauendiener whispered to us not to trust him but to scatter into the forest toward the north-northwest.

We ran for it, followed by cannon and machine gunfire. Running deep into the forest, we desperately tried not to lose sight of each other. After a while, hearing no more sounds, we stopped and gathered in a small clearing, waiting and waiting with increasing anxiety for the whole squad to arrive. But only seven of us had made it, including the *Hauptsturmführer.* He gathered us around him, pulled out a slip of paper from his camo tunic, and read its contents: "I have been authorized by the commander of our Waffen-SS signals officers school to release you from your honorable service for your fatherland, Germany. Signed, Lieutenant Colonel Willy Kruft." We kept on running until sundown, hid in the densest part of the forest, boiled a saltless nettle soup, and posted guards but were unable to sleep. At sunrise, we were ordered to bury our weapons and to burn our *Soldbücher* (personal ID booklets) and then to take off toward the north into Saxony.

Just before noon, we suddenly came across what looked like a female person half buried under a pile of leaves, bleeding. Frauendiener approached her silently, touched her, and lifted her up. Waking up, she started sobbing and begging the officer to kill her, "I was a German Red Cross nurse, was caught as I was running toward the west, was raped many, many times, beaten, and left to die." We carried her gently to a little creek. Frauendiener washed her face, took off his tunic, and wrapped her into it. Then we continued carrying her along until the late evening, putting her on a bed made of dried oak leaves, and trying to feed her with a bit of hot nettle soup; but she wouldn't eat. We had a few hours of sleep with our eyes held open. When we got up, we discovered that she had died. Having no digging tools, we placed her into a very shallow grave. We saluted her—not anymore with the *Hitler-Gruß*—because she had become yet another innocent and totally guiltless victim of the madness of Adolf Hitler's totalitarian dictatorship.

Arriving in *Marienei*, a small village not far from the town of *Ölsnitz*, Frauendiener advised us to split up and then to go on individually in our own chosen direction. Only three of us decided to remain in the village as it was plowing and seeding time. Each of us was instantly hired by local farmers who gave us civilian clothing and fed us well to make up for our meager rations at officers' school. This part of Saxony was known as *Vogtland*, an area that, by the treaty of Yalta, was supposed to be occupied by the Soviets. But the Americans had arrived there first. Rumor soon had it that the Americans would be leaving before the end of June 1945. Having absolutely no desire to live in a communist regime and having recognized that the *Reichsdeutschen*—whether the military or the farmers—were not *my* people, I decided to take off early in July toward the west, stealthily trying to cross the armistice demarcation line between the Soviets in the east and the United States in the west. In the middle of the forest, I was suddenly stopped and accosted by a Red Armist who did not threaten me but asked if I had any watches.

I did indeed have one hidden deep in my pants pocket, my last souvenir from back home. I had no choice but to hand it over to him. In exchange, he let me go—possibly because I was dressed like a farm worker. After several hours of running west through the forest, I found myself facing a couple of US tanks on a two-lane road. I raised my arms, yelling *Fremdarbeiter* (foreign worker), and stopped. It was the first time in my life that I saw Americans. A couple of them looked at me up and down, made some comments about my dark eyes and dark hair, noticed my non-*Herrenmensch* appearance, and frisked me—found nothing, no papers. Then they ordered me to get up into one of their army trucks with several foreign worker types already seated. The trucks soon took off in the direction of the city of *Hof* (in Bavaria). They stopped at what seemed a major assembly point, unloaded us, and handed each of us a transit voucher (in my case, with my name on it from Hungary). It took me almost two weeks of hitchhiking, usually in US army trucks, to make it to *Salzburg*, where I stopped in one of the refugee camps, seeking to decide what to do. With the Red Army all over Eastern Europe, returning to the *Bánát* or the *Bácska* was out, as was the alternative of joining my remaining relatives in Budapest.

I remained for several days in the refugee camp, and having heard that the Tito partisans had invaded parts of southern Austria, I decided to continue to *Graz* to see what might happen, possibly even helping me to return home. Arriving in *Graz*, I learned that in one of its suburbs, *Wetzelsdorf*, the Brits had set up a POW camp for former *Waffen-SS* officers and soldiers. I also learned that they were treating the captured Germans very well, especially the *Waffen-SS*, apprehensive that there might be a war against the Titoists should the latter decide to push deeper in Austria (then the British occupation zone). So I decided to give myself up and, if necessary, partake in the defeat of Tito's godless communist regime. The Brits took me in, interrogated me, apparently found me innocent of any war crimes, fed me well, and let me partake in the daily physical exercise with the other POWs, most of whom *Reichsdeutsche*, including quite a few unrepentant Nazis. Having learned that I had been a ranking high school graduate and, unlike the *Reichsdeutschen*, also spoke several other languages and therefore potentially of use as a translator, one of the British sergeants encouraged me to start learning English. They even let me into some of their lectures on Britain's government and institutions. With their treatment always civil, I began feeling *free* for the first time since being drafted against my will into the *Waffen-SS*. There was no more *Lochkopf, Vollidiot, Zigeuner, Speckfresser*, and *Balkaneser*. Eventually, the Titoists backtracked, and I was released in August 1946. Since I didn't desire to return to Hungary and was also unwilling to go back to the *Bánát*, fearing that I would likely be shot by the Tito communists, the Brits decided to send me to the city of *Bamberg* in West Germany, even though they knew that I was not a *Reichsdeutscher* and that I did not consider them my people. Letting me go, the British POW release officer advised me that after arriving in *Bamberg*, I should report for reeducation to the local US military authority.

Arriving in *Bamberg*, I discovered that former *Waffen-SS* soldiers had become unemployable since the war, the local Germans desperately attempting to sever their (previously enthusiastic) past linkages with the Nazis. To my good fortune, during the course of my first appearance at the US military command, I was met by an officer, who shook my hand, introduced himself as Major Brown, CIC, and invited me to sit down. After several lengthy debriefings, he offered me a job as stove man in the kitchen of the local US Army company, which I happily accepted. Many more interviews followed, as did my denazification by the West German *Spruchkammer* (Denazification Board) late in 1947. Henceforth, I was permitted to enter the local university and to inscribe in law, economics, and political science while continuing my job as stove man and also in a hurry to improve my command of English.

However, deep inside myself, I was feeling unhappy about living in West Germany, longing more and more for my place of birth, even though I knew that I would never again return to it. By March 1948, I was ready to compromise. I'd leave *Bamberg* and its university and move to *Vienna*, where I would finish my studies, settle down, and really begin my new life (in spite of the fact that my family's prewar house on the Danube Canal had been totally destroyed). Having become a stateless refugee who had to wait for his Austro-Hungarian citizenship to be reconfirmed, I had no passport and was therefore forced to cross illegally the German-Austrian border. I arrived in Vienna, and my grandmother's pre-WWI *k.u.k.* linkage helped me to obtain a temporary work permit, enabling me to sustain myself while continuing my studies in *Vienna*'s world-renowned *Hochschule für Welthandel* (university for world trade).

Since I had already completed two years and had only one year left before graduation, I was becoming more and more willing to remain in *Vienna*. However, suddenly, my life took a change into a completely different, unanticipated direction.

CERTIFICATE OF DISCHARGE
Entlassungsschein

CONTROL FORM D.2.
Kontrollblatt D.2.

ALL ENTRIES WILL BE MADE IN BLOCK LATIN CAPITALS AND WILL BE MADE IN INK OR TYPESCRIPT.

I
PERSONAL PARTICULARS
Personalbeschreibung

Dieses Blatt muss in folgender Weise ausgefüllt werden:
1. In lateinischer Druckschrift und in grossen Buchstaben.
2. Mit Tinte oder mit Schreibmaschine.

SURNAME OF HOLDER: Lallier
Familienname des Inhabers

DATE OF BIRTH: 7.5.1925
Geburtsdatum (DAY/MONTH/YEAR)
Tag/Monat/Jahr

CHRISTIAN NAME: Albert
Vornamen der Inhabers

PLACE OF BIRTH: Botosch, Ungarn.
Geburtsort

CIVIL OCCUPATION: Student
Beruf oder Beschäftigung

FAMILY STATUS—SINGLE / Ledig
Familienstand
MARRIED / Verheiratet
WIDOWER / Verwitwet
DIVORCED / Geschieden

HOME ADDRESS Strasse: D.P. Camp
Heimatanschrift Ort: Salzburg
Kreis:
Regierungsbezirk/Land: Salzburg

NUMBER OF CHILDREN WHO ARE MINORS
Zahl der minderjährigen Kinder

I HEREBY CERTIFY THAT TO THE BEST OF MY KNOWLEDGE AND BELIEF THE PARTICULARS GIVEN ABOVE ARE TRUE.
I ALSO CERTIFY THAT I HAVE READ AND UNDERSTOOD THE "INSTRUCTIONS TO PERSONNEL ON DISCHARGE" (CONTROL FORM D.2. †)

Ich erkläre hiermit, nach bestem Wissen und Gewissen, dass die obigen Angaben wahr sind. Ich bestätige ausserdem dass ich die "Anweisung für Soldaten und Angehörige Militär-ähnlicher Organisationen" u.s.w. (Kontrollblatt D.1) gelesen und verstanden habe.

SIGNATURE OF HOLDER
Unterschrift des Inhabers

II
MEDICAL CERTIFICATE
Ärztlicher Befund

DISTINGUISHING MARKS
Besondere Kennzeichen

DISABILITY, WITH DESCRIPTION
Dienstunfähigkeit, mit Beschreibung

MEDICAL CATEGORY: Dienstfähig
Tauglichkeitsgrad

I CERTIFY THAT TO THE BEST OF MY KNOWLEDGE AND BELIEF THE ABOVE PARTICULARS RELATING TO THE HOLDER ARE TRUE AND THAT HE IS NOT VERMINOUS OR SUFFERING FROM ANY INFECTIOUS OR CONTAGIOUS DISEASE.

Ich erkläre hiermit, nach bestem Wissen und Gewissen, dass die obigen Angaben wahr sind, dass der Inhaber ungeziefervrei ist und dass er keinerlei ansteckende oder übertragbare Krankheit hat.

SIGNATURE OF MEDICAL OFFICER
Unterschrift des Sanitätsoffiziers

NAME AND RANK OF MEDICAL OFFICER IN BLOCK LATIN CAPITALS: Dr. Jeny, Lagerarzt
Zuname/ Vorname/ Dienstgrad des Sanitätsoffiziers
(In lateinischer Druckschrift und in grossen Buchstaben)

P.T.O.
Bitte wenden

† DELETE THAT WHICH IS INAPPLICABLE
Nichtzutreffendes durchstreichen

Chapter VI
The United Nations Refugee Organization and the Holocaust Survivors

Working for almost a whole year in construction, I heard that the *Vienna* headquarters of the International Refugee Organization (IRO) had been urgently looking for a multilingual person able to communicate preferably in Hungarian, German, French, at least one of the Slavic languages, and also some English to assist with the processing and emigration of many thousands of persons who had escaped from the countries under Soviet occupation and their imposed communist rule. I quickly dropped off my credentials (including my high school graduation diploma, the release form from the British POW camp, and the denazification certificate). Within two days, I was granted an interview with the IRO chief in *Vienna*, the US two-star general Woods. As I entered his office, he greeted me with "Ah, you're the former SS soldier, but I've received a report from Bamberg that you were trustworthy and willing to work for the United States government. If you really speak all those languages, I'd be willing to employ you as the officer responsible for the Canada desk with its huge backlog of applicants. If you really wish to redeem yourself, try by helping the Holocaust survivors find a new home. I'll give you permission to prove it to me, followed by a contract. If you do and are successful, I'll forgive you your wartime adventures. I might even consider you for immigration to the United States."

Suddenly, my six years of misery and hopelessness had come to an end. I had not only become a free person but had also been offered the trust of an American two-star general. Grateful for the opportunity, for almost two years, I devoted all my energies not only to earn the general's trust but also to secure visas for more than one thousand refugees, mostly Jewish, from Hungary and Czechoslovakia. Most cases involved Holocaust survivors, a large portion of whom had never been manual laborers but white-collar employees or independent businessmen. In quite a few cases, I faked their professional qualifications to read textile workers, shoemakers, and woodworkers, else they would not have received their immigration visas. In several cases, I had to find means and ways of getting the applicants to Salzburg for concluding interviews with the two Canadian immigration officers, Mr. Classen from Toronto and M. St. Laurent from Montreal—a dangerous undertaking because we had to swim or take a boat across the river Enns, the Soviet-American demarcation line, risking to be shot by the Red Army border guards. An alternative would have been across the Danube Bridge at Linz. It was also well guarded by the Soviets who were forever on the lookout for "capitalists" seeking to flee from Czechoslovakia and Hungary and make it to Canada or the United States.

I recall two occasions in which I had organized the smuggling out of two highly specialized experts in steelmaking and was lucky to barely ferret them across the demarcation line. Once in Vienna, both of them were within two days on their way to the United States, which earned me a high commendation from General Woods. He called me in, complimented me for my work, asked me to describe to him exactly how I had managed to get them across, and promptly suggested to me that I should start working for the OSS, which I refused. But he also asked me to describe what had happened in the antitank ditch and my role in it as a witness. I gave him my full account, describing my feelings of shame and guilt for not having had the courage to stop Viel's shooting. His answer was twofold, "You do not have to feel guilty, since you'd have been shot if you had intervened. Leave the killing at Leitmeritz behind you and continue doing your good work of helping the Jewish survivors of the Holocaust." I still fondly remember Mr. Goldstein, a former jeweler from Budapest, whom I classified as textile worker. I got him to Salzburg, got him the immigration visa, and—both of us back in Vienna—was surprised when he asked me if I could postpone his departure for at least three months since he still had some business to conclude.

"What kind of urgent business?" I asked.

He answered, "Importing Leica cameras from East Germany to get some capital for a jewelry store in Montreal." He got the extension. Upon my own arrival in Montreal, I discovered that he had not opened a jewelry shop but, instead, the coffee shop Pam-Pam on Stanley Street that soon became a very popular place for Jewish refugees from Budapest. Overall, most of my Holocaust survivors immigrated to Toronto, one of them an ultra orthodox rabbi with a family of seven children originally from Miskolc.

With Hungary, Czechoslovakia, and Yugoslavia having turned communist—and my entire family having lost all its possessions—I had no choice but to emigrate. I had finally become a free man, but one who was to remain burdened for the rest of his life with the feelings of shame and guilt and their cause: Hitler's *Herrenmensch* Nazis. Living in Canada and eventually highly educated, I was grateful to have been accorded the opportunity to redeem myself and to proceed to share in the joy of individual freedom as guaranteed by its Charter of Human Rights. It was in Canada that I realized that "man is only free if he has cleared his conscience," which I had attempted twice while still in Vienna. Before Christmas 1948, I revealed Viel's war crime to Dr. Sekyra, the abbot of the Benedictine monastery in *Vienna*, who advised me to stop thinking of the seven dead Jews, since my primary obligation was to start rebuilding my life. In April 1951, when Mr. Classen, the Canadian visa officer in Salzburg, offered me the chance to immigrate to Canada, I revealed Viel's crime a second time, even though fearing that he might refuse me if I did not but also fearing that he might refuse me if I did. However, wishing to be completely honest, I did tell him. He listened, took some notes, and said that he would pass on the information to the proper Canadian agency.

In October 1951, having completed my task as officer for the Canada desk, I resigned from the IRO; boarded the ship TSS *Nelly* in *Bremerhafen*; landed in *Quebec City* on November 11, 1951; took the train through *Montreal* to *Ajax*, Ontario; transferred to *London*, Ontario; and started rebuilding my life. Having no funds to spare, I was forced to leave behind in *Vienna* my wife, Henrietta, and our baby daughter, Renée. After working day and night for the first nine months in a factory, first in Ajax, Ontario, then in Montréal, I was able to pay for their flight. Happily settling down in Montreal, I undertook to attempt to prove to the government of Canada that its forgiveness and trust will be repaid in full. Working my way through university education, first at McGill, then at Columbia in New York City, and finally ending up with *le doctorat en sciences économiques* at *Sorbonne/Paris2*, I commenced my career as university professor. The academic highlights during thirty-six years of teaching were several books, promotion to full professor, and receiving Concordia's Certificate for Teaching Excellence.

Hitler's *Reichsdeutschen* had cost me first three lost years of my life in a war that they had forced upon me, then more than one year of POW status with the British, and then another two years of a desperate quest to survive the loss of my home and of my brother. The first four of those years had robbed me of the opportunity to develop my nascent intellectual ability and to earn the appropriate university degrees. Instead of permitting my brain to experience the joy of studying the writings of the great philosophers, it had been subjected to the repeated attempts by my *reichsdeutsch* Nazi superiors to inculcate it with the dehumanizing tenets of their *Herrenrassen* ideology (ideology of the master race), even though I had never been a member of the German *Volksgemeinschaft*. Instead of attempting to raise the innate quality of my ability to reason to its highest intellectual potential, they forced upon me (and millions of other adolescents) the war cries of their ideology, expressions of Adolf Hitler's absolute totalitarian power: *Ein Volk, ein Reich, ein Führer* (one people, one nation, one leader) and *Ich schwöre dir, Adolf Hitler, Treue und Gehorsam . . .* (I swear to you, Adolf Hitler, fealty and obedience . . .).

Instead of enabling me to bring my innate qualities as a human being to full bloom, the Hitlerites inducted me, only seventeen years old—totally against the Hague laws on war—into their *Waffen-SS* and forced upon me three darkest years of spiritual misery. In comparison with the dehumanizing treatment of my person by the **Waffen-SS superiors, becoming a POW in a British camp offered me the promise, for the first time since April 1942, of individual freedom and respect for my person.**

After my arrival in Canada (November 1951), looking for my brother has remained one of my continuing priorities. I approached several times the German Red Cross, the German war archives, and have even written pleading letters to several officials of the *Bundesrepublik*. The German Red Cross had not heard anything about my brother's fate. The officials of the German *Waffen-SS* archives claimed that no file containing the name of my brother had been found, as if he had never existed. But I doubted the veracity of this totally unexpected answer. It could not possibly be true because my brother had shown me at our last meeting at the end of December 1944 his copy of the *Soldbuch* (payment booklet) that contained all his personal data taken from his original *Waffen-SS* registry file. The answer by the archives office, if it was true, made me worry even more because my brother's missing or nonexistent personal file revealed the possibility of an absolute tragedy: death by hanging or shooting. The files of *Waffen-SS* personnel who had gone AWOL but were caught, tried, and promptly executed were usually destroyed—the ultimate revenge for such treacherous behavior by officers and soldiers of the *Waffen-SS*.

Thinking that my brother may have been shot dead by the SS military police—very same soldiers of the *Herrenrasse* (master race) who had drafted him against his will—has caused me prolonged agony and increasing frustration with the Germans. Trying to cope with it, I finally decided early this year to address formal personal letters to four of the most senior federal ministers of Germany, asking for an official search and confirmation. So far, I have yet to receive an answer from any of the four, which reminds me of the high-handed, aloof, disdaining behavior of their Nazi predecessors. The only other information about the possible fate of my brother had been a rumor in the mid-1970s that the remaining pitiful remnants of the *Prinz Eugen*, numbering fewer than two thousand, had capitulated to the Titoists at the city of *Celje* (in Slovenia) and were disarmed and that most of them were shot on the spot while the remaining several hundred had been tied together and driven into the river *Sava*, where they drowned. The remaining few dozen, possibly including my poor brother, were rumored to have been shipped to *Vršac* (*Bánát*'s third-largest city) and tortured to death.

The major effects of this forced recruitment and use of the *volksdeutsch* men as cannon fodder mainly on the eastern front was the destruction during 1944 to 1946 of almost the entire community, in particular in Tito's Yugoslavia. It involved the following numbers starting with the prewar count of about 1.5 million: more than 300,000 were recruited, of whom more than 200,000 were KIA, literally destroying most men in the age group of eighteen to forty; an estimated 250,000 perished in postwar Yugoslav concentration estimated 400,000 managed to escape to West Germany and Austria, of whom 200,000 were eventually permitted to emigrate as good, honest Christians to the United States and Canada.

INTERNATIONAL REFUGEE ORGANIZATION
AUSTRIA

Letter of appointment Local Employees
Angestellte

Wien IV.
11 Stalinplatz. Tel. U 46-5-80
1st January, 1951.

To: Mr. Adalbert Lallier

Dear Madam, (Sir),

1. This is to confirm your appointment with I.R.O. Headquarters Vienna as a *re-establishment* Clerk at a salary of ANS 650,- per month.

2. The hours of duty are 48 hours weekly. As the salaries are based on a 48 hours week, overtime will only be paid in excess of 48 hours.

3. Your appointment is subject to
   a) a probationary period of 1 month during which it may be terminated immediately. Thereafter it will be terminable on the last day or 15th of each month with 6 weeks notice in writing on either side.
   b) the clearance of Military Security Authorities. If a favourable clearance cannot be obtained your appointment will be terminable immediately even after expiration of the probationary period.

4. You will be eligible for annual leave after 6 months of employment with I.R.O. in accordance with the Austrian Labour Law (Angestelltengesetz).

5. If you are absent from duty on account of sickness you must report immediately. If absent more than 3 days a medical certificate must be produced, otherwise deduction will be made from your salary.

Yours faithfully

Chapter VII
Canada, My Destiny: Conscience and Redemption

My arrival in Canada—finally forever liberated from the horrors of Nazism and its claims to the racial superiority of the Germans— offered me the opportunity to make up for those lost years of intellectual striving: university and its emphasis on the development of creative, objective, but also critical reasoning. At first, with only my own urge to succeed to rely upon, I needed not only to secure the necessary funds but also to raise my knowledge of the English language to the required level of academic excellence, a task that would eventually involve another three years of undergraduate study. Just twelve years earlier, I had been labeled as *Lochkopf* and *Vollidiot* by my *Waffen-SS* superiors. However, in August 1954, the dean of admissions to McGill University (Dr. Solin, at that time, the only Jewish-Canadian dean at McGill) admitted me into the honors BA program in economics and political science at McGill University, thus offering me a long-coveted opportunity to make up for the ten intellectually lost years and an opportunity to demonstrate my gratitude to Canada for letting me in and granting me, in 1957, the citizenship.

Filled with enthusiasm and the desire to catch up, I worked part-time and studied day and night, devoting the required three undergraduate years to the joy of learning what I had completely missed out on: commencing with Plato and Aristotle, to evolution of the thoughts and propositions of the great thinkers of Western civilization; exploration of its economic, social, and political structures; as an honor student, delving into the many mysteries concerning its so-called Dark Ages, AD 850 to AD 1350; reflecting upon the causes and consequences of the emerging absolutisms, religious as well as monarchic—the holy church, papacy, *universitas*, the divine right to rule; Luther, Calvin, and the Huguenots, Grotius; Pufendorf's incipient views on human rights; the Enlightenment, with its emphasis on individualism, free will, and the propagation of constitutional government and democracy; the optimists and the pessimists concerning human nature of the British (Locke and John Stuart Mill and Hobbes and Malthus), the French (Montesquieu, Descartes, Voltaire, and Rousseau), and even quite a handful of Germans (Kant, Goethe, Hegel, and Karl Marx); nation-states and power politics versus the higher ethics and morality of regional alliances and the League of Nations; mythologies, ideologies, and indoctrination (communism, fascism, Nazism); the alternating duality of war and peace; the United Nations and the Charter of Human Rights.

I devoted three years of my life not only to obtain my first academic degree but also in attempting to find answers to the following question: How can we link the God of the Christians to the rise of Hitler's racist, evil empire of the German master race? How do we explain the rise of the USSR, the godless homeland of communism, to the status as the world's second most powerful state for forty years? How do we explain the tragedy of the Holocaust? How do we explain religious wars starting with the Reformation, right up to contemporary radical Islam? More personally speaking, how could God have possibly ever decided that I should be drafted into Hitler's *Waffen-SS*?

Among the numerous main themes that commanded my attention at both the undergraduate and the graduate level, the study of the evolution of human rights had become my primary interest. Its understanding and acceptance were not only necessary as one of the three bases of the formation of my character as an adult, but also because they might also enable me to recognize and better understand the absolute evil in Hitler's insane ideology of the *Herrenrasse* and his pathological quest to create the *Eintausendjähriges Reich der deutschen Nation*, the main purposes of which were to be the destruction of the Jewish people and the enslavement of the other *Untermensch* nations.

I graduated high enough on the dean's list to be offered by Columbia University in New York City a three-year graduate fellowship in economics, political science, as well as its world-renowned Russian Institute (the Cold War had moved to its apogee, requiring the training of a huge number of US-trained specialists on the USSR). At Columbia, in June 1959, I earned my MA in economics; in June 1960, my graduate diploma in international politics, Soviet studies; and in June 1961, a doctoral candidate in economics.

With my graduate diploma in Soviet studies, I was invited by the RAND Corporation, the spy agency of the United States Air Force, to accept a research post. I refused for two reasons: (a) after my release from the British POW camp, I swore never again to take any weapons into my hands; and (b) as a citizen of Canada, a peace-underwriting country, I couldn't help comparing America's undeclared war against Vietnam, an impoverished and underdeveloped country, with Nazi Germany's invasion and occupation of Yugoslavia, also an impoverished and undeveloped country, a serious breach of international law, a major war crime. My conscience—making me forever recall that I had had to wear the uniform of the *Waffen-SS* and also to witness Julius Viel's murder of those seven helpless Jewish *KZ* prisoners—had left me with no other choice. Even though I had already been offered a teaching post at Columbia College, I decided to postpone writing my doctoral dissertation and to return to Montreal, following an offer to teach both economics and politics at Loyola College. As an honors McGill graduate, I was also hoping to raise Loyola's academic standard to that of my *alma mater*.

Into my second year at Loyola, as behooves a university professor, I was already being offered research contracts by the federal and the provincial government, as well as by one of the major banks, one well-known international corporation, and UNCTAD (of the United Nations). Into my third year at Loyola, I was appointed dean of the evening division, with the mandate to create a complete BA and BCom undergraduate program for adults, a challenge that I was expected to accomplish within two years, after which, I would be granted a sabbatical to obtain my doctorate and to return to full-time teaching.

It was during my mandate as dean of the evening division that I was able to pay special attention to the next-door neighbors of Loyola College, the large number of Jewish persons living just a couple of bus rides away, many of whom veterans in their midtwenties who hadn't even graduated from high school. Having returned in one piece from the war, they were wishing to get a degree in commerce or in arts. Quite a few of these adults were Holocaust survivors who had immigrated to Canada and were trying, just like me, to complete their education that had been disrupted by Hitler's Nazis. Not having obtained a high school matriculation diploma, they had been refused by both McGill and Sir George University. To induce them to come to Loyola, a Catholic college that still insisted on four undergraduate courses in philosophy and four in Catholic theology, I appealed to the then rector Father Malone for permission to create a new admissions condition that would allow the young men and young women without a high school diploma to take up formal undergraduate studies toward a BCom and a BA. It was a "conditional admission" for applicants who lacked such a diploma but were at least twenty-one years old, with special consideration for veteran, an academic innovation that would soon spread all over Canada. The applicants were allowed to take two full-year courses on probation and would have to obtain at least a B grade in each in order to be granted full credit and to be admitted to their full undergraduate program. Aware of their not having been for years in formal schooling, I also arranged special tutors and tutorials that would enable them to catch up and to qualify for their degrees. After obtaining approval and making it public, the enrollment doubled within the first year.

My innovative and liberal program was receiving accolades from the Jewish community and provided the basis for an evening studies in BCom, especially in accounting, assisted by Professor Larry Bessner, chair of the day program of the Accounting Department. However, my attempt to develop the evening BA degree program was lagging behind until I discovered the main reason. Persons of the Jewish faith were having problems being forced to take Loyola's required four courses in Catholic philosophy and Catholic religion. So I again went to Father Malone to ask for permission to introduce two electives in the Jewish religion and to engage a rabbi as their teacher. His reaction was to accuse me of sabotaging the well-established program in Catholic education, but he relented after I was able to convince him that the evening division's enrollment was bound to increase by another 50 percent and that the local Jewish community would show itself appreciative and would respond positively to Loyola's need for funding. So my rapidly increasing number of Jewish students got their first rabbi and was eventually exempt from those eight Catholic religion courses, which were soon replaced with electives including Jewish religion courses. Many of my initially admitted mature Jewish students on probation had successfully graduated, and I have developed a longtime friendship with quite a few of them.

One particularly interesting case had been that of Dr. Steven Korda, son of Hungarian Holocaust survivors, who had come to me in August 1964, begging for admission as he had been prevented from high school graduation. He was working full-time in his father's photo store. I granted him conditional admission into political science. Four months later, he obtained grades of A in both initial courses and was admitted to the BA in political science, first taking courses at night and finishing full-time in his senior year—a brilliant and highly promising young man. After his graduation, I wrote for him a personal letter of recommendation to the law faculty of Université de Montréal, even though his French was poor. But working very hard, he obtained his bachelor in law, passed the Quebec bar exams, and entered the law profession. With his extraordinary intelligence, sharp mind, and desire to learn, he asked me, about twelve years later, for assistance for his admission to the doctoral program at the Sorbonne/Paris2 in Paris, France. Once again I personally recommended him and stood by him when he wrote his doctoral dissertation, went on to defend it successfully, and succeeded in obtaining a *docteur en droit*—truly an extraordinary achievement by a young man whose parents had barely survived the Holocaust, finding their new home in Canada.

A second remarkable achievement following his admission on probation into the BCom involved a seventy-five-year-old Canadian-born Jewish gentleman, CEO of one of Canada's most renowned chains of women's fine clothing, also a millionaire. He had heard of my interest in helping Jewish people and, not having finished high school, arrived literally begging for admission, saying that he wished to die as holder of an undergraduate degree. He was admitted on probation (with lots of help and encouragement), did well enough to continue through seven years of evening courses, and got his BCom, the happiest and most grateful rich man that I had ever seen. Very much to my regret, he died soon after realizing the great dream of his life.

Devoting all my energies to fulfill my mandate within two years, I increased the evening division's enrollment from the initial two hundred to more than one thousand, securing significant funding from the Jewish community, and took my academic leave in 1965–66. Upon returning from Columbia University, having passed all my doctoral work except for the dissertation, I rejoined the Department of Economics and added, part-time evenings, political science, involved in teaching, administration, and research. During the 1970s, I was promoted to associate professor, followed by several major senior-level research contracts with banks, with Alcan Shipping Limited, and with UNCTAD, the economic development division of the United Nations.

In the mid-1970s, upon the recommendation to the Hungarian Orthodox Jewish community by Hirsh Cohen, who had been my assistant as dean of the evening division, I was invited by the directors of the recently formed Yeshiva Gedolah Merkaz Hatorah to become the school's director of lay studies, required by Quebec's Department of Education if the school was to become fully accredited—speaking French in order to negotiate with the department officials being a primary consideration. My assignment would be part-time, five days per week in the afternoon. I was delighted to accept for two years and had a wonderful time watching the kids devote themselves to the Jewish studies in the morning and taking on the lay courses in the afternoon. Evidently, hiring the teachers for the lay program studies, especially for English, history, and mathematics, was a challenge that I was able to cope with because many young Americans with appropriate graduate degrees had escaped from being drafted into the Vietnam War and were available.

Yet watching the kids study an average of eight hours a day with only a tiny luncheon break, I got worried about the complete lack of physical education but was finally able to convince the rabbi who

was in charge to set aside one hour per week for sports. In no time, the Americans and I were able to create a baseball team right there behind the buildings, watching with delight the happiness of the kids when hitting and chasing the baseball. It was the most memorable time in my desire to contribute to the local Jewish community's ability to ease the memory of the horror of the Holocaust and to strengthen their desire to overcome it.

During the early 1980s, I was engaged as professor, researcher, and international consultant. I had also decided to complete my doctorate in economics by transferring my Columbia doctoral credits to the Sorbonne/Paris2, France's most renowned university, during my sabbatical year, 1977–78. My dissertation, *L'Intégration et la désintégration économique: L'histoire, la théorie, la politique,* two volumes, 710 pages, was adjudged "excellent," enabling me as a fifty-five-year old candidate finally to realize my lifelong dream. During 1982–83, I was then engaged in postdoctoral studies at the London School of Economics and Political Science, exploring the economics of one of Karl Marx's most difficult books, *Die Grundrisse* (*The Foundations*), and had it published under the title *The Economics of Marx's Grundrisse,* by Macmillan, London, in 1982. But the murder in the antitank ditch had remained anchored in my conscience.

Back in Montreal, I phoned Steven Korda and asked him to help me find Julius Viel. He warned me again about the most likely repercussions, especially within Montreal's Jewish community.

But I kept on insisting until he promised me to invite a well-known American Jewish Nazi hunter to come to Montreal and to listen to my story. While waiting, I resumed my full-time teaching.

It seemed to me that I was the only former *Waffen-SS* soldier who had been granted the privilege of studying at several universities of universal renown, not only in Canada, but also in the United States, in England, and even in France. My lifelong quest to catch up with the lost years that the *reichsdeutsch-Herrenrasse* had forced upon me had *almost* come to full fruition in Canada, my chosen home, the country that had given me its trust and had offered its welcome. The top-level Concordia University's administrator and most of my professional colleagues at Loyola College and Concordia University had rewarded me for my commitment and contributions. In August 1986, I was promoted to full professor and was also happy and proud to have received one of the only five Certificates for Teaching Excellence.

But why *only almost*? Even though professionally highly recommended and socially very engaged (e.g., I served for four years as president of the Montreal Austrian Society, but I had never been a member of Montreal's Society of the Danube Swabians, a postwar polite substitute term for the designation *Volksdeutscher* during World War II), during the almost four decades of striving to make up for the lost time as well as to redeem myself, my conscience would never leave me alone—not only because of the tragic loss of my brother, but also because of recalling, especially during the night hours, the anguished, frightened faces of those seven Jewish victims who were killed by Julius Viel without my being able to save them. These repeated pangs of conscience had at times turned into pure agony that involved the trade-off of the question of natural justice for those that had been murdered versus the security of my own person.

I had been advised by the Canadian immigration officer, Mr. Classen, that, living in Canada, I should not reveal my *Waffen-SS* past. However, by the mid-1990s, my conscience succeeded in convincing me to turn to my former student Steven Korda, the Canadian-educated lawyer and son of Hungarian Jews who had survived the Holocaust. He was very surprised about my story, but as a close friend, he felt obliged to remind me—if I did make it public—of the possible threat to my academic standing and even my retirement. He urged me to have my reason prevail over my conscience.

However, in July 1995, fate intervened once again. In the wake of the Soviet pullout from Eastern Europe and the ensuing establishment of Western-style democratic governments in that region, I was sent by CESO (Canadian Executive Service Organization), a branch of CIDA (Canadian International Development Agency), as a senior financial adviser to the government of the Czech Republic for a six-week series of seminars on the operation of commercial banks and financial institutions in Canada, with the purpose of providing assistance in their attempts to change from the Soviet-style system of banks to our system of financial capitalism. By mid-July, I found myself in Prague, a distance of only eighty kilometers from *Theresienstadt* (renamed *Teresin*) and *Leitmeritz* (renamed *Litomerice*) and the antitank ditch. I wasn't surprised at all to find myself, as early as on the second weekend, taking a bus for the two-hour ride and stepping out at the main gate of the former concentration camp that had been converted into a permanent memorial. All my instincts were urging me to attempt to find the exact site of the killing so that I could kneel down and beg for forgiveness. I returned two more times, really resolved that upon my return, I would follow my conscience and go public with Julius Viel's war crime. But I first had to discover if Viel was still alive.

Early in January 1996, CESO/CIDA once again got in touch with me, with a mandate to proceed to Thailand's Sripatum University in Bangkok, to study the feasibility of creating an English-language undergraduate degree program in international business and communications—a six-week mandate—and to submit the respective recommendations. I submitted a positive evaluation before the end of August 1996 and returned to Montreal to resume my teaching. Early in 1997, Steven Korda phoned me, reporting that Steven Rambam, American citizen and already a renowned Nazi hunter, would like to meet with me about Julius Viel.

In February 1997, I received a letter from the president of Sripatum University confirming their approval of my recommendations concerning the creation of the new program and offering me the post as its first director on a one-year contract. Even though I had been assured of a two-year contract renewal at Concordia University, I was quickly granted a one-year leave of absence and was planning to leave early in June. Late in May, Korda phoned me about Rambam passing through Montreal at the end of

May and wishing to talk to me at Montreal Württemberg Airport, which we did. Listening to my description of the killings in the antitank ditch, Rambam agreed to look for Julius Viel. At the end of September 1997, Rambam phoned me urgently in Bangkok. He had discovered Julius Viel still alive and living in Württemberg.

My moment of truth had finally arrived. Do I prefer continuing the struggle with my problems of conscience? Or do I sue Julius Viel for the multiple murders of those seven Jewish KZ prisoners? After my final soul-searching, I decided in favor of my conscience and promptly asked Rambam to continue his investigation and to report back to me. A couple of days later, I also phoned the Simon Wiesenthal Holocaust Center in *Vienna*, informing Mr. Wiesenthal about Julius Viel and asking him to contact the German (*Bundesrepublik*) war crimes office and to initiate the proceedings. I also wrote a letter to the former *Waffen-SS* Brigadier Otto Kumm, the second-to-last former commander of the *Prinz Eugen*, describing to him the tragedy in the antitank ditch and asking about his views on war crimes. Surprisingly, he answered, averring that *Kameradschaft endet, wo Kriegsverbrechen begangen werden* (comradeship ends when war crimes are committed, thus, in fact, lending his support to my decision to sue.

At the end of November 1997, I asked for and received a one-week furlough from Sripatum, flew back to Montreal, and had a final session with Steven Korda. On this occasion, he once again emphasized the potential threat to my person if I went public: upheavals in the Jewish community demanding my removal from Canada, possible loss of my senior teaching post at Concordia, loss of many friends, material and property losses, neo-Nazi threats (*Verräter*, traitor), being branded a liar, and the ensuing social ostracism. Instead of listening to him, I asked him to arrange a private but recorded interview in the presence of Rambam, Poupko (one of Montreal's chief rabbis), an Israeli secret service agent, a member of the press, and Korda. An official public announcement followed the next day.

The principal considerations that made me decide to go public no matter what might be the consequences emanated from two fundamental concerns that both my reason and my conscience had struggled with since the terror in the antitank ditch: (1) Which apparently embedded forces in the nature of the German nation had caused them to act as history's most destructive savages? And under which circumstances would they be most likely to reemerge?

(2) What kind of punishment would be required in order to ensure that the perpetrators of massive war crimes like the Holocaust will be tried according to the principles of natural justice?

With the press releases in Montreal's and Ottawa's newspapers of my "confession," Steven Korda's apprehension was confirmed: massive uproar in the Jewish community, including the demand that I should be deported and phone calls by former friends who had suddenly given up on me. There were no messages from Concordia, but there were also a few laudations, including Rabbi Poupko's, who referred to me as a "man of courage and conviction." Neither was there a response from the federal government (as a matter of fact, upon my inquiry a few days later with the Canadian War Crimes Commission in Ottawa, I received a confirmation that "Adalbert Lallier's name had not shown up in any of the submissions to the Commission").

Convinced that my promised two-year contract with Concordia would be renewed, I returned to Bangkok. Several weeks later, I was informed (Rambam, Wiesenthal Center) that the Viel case had been taken up by the *Bundesrepublik* war crimes court.

Having completed my mandate at Sripatum, I received a letter of acknowledgment from its president and returned to Montreal, end of May

1998. A few weeks later, I was invited by the German consulate in Montreal to appear for my first hearing, with the purpose of confirming the identity of Julius Viel and of proceeding to the next legal stage—his trial.

In August 1998, I was hit by a totally unexpected catastrophe. In an official letter, the Concordia academic vice rector (Canadian of the Jewish faith) informed me that my teaching contract would not be renewed, thus unfairly ending my teaching career of almost forty years and forcing me to retire against my will. My pleading even at the highest level remained unsuccessful. However, a few days later, the *Ottawa Citizen* published an article that claimed that "Professor Lallier's contract had not been renewed in response to a letter from several members of the Economics Department that he may be presumed to have been a war criminal and that his presence in the department was therefore not wanted." Regaining my confidence, I attempted once again to have my contract renewal confirmed, but to no avail. I turned to my lawyer for a possible court action. Soon a compromise solution was agreed upon: I would receive an official apology as well as a small compensation. Eventually, a final negotiated settlement—that included an official statement by the university that I had been a "valuable member of the community"— was arrived at, leaving me disheartened yet also proud to have been bestowed the Certificate for Excellence in Teaching.

In August 1999, I was invited by a German TV documentary station to return to *Theresienstadt*, accompanied by a German television of three, paid for the trip but without any other compensation. The purpose was to find the antitank ditch and the site of the killing, to visit the Small Fortress, to contact available witnesses, and to visit the museum of the former concentration camp, looking for written evidence—the whole to be accomplished within two weeks, including a visit to Prague. Evidently, I consented and returned to the plains, looking for the tragic site, finding it, and then visiting the cemetery of the murdered thousands of Jewish victims, expressing homage and praying. While no witnesses were found, we were lucky to discover in the museum a little black book that had been written by one of the Czech prisoners of the day-in, day-out events since 1941, including accounts, in names and numbers, of the prisoners who had been killed.

The booklet had been hidden for years by its writer but was eventually returned to the museum, a forever reminder of the Nazis Final Solution. I took the book into my then shivering hands, quickly leafed through to mid-March 1945, and discovered, dated March 19, 1945, twenty-six entries for murdered *KZ* prisoners, including the names of the seven that I had witnessed being shot dead by Julius Viel exactly at 2:00 p.m. Several photos of the antitank ditch were also in that little black book. The documentary crew took photographs of the entries, of the museum, of the graves, and of the antitank ditch as proof for the war crimes court that the murder had really happened and even listing the names of those who were killed: Baruch Joshua, born 25 November 1921; Friedmann Robert, born 8 November 1899; Kaufmann Wilhelm, born 9 September 1915; Kras Ladislav, born 1 September 1917 (the giant); Schütz Victor, born 1 July 1902; Severin Klastimir, born 15 December 1898; and Stern Victor, born 19 September 1891. Copies of these names were instantly faxed from the director of the museum to the German war crimes court in Ravensburg. All in all, I had obtained recorded proof of the murder, confirming that I was not imagining and was not lying.

The timetable of my involvement in the war crimes trial of Julius Viel was as follows:

August 1995: My CESO research mandate in Prague, six weeks, including my weekend trip to the *KZ Theresienstadt*.

August 1996: My first visit to Bangkok, Thailand, on behalf of CIDA, two weeks.

May 30, 1997: My first meeting with Steven Rambam at Montréal's airport, arranged, upon my request, by Steven Korda.

June 4, 1997: Rambam phoned me that Julius Viel was still alive in Germany.

June 5, 1997: My departure for Bangkok to set up for Sripatum University its first English undergraduate program in international business, a one-year mandate.

Mid-July 1997: My phone call from Bangkok to Mr. Wiesenthal in Vienna about Julius Viel.

End of November 1997: My three-day return to Montreal for the official interview about Julius Viel. Present were Rabbi Poupko, Steven Rambam, Steven Korda, a Mossad agent, and a video specialist.

End of April 1998: Return from Thailand, mandate accomplished.

Mid-May 1998: First official interrogation about Julius Viel at the German consulate in Montreal.

End of May 1998: Informed by the VP academic that I must leave Concordia University.

Mid-September 1998: From a journalist in Ottawa, I received a copy of a letter that five professors from the Department of Economics had written at the end of April to Concordia's academic VP, asking for my immediate release for "being a war criminal." To me, this letter was proof why I had been "fired" in May. I confronted the VP academic, but he denied to have even seen the courses that I had been offered after my return from Thailand but was not allowed to teach. In return, I had to agree to my formal retirement, causing me much disappointment and anguish.

Summer 1999: Two official witness appearances in Ravensburg, Germany. The trial was just about to begin.

September 1999: Second visit, accompanied by a German TV crew, to the *KZ Theresienstadt* and the site of the murder.

October 1999: Confrontation in Stuttgart with Julius Viel, required for beginning of the trial.

Years 2000: Two appearances as chief witness at the war crimes trial of Julius Viel.

April 3, 2001: Julius Viel's trial ended with the verdict of twelve years of imprisonment.

THE TRUSTEES OF COLUMBIA UNIVERSITY
IN THE CITY OF NEW YORK

TO ALL PERSONS TO WHOM THESE PRESENTS MAY COME GREETING
BE IT KNOWN THAT

ADALBERT GUILLAUME LALLIER

HAVING COMPLETED THE STUDIES AND SATISFIED THE REQUIREMENTS
FOR THE DEGREE OF

MASTER OF ARTS

HAS ACCORDINGLY BEEN ADMITTED TO THAT DEGREE WITH ALL THE
RIGHTS PRIVILEGES AND IMMUNITIES THEREUNTO APPERTAINING
IN WITNESS WHEREOF WE HAVE CAUSED THIS DIPLOMA TO BE SIGNED
BY THE PRESIDENT OF THE UNIVERSITY AND BY THE DEAN OF THE
FACULTIES OF POLITICAL SCIENCE PHILOSOPHY AND PURE SCIENCE AND
OUR CORPORATE SEAL TO BE HERETO AFFIXED IN THE CITY OF NEW YORK
ON THE FIRST DAY OF JUNE IN THE YEAR OF OUR LORD
ONE THOUSAND NINE HUNDRED AND SIXTY

McGill University
MONTREAL, CANADA

obtained the degree of

M. A.

from McGill University

Signed on behalf of the Faculty of Arts and Science and the University.

THE TRUSTEES OF COLUMBIA UNIVERSITY
IN THE CITY OF NEW YORK

TO ALL PERSONS TO WHOM THESE PRESENTS MAY COME GREETING
BE IT KNOWN THAT

ADALBERT G. LALLIER

HAVING SATISFIED THE REQUIREMENTS OF THE TWO YEAR GRADUATE
COURSE PRESCRIBED BY THE RUSSIAN INSTITUTE WITH
A MAJOR CONCENTRATION IN

ECONOMICS

HAS ACCORDINGLY BEEN GRANTED

THE CERTIFICATE OF THE RUSSIAN INSTITUTE

IN WITNESS WHEREOF WE HAVE CAUSED THIS CERTIFICATE TO BE
SIGNED BY THE DIRECTOR OF THE RUSSIAN INSTITUTE AND OUR
CORPORATE SEAL TO BE HERETO AFFIXED IN THE CITY OF NEW
YORK ON THE NINETEENTH DAY OF DECEMBER IN THE YEAR
OF OUR LORD ONE THOUSAND NINE HUNDRED AND SIXTY TWO

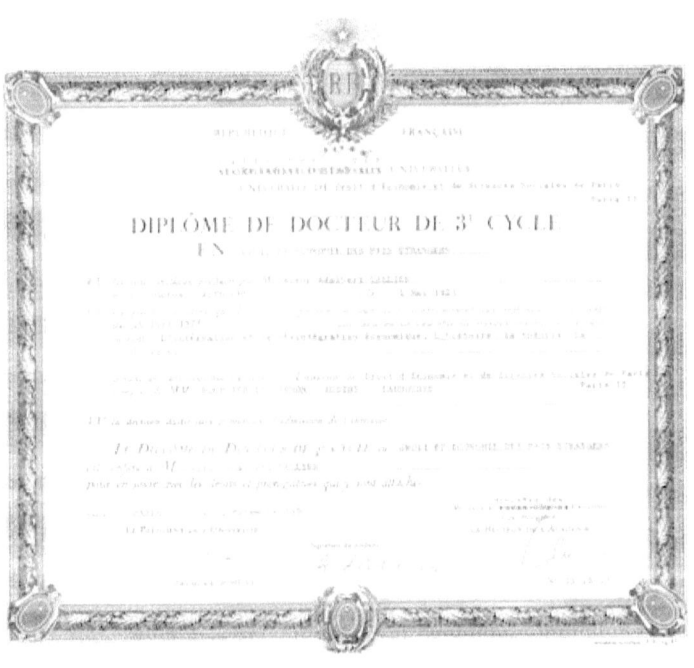

PROMOTION TO THE RANK OF PROFESSOR

ADALBERT G. LALLIER Doctorat (Paris II) joined the Department of Economics in 1960. He was promoted to the rank of Associate Professor in 1969. Dr. Lallier is regarded as one of the best teachers in the University. In 1985, he was a recipient of the J.W. O'Brien Distinguished Teaching Award. His teaching methods and his innovative curriculum developments have marked him as a superior example of a university teacher. In addition, Dr. Lallier has done important research in the area of applied economics, especially in the fields of trade, transportation and international finance. In his twenty-six years at Concordia, Dr. Lallier has also served on numerous committees and decision-making bodies within the University.

Chapter VIII
The "Eye for an Eye": Revenge versus Retribution

According to Professor Gary Evans, of Ottawa University, the four references to the "eye for eye, tooth for tooth, hand for hand, foot for foot" are found in the following phrases in the Old Testament:

1. Exodus 21:24—"Eye for eye, tooth for tooth, hand for hand, foot for foot"

2. Leviticus 24:20—"Eye for eye, tooth for tooth, fracture for fracture"

3. Deuteronomy 19:21—"Eye for eye . . . show no pity"

4. Matthew—"An eye for an eye . . ."

In Professor Evans's view, the private and highest-level viewpoints had come from the offices of the chief rabbi of Jerusalem and the minister of justice. Their messages were almost identical. For many centuries, Jewish teaching has emphasized that the literal biblical reference has lost its value, having been replaced by the idea of justice as the victim receiving the value of his loss she or he had sustained, the indemnity payments by postwar German governments and distributed by the Israeli Ministry of Welfare. This process of humanization has found its expression in Israel's contemporary legal system: the law is how our society operates. It has to prevail, even though it seems an unfair burden upon those who are victims or relatives of victims. It was the suspension and perversion of law that made the Nazis possible. When the Nazis were crushed, law reasserted its rightful place in the world. To allow the killing by an Israeli, to wreak vengeance, is to deny the law.

Reflecting upon the dictum in the Old Testament, one may ask if retribution has indeed replaced vengeance in all cases, including the killing, by agents of the various government secret services, of persons who are suspected as terrorists who had killed local citizens. If it is presumed that (financial) retribution is morally acceptable even in such situations, the presumed killer, when caught, would get away with a prison sentence no matter how many victims he had killed. But what if the killer is caught in the act of killing by a secret service agent who is armed but needs to abide by the *law*, probably at the cost of losing his own life? Interpreting carefully the meaning of modern Israeli jurisprudence, the *law* actually means that the Jewish person that is seeking to take revenge on a Nazi killer of her father is viewed as having broken *the law* and must expect to be severely punished. Also, what if the presumed killer is set free for lack of conclusive evidence and the victim's relative is punished by not receiving any retribution payments? Will she or he really consider letting the verdict that will let the presumed killer go free, to be a *just* verdict, the result of the process of natural justice?

With these reflections in my mind, I was getting ready to travel to Ravensburg and to act at the German war crimes court as its principal witness, wondering not only about the length of the trial but also about the final verdict. I knew that death penalties had been abolished in the European Union. But personally, having witnessed the cruelty in Viel's murder of those seven Jewish prisoners, in my mind the only just verdict would be imprisonment for life without any chance of parole, plus full restitution to the heirs for the loss of life and for loss of income.

I must confess here that my teaching career and accomplishment had filled me with a meaningful purpose in life that made me feel as having received the joy of a partial compensation for the bitter years under Hitler's *reichsdeutsch* whip during the war, even though the feelings of shame and guilt about the killing of those seven innocent Jewish prisoners had continued unabated. In intellectual response to these painful subjective pressures, I decided to take some time to study the system of jurisprudence of ancient Israel, in particular, the era of Kings David and Solomon, and its correspondence with the system of jurisprudence in modern Israel, hoping that reading them might help me answer more rationally the question, what would be the appropriate verdict for Viel's murder of the seven Jewish prisoners?

Chapter IX
The Trial of Julius Viel: Anticipation versus Reality

The several pretrial interrogations by the Chief Prosecutor Kurt Schrimm and his team had prepared me both spiritually and mentally for the trial, an important condition for someone who had been before a court only three times in his long life: in 1948, in Bamberg's denazification court; in 1957, in Montreal's citizenship court; and in 1985, in Montreal's municipal court, for a traffic violation. Each time, I received a favorable verdict. In Bamberg, I had been quickly denazified for two reasons: I had been drafted against my will and was still a minor; and not having been a true volunteer but being *forced* to serve in the *Waffen-SS* by the Nuremberg judgment, I could not be considered a war criminal. In Montreal, the traffic cop had erred in filling in his summons. As already demonstrated, in the summer of 1944, I had also been an involuntary witness at the trial of a *Volksdeutsher Waffen-SS* soldier who had gone AWOL, had returned, and was condemned for instant execution by shooting—all of it a reflection of the Nazi system's perversion of the process of natural justice.

In Bamberg, since my release from a British prisoner of war camp in July 1946 and even though already inscribed to study law, politics, and economics at the local university, I had very little knowledge of how the system of law in West Germany, which was still occupied by the Western allies, was operating. But I was told that it was indeed "democratic" and that its judges, its public prosecutors, and the involved attorneys were all dressed in black. But by 1999, I had taken at the Sorbonne/Paris2 several courses in law and international law, convinced that my academically trained intellect was at the very least equal to that of the judges, the prosecutors, and the defense lawyers at the war crimes court in Ravensburg. I did not have to feel insecure or even frightened during the entire course of the trial of Julius Viel. I also knew that the truth was on my side, as was my honesty.

Neither would the numerous audience bother me, a professor who had usually been facing classes of well over one hundred students. But I was somewhat disturbed by the fact that most of the persons in the audience were expected to be Germans, recalling how unfriendly and even hostile they had been after my arrival as a refugee in Bamberg. However, they might have changed, recognizing that to try a presumed war criminal— especially a former *Waffen-SS* officer— was the right, moral thing to do. In the worst possible setting, I'd be surrounded and protected by the cops from the *Sicherheitsamt* (security office), the same officers who had been watching over me since my previous two arrivals. Last but not least, I'd also been told that members of the audience would involve Holocaust survivors and officials from Jewish organizations, as well as a small group of *Waffen-SS* veterans and, most likely, several neo-Nazis.

Overall, I was feeling motivated and optimistic, trusting the integrity of the judges and the chief prosecutor, for even though they were speaking the German dialects of their Nazi forefathers, they were representing the new democratic *Bundesrepublik* member of the European Union and a fully fledged partner in NATO (and therefore a friend of Canada).

The war crimes trial of Julius Viel lasted for almost two years, requiring my presence on two occasions. On both occasions, federal security agents were waiting for me at the airport and brought me in an official car to my "safe" hotel in Ravensburg, with agents up front day and night (since I had received two telephone calls that threatened that I would be killed: one, if I did talk, and the other, if I did not).

On the first day of the trial, the Great Hall of the Court of Justice in Ravensburg was jammed full with a half dozen Holocaust survivors, several white-haired old men but blue eyes who looked like *Waffen-SS* veterans, a much larger group from the media, several male and female lawyers who were observing the goings-on, and many younger women and men who seemed curious to find out what real *Waffen-SS* officers might have looked like back in 1945.

The chief judge, *Herr* Hermann Winkler, did not seem to mind photos being taken by the audience. The chief prosecutor, Kurt Schrimm, was shuffling his documents, while the chief defense counsel, Ingo Pfliegner, was busy shifting his eyes back and forth from Viel to Lallier. From reading the charge—*the wanton and unprovoked murder of seven Jewish KZ prisoners*—to asking Lallier to describe the murder, the atmosphere in the hall remained tense but respectful, to be repeated during the two-week deliberations during December. Not having, since the end of the war, ever been in a German court (even though I had witnessed one of the *Waffen-SS Schnellgericht* trials), I gained the impression that the chief judge would treat me fairly and with respect, emulated by *Herr* Schrimm's reading parts of my testimony and asking that I confirm or be more specific and eventually referring to me as highly intelligent and granting me full credence.

On the contrary, most of the journalists and the other members of the media were either unsympathetic, if not outright adversarial. For example, a male journalist, Willy Roos, expressed himself very sarcastically about the veracity of my testimony; while yet another male journalist, writing for the *Frankfurter Rundschau*, went to great lengths to disparage my character and presence, again referring, using Nazi terminology, to me as *Volksdeutscher*, a second-class person, without any reference to my academic degrees from several of the world's top-ranked universities: (The accuser) is "theatrical, pretentious, narcissistic, with a foaming mouth, badly in need of recognition . . . all of it fiction, a process about an event that had never happened." A third journalist, Gisela Friedrichsen, having a reputation as democratic Germany's foremost criminal court reporter, appeared particularly prejudiced and even vile in her report on my presence at the court. Here's a brief summary, point by point (derived from her articles in *Der Spiegel* on March 5, 2001, and February 25, 2002):

- Friedrichsen referred to me as *Donauschwabe*, even though my mother was Hungarian and I graduated from a Hungarian high school and had never been a member of the German minority.

- She insisted that "*Lalliers Lebelslauf ist unübersichtlicher*" (Lallier's CV is suspiciously unclear).

- She insisted that "*Lallier sei zur Waffen-SS gekommen*" (that Lallier had come to the Waffen-SS), instead of acknowledging that I had been drafted against my will and was only seventeen years old.

- She referred to my feelings of *Schuld und Schande* (guilt and shame) as *literarischer Stoff* (literary stuff).

- She insisted that no other witnesses confirmed the killing, even though Manfred Obst did.

- She used the phrase "*der angeblich einzige Tatzeuge und möglicher Tatbeteiligter*" (the allegedly only witness and therefore as possible accessory to the murder).

- She used the really insulting phrase "*schäumende Wortkaskade*" (foaming froth cascade of words).

- She stated that *"Lallier entkam nach Kanada"* (Lallier *"escaped"* to Canada), as if I had been a war criminal, even though I had obtained a legitimate immigration visa.

- She asked, *"Wie wurde er vom Mulifűhrer zum Offiziersanwärter?"* (How would he have made it from mule attendant to an officer candidate?) It implied that I must have been an ardent Nazi or officer's pet.

- She insinuated that I had "contacted Dr. Korda *after* having heard of Steven Rambam's ads in Canada looking for German war criminals," which was a lie because it was I who contacted Rambam.

- She insisted that "Lallier invented the story about *Julius Viel* in order to save himself from being declared a war criminal in Canada, the loss of his citizenship, and deportation," which was a lie and was definitively refuted by the chief judge and the chief prosecutor.

- Her overall biased behavior was typical of Nazi Germans toward the "subraces," without even having the fairness to interview me and do some real fact-finding. Noticing my Hungarian accent when speaking German alone would have had her recognize that I couldn't possibly have been a *Donauschwabe*.

All in all, at the court in Ravensburg, I wasn't impressed—except for the judges and the chief prosecutor—about the Germans who were present, especially the media's haughtiness and unfair accusations that reminded me so much of their Third Reich predecessors.

During the entire course of the trial, the most insulting and the most disparaging words and expressions were thrown against my person by

Viel's senior defense counsel, *Herr* Ingo Pfliegner. In his final summary, he accused me of lying about Viel and the murder in seeking to save myself from being brought to court for having been the "real killer," who, as a former war criminal, was about to be expelled from Canada—an artificial construction I had been engaged in after having been approached by Steven Rambam. Pfliegner's summary also emphasized that I had been the only witness claiming to have *seen* the killing while all the former officer candidates who had been summoned before the court were claiming to have seen nothing and heard nothing.

Over and beyond these specific accusations, there were also many moments in Ravensburg during which I was feeling treated as if I had been the murderer. But the chief judge and the chief prosecutor had believed my testimony and gave me full credit for my testimony, afterward themselves being accused by the two defense attorneys, by most of the German press, and by neo-Nazis as "accomplices in a trial that should never have taken place."

DE LA LIEUX

UNFORGIVEN

Chapter X
Insights into Hitler's Nazism versus the Ethics of Natural Justice

After my last presence in Ravensburg, I returned to Canada feeling like a pariah accused of breaking Hitler's oath and thereby betraying my former comrades who were still hanging on to it. The disparaging of my person was continued even after the final verdict of twelve years in prison. Viel's defense counsel, supported by most German media, filed an appeal claiming that I had not only lied but also managed to convince the judges and the prosecutor that the killing had taken place even though it had never happened, that I had been the criminal and Viel the innocent victim of my accusation. In consequence, my return to Montreal was wrought in uncertainty, for not only had I lost my teaching job, but I also didn't have any idea how the Jewish community would react. Would they give me full trust for having brought Viel to his well-deserved and long-overdue trial? Or would they look at me with continued and even growing suspicion, since once a *Waffen-SS* man, always a *Waffen-SS* man, even though I had committed myself to keep the candles lit by appearing in public, ready to debate the Holocaust deniers and to -continue proving by my presence and experience that the Holocaust *did happen*? In 2005, I consented to have a documentary made of my participation in the Viel trial, *Once a Nazi . . .,* for the producers (two Jewish students), which was a success, both artistically and financially. However, since then, even though always ready, I haven't received even *one* invitation by any of the

Jewish organizations to appear in public and take on the neo-Nazis and the Holocaust deniers. Neither was I informed by any Jewish person (e.g., Steven Rambam) or any Jewish agency that several surviving relatives of some of the murdered Jewish prisoners had called, grateful to have finally discovered what had happened to them. It appears to me that for the Jewish people, I had become an unwelcome part of the tragedy of the Holocaust.

After being dismissed from Concordia, I retired to my farm. After almost fifty years of spiritual anguish, my conscience had finally prevailed over my reason, inducing me to believe that my feelings of guilt and shame would finally disappear forever—effect of the process of natural justice having been brought upon the accused. However, still recalling Viel's war crime, the arduous course of the trial with its surprisingly mild verdict, the accusations against my person, my dismissal from the university, and the accusation that I had become a "traitor" have made me realize that I had paid a very heavy spiritual and material price. It has also still left me, during and after the trial, with the public sigma of having been a soldier in Hitler's *Waffen-SS*, a criminal organization. Even though my presence at Viel's trial had been lauded as a "courageous moral act" even by several leaders of the Jewish community, the approval has yet to prevail over that still remaining deep in my psyche that had been caused by my own mistreatment on the part of my *reichsdeutsch Waffen-SS* NCOs and officers. And I remain still unable to cope more successfully with the accusation by most of the German press, the defense attorneys, and the German neo-Nazis that "I had been the real killer who had desperately tried to shunt his heinous act upon the 'innocent' person of Julius Viel."

The verdict of twelve years in prison raises the question whether the decision by the senior judge, Dr. Winkler, had fully complied with the principle of the course of natural justice as agreed upon in the United Nations, *viz* not revenge but retribution (restitution). In my opinion, the answer is partly yes, partly no. Why so? Let us first have a look at the murderer, the *Waffen-SS Untersturmführer* Julius Viel as an "officer who is presumed to be a gentleman." As officer, he may be presumed to have been fully informed about the meaning and relevance of the Den Hague Conference of 1899; yet he still did proceed to commit in cold blood the war crime. At the time of the Nuremberg trials, the verdict would have been death by hanging. But death sentences had been abolished after the mass hanging during 1947 of the *hauptschuldige* criminals, except for Eichmann. *Restitution* had become the new morality, which means "cash payment for damages that had been inflicted" by the killing as well as upon the victim's property. Julius Viel's verdict had failed to spell out any restitution payments to any of the relatives of the seven murdered Jews.

Given this fact, the sentence of only twelve years of prison did not reflect the course of natural justice. In my view, it contradicted it! Had Dr. Winkler wished to comply *fully* with the requisites arising from the Den Hague treaty, in my mind as an economist, the following financial compensation would have had to be arranged: twelve dead Jews, reflecting their ages on the day of their murder—24, 30, 32, 43, 46, 49, and 54. Statistics bear out that before 1939, men had been working up to fifty hours per week until the average age of sixty-five, with some retiring with pensions, while others had not been so fortunate. Bringing the prewar stats up to date to present-day income levels, I estimate that the average annual income of these Jewish men would amount to about $40,000 per person, which adds up to the following totals for all seven:

Joshua Baruch, forty-one working years left, total restitution payment	$1,640,000
Wilhelm Kaufmann, thirty-five working years left, total payment	$1,400,000
Ladislav Kras, thirty-three working years left, total payment	$1,220,000
Victor Schütz, twenty-two working years left, total payment	$880,000
Robert Friedmann, nineteen working years left, total payment	$750,000
Severin Klastimil, sixteen working years left, total payment	$600,000
Victor Stern, eleven working years left, total payment	$450,000
Grand total	**$6,940,000**

For full justice to have been rendered, the chief judge, Dr. Winkler, would have had to rule that with his twelve-year prison sentence, Julius Viel (or the German government) would have to pay to the heirs of the seven murdered Jewish prisoners the total of almost seven million dollars in full compliance with the restitution payment agreement between Israel and West Germany.

In his particular sense, I also wish to refer to the totals that have been so far paid by the Germans to Israel, the estimated amount being about $90 billion. By the agreement in 1952, those payments were meant for the Holocaust survivors and their heirs. Unlike my calculations, they did not involve estimates for the lost lifetime earnings of the victims. My estimates do: six million Holocaust victims, men (3 million), women (2.5 million), and children (500,000). Average age of the adults is thirty-five years, which means thirty years of loss of income by not living until the age of sixty-five.

The children, if they had survived, would have worked an average of forty-five years. Average income for the adults (in today's dollars) is $40,000, assuming that of the total of six million Holocaust victims, at least four million would have been actively working. So we have a total of four million Jewish persons working for an average of thirty years each at $40,000 per year, which makes for a grand total of income that had never been generated because of the Holocaust, which means income which at least a part would have been received by the heirs: $4.8 *trillion of lost Jewish income because of the Holocaust*. With the restitution payments of $90 billion, the author thinks that the Germans got themselves a fantastic deal.

Overall, with my experience and seeking to respond to my conscience, I am left with the need to ask the following questions, attempting to find what seem to be, at present, impossible answers:

- How do we explain that the Germans—an intelligent, talented, hardworking, law-abiding, and even overall friendly people— fell with such apparent ease under the studded boots of the absolute dictatorship of Adolf Hitler, originally hailing from Vienna's *Lumpenproletariat* (riff-raff)?

- How did Adolf Hitler, with his colloquial Austrian accent, succeed in bewitching and seducing the traditional German power elite with its use of *hochdeutsch* (high German) and make it fall for Hitler's promise of the *Eintausenjähriges Reich* (thousand-year empire)?

- How was Adolf Hitler able, by the cunning application of their tradition of *Ehre, Blut und Boden* (honor, blood, and soil), to con the kaiser-loving Prussian aristocracy into accepting his *Wahnidee* (delusional idea) of the *Eintausendjähriges Reich,* reminiscent of feudalism?

- How do we explain the fact that people with the highest relative percentage of doctorates in philosophy, in law, and in the sciences, subjected during the course of only six years of Hitler's dictatorship, consented to being debased to the lowest level of morality by Hitler's ideological delusion, a regime that even went on, during the last phase of the war, to commit mass murder upon its own *Herrenrassen* armed forces—the hanging and shooting of thousands of battle-weary Third Reich soldiers and officers charged with cowardice and desertion?

- How do we explain the fact that all Western powers had enthusiastically sent their athletes to the Berlin Olympics of 1936, even though they knew that Hitler had already opened concentration camps and had ordered the mass killing of Jews and of his political opponents?

- How will the signatories of all Geneva agreements and other treaties concerning the "proper conduct" of war view and interpret the officers of Hitler's *Wehrmacht* and the *Waffen-SS*—as extensively documented by thousands of photographs—standing up with their revolvers on the top of ditches and shooting dead one at a time the prisoners standing below at the bottom? While openly professing to be *Gott-gläubige* (believers in God), the Hitler Germans were proclaiming to fight for two nationalistic causes: a "just war" that was needed to undo the "shame" of the Treaty of Versailles, and a "necessary war" that had to be fought with the moral purpose of saving "Western civilization" from the Stalinist-Bolshevik threat. But turning into a war of ideologies that seemed interminably long, the fighting soon degenerated into prehistoric forms of savagery in which the notion of just war was soon replaced by an infinite number of war crimes: plain murders, so-called official acts of execution, racial-hatred-induced acts of revenge, physical torture, and massive rapes. Each and all perpetrated upon orders from the very top (*OKW, Oberkommando der Wehrmacht*) down and enforced by the Oath of Fealty to the *Führer*. Toward the end of the war, thousands of German officers and soldiers, who had initially been very much willing to serve the cause and goals of Hitler's *Eintausendjähriges Reich,* were accused of *Feigheit vor dem Feinde* (cowardice before the enemy) and *Wehrzersetzung* (impair the will to fight) by the roving *Schnellgerichte* and condemned to instant execution. Certainly not officers and gentlemen but war criminals from the top down.

- How do political theorists explain Adolf Hitler's behavior and decisions after the Third Reich's victory in France? Invoking the brilliant statesmanlike performance of Count Metternich, sanity would have preferred an offer of peace and friendship to the conquered but proud French and a firm invitation to create an alliance of Europe's Christian countries that would wage a winning war against the godless Bolsheviks of the USSR and thus save Western civilization. However, Adolf Hitler, in his *Größenwahn* (delusional grandeur) and also totally lacking the statesman's genius of Talleyrand and Metternich, opted for crude revenge, supported by his ranking *Parteigenossen* (members of the *NSDAP*) and his mainly Prussian field marshals. Enforcing his slogan of *Macht ist Recht* (power is the law), he proceeded to demonstrate the racial superiority of Nazi Germany over France by subjecting France to a dehumanizing occupation—most likely inducing his famous peacemaking countryman Count Metternich to turn around in his grave in the face of such idiocy. Relying on his passion as painter and driven by resentment instead of using his brains, Hitler but inevitably aroused the opposing nations into quickly forming an emergency "unholy" alliance— the Christian United States with the godless USSR—with the aim of destroying Nazi Germany but which also empowered the Soviet Union to enslave Eastern Europe until 1989. Filled with their hatred of Jews and Stalin's Bolsheviks, Hitler and his foreign minister, Joachim von Ribbentrop (a former wine merchant), were lacking the intellectual capacity and the vision to propose the creation of a European Union of equally ranked nations, which would together thwart Stalin's plans. Instead of demonstrating remarkable statesmanship, Hitler had foolishly convinced himself that the *Herrenmensch* muscle rather than human reason was sufficient to enable the Third Reich to win his war by banging down his crude Prussian iron-and-steel-enhanced fist—the blitzkrieg.

- How do social scientists explain Adolf Hitler's *Endlösung*, the planned destruction of the Jews of the world? Exclusively as consequence only of racial hatred? Or of his ambition to unseat the Jewish people from their historical primary role as G-d's "chosen people" and to replace them with the Thousand-Year *Reich* ruled by the *real* "master race"? In his futuristic plans, Hitler had numerous times referred to the image/being of *Die Vorsehung* (Providence) as the heavenly force and influence that had ordered him to create his *Eintausendjähriges Reich*.

Before WWI, Adolf Hitler was living in Vienna, poverty-stricken and developing feelings of anti-Semitism from unsuccessfully attempting to sell his paintings to Jewish dealers in art. In 1914, he volunteered to serve in the army of Imperial Germany, got a EK1 for bravery, and even though severely wounded, managed to survive living in a Germany that had by the late 1920s been rapidly sinking into the abyss of a fallen state and nation—massive unemployment, evidence of starvation, chaos instead of law and order, threat of a communist revolution, and rapidly spreading anti-Semitism, each and all of which were crying out for a strong-willed leader who would credibly promise salvation. Over the course of just a few years, Adolf Hitler's presence and pretentions had become overpowering, supported not only by the masses but also by men of great repute, politicians, industrialists, bankers, former military commanders, and men of the collar, both Catholic and Protestant.

Hitler's message had been revealed by heaven: Adolf Hitler showed up:

I am the trusted envoy of Providence, with the authority to save Germany and you, my beloved German people. Providence has passed on to me some of its absolute power that is needed to restore law and order and to restore the greatness of our fatherland. In exchange for your total obedience and lifelong fealty, *I promise* you delivery from all the evils that you have had to endure because of the cruelty of the Treaty of Versailles. *And I shall also liberate* you from the real causes of your misfortune: the Jews. With my direct linkage to *Providence*, as a strong leader I guarantee you law and order as reflecting the will of Divine Providence; we shall therefore, acting together, even using force whenever necessary to save our nation from becoming a "failed state." We can accomplish this enormous task if the powerful image of the absolute Ruler in Heaven is replicated with an equally powerful presence of the ruler of our nation on earth. To save Germany, we shall need a highly centralized system of government. To save Germany, its people, its state and its and government, we must become *rassenrein* [purified race]. Providence had ordained that in the long run only one nation is destined to become the ruler of the world: *der rassenreine Staat der Deutschen* [the racially pure German state], successor of the Holy Roman Reich of the German Nation, as per the will of Providence.

The creation of Hitler's Third Reich will live up to Providence's mandates "to do the good" by confirming God as possessing and exercising absolute power over human beings, at present and in the future. However, the creation and historical continuity of the Third *Reich* will be conditional upon the disappearance of the ancient state of the pure race Hebrew tribes, referred to by their Old Testament as being their G-d's own "chosen people."

Evidently, as a social scientist, the author thought that trying to make an objective sense of Adolf Hitler's often announced mission of "having been the appointed messenger of Providence [*Vorsehung*]" would enable him to discern whether his utterances had been received directly from Providence, or whether he had imagined, Moses-like, to have received them in form of revelations. As early as 1929, he had already succeeded to convince his most devoted *alte Kämpfer* (the first one hundred thousand Germans who had already joined the *NSDAP*) that he had been entrusted by Providence to repurify the Aryan blood of the German nation that had been contaminated by Jewish blood and thus to replace G-d's own chosen people as savior of the world's sins with the pure-blooded Aryan-German *Herrenrasse*.

Adolf Hitler appears to have viewed the revelation by Providence as a *moral* mandate: the task of making Germany the world's ruling nation by applying absolute power. Influenced by his chief ideologue, Rosenberg, Hitler, upon his appointment as chancellor, proclaimed the fundamental motto of Third Reich's National Socialism: *Macht ist Recht* (power is the law).

We will never know if Adolf Hitler had ever received such a mandate as an order or only as a revelation. But if he did, and if we believe in God (Providence), then we are faced with an intellectual problem concerning ethics and morality, but also with the practical question as to who, in fact, rules the world and us, the humans.

Wikipedia's definition is as follows: "Providence is God's intervention in the world." More specifically, Saint Augustine spoke of "God's governance in the universe . . . his foresight and care for its future." According to Calvin, "God's plan for the world and every soul that he has created is guided by his will." Referring to Luther, we have the following explanation: "Divine providence began when God created the world with everything needed for human life." In Jewish thought, emphasis is put on the "divine supervision of the individual: Divine Providence means that God is directing (or even recreating) every minute detail of creation." Each and all these definitions—the Catholic, the Lutheran, the Calvinist, and the Jewish—speak of God/Providence as the absolute master of the universe but with a personal commitment to the welfare of *all* human beings: "Divine Providence began when God created the world with everything that is needed for human life."

In the author's view, Providence is about creating life, not destroying it. Yet there came Hitler professing his mandate from Providence to proceed with the creation of a worldwide German empire by applying *absolute* power upon the *Untermenschen*, in particular the Jews, which means by enforcing the Holocaust. It does not take much intellect to recognize that Hitler was inferring that Providence had granted him *absolute* power over all human beings, over both their lives (e.g., the racially pure Aryans, especially the Germans) and their deaths (the *Untermenschen*, in particular the Jews). Intellectual reflection suggests that Hitler's reference to Providence as God's mandate that he should proceed with the creation of his *Eintausendjähriges Reich* at the cost of six million Jewish people and additional millions of *Untermenschen* could not possibly have been ordained by Providence, as defined above. Why not? Because each and all of them stated clearly and emphatically that "Divine Providence began when God created the world with everything that is needed for human life," which means not for the destruction of human life—as prescribed and implemented by Hitler—but for the preservation of human life.

Viewed as a mandate by God, this interpretation of the racist essence of Nazi ideology and its implementation as a moral act that had been sanctioned by the *Vorsehung* adjoins to the tragedy of the Holocaust with an explicitly religious connotation: it elevates Hitler's *NSDAP* ideology upward into the realm of the spiritual, of faith, of a personal commitment to God, a vertical dimension that is fused with the secular, earthly, political realities of the German nation. The ideology of National Socialism is thereby, in fact, converted into a religion for those who (are brainwashed to) believe in it.

Let us recall at this point that Cardinal Innitzer of Vienna had personally given his benediction to the Nazi troops that were about to invade the USSR. Let us also recall that neither of the two popes (Pius XI and Pius XII) during Hitler's reign had ever hinted at the possibility of excommunicating Hitler, even though they had been informed of the tragedy of the Holocaust.

In the author's view, history was once again repeating itself. As throughout human history, *killing in the defense of one's faith* was not subject to moral approbation because it had been willed and sanctified by the (respective) Gods of Christians (Christian, Jewish, or Muslim). All that we need to do is to recall the dictum at the conclusion of the Synod in Nicaea in which by the decision of the Roman emperor Caesar Flavius Constantine and with consent by then pope, Saint Sylvester, the Christian church had been declared as the Byzantine empire's only official religion, with the mandate that "henceforth, the Holy Church will wage war in its defense," thereby betraying hundreds of years of previous attempts to establish itself as the worldwide "religion of peace and love."

While each of the above definitions of *Providence* emphasizes his absolute power, which is not shared with the humans—who are granted only free will—Adolf Hitler interprets his mandate as the willingness of Providence to delegate some of his power over both life and death to Adolf Hitler. The *absolute* ruler in heaven shares his power with Adolf Hitler, the *absolute* ruler on earth.

So here we have it, from Divine Providence and its absolute heavenly power over human beings to Adolf Hitler's totalitarian ideology that was promising down-to-earth, loving care, good governance, and thereby restoration of the pride of the nation. All that was needed was a leap of faith toward a leader who claimed that he had been entrusted by Providence not only to secure a speedy economic recovery but also to purge those who had brought that misery upon the German people—the Jews. The presumed absolute heavenly power of Providence/God in both Christianity and Jewish thought revealed onto Adolf Hitler the mandate to lift Germany up from its dismal state of hopelessness by subjecting it to the absolute, secular, totalitarian power of Adolf Hitler's National Socialism and then to proceed with the Final Solution as sanctioned by (Hitler's view of) Providence as the expression of its loving care for the pure Aryan-German people—the Holocaust.

Let us here emphasize once again that neither the Catholic nor the Protestant-leading churchmen had engaged in massive open rebellion after Hitler passed his first enabling act. Even if they had attempted it, they wouldn't have been allowed to because in so doing, they would have denied the absolute will of Divine Providence as claimed by Adolf Hitler.

In Adolf Hitler's system of Nazism, the spirituality of Providence and its designs on the Nazi heaven as viewed by Hitler induces us to believe that God had revealed to Adolf Hitler how to create a totalitarian ideology whose organizational structure would emulate that of the Vatican's long-aspired *Universitas*. If so, then we are according a religious symbolism to the myth of the racial purity of the pure Aryan-Germans. Adolf Hitler, as the single highest authority on earth acting in the name of Providence, commands absolute obedience for *Der Führer*, absolute respect for the credo of National Socialism and its ideological tenets; exerts total control over the lives and thoughts of his believing and faithful subjects; and imposes extreme penalties for doubt, disobedience, and disloyalty—each and all recalling the Inquisition, of which had always been practiced and applied in religions that claimed to be messianic and aspired to world totalitarian dominance.

According to Adolf Hitler, the revelation from Providence involved both the God-decreed purification of the race of *Herrenmensch* and the mandated creation of their *Eintausendjähriges Reich* that applied exclusively to the German nation: the members of the *NSDAP* as its standard bearers, the *SS* organisations, the government officials, and the sixty-five million obedient Germans (labeled *Mitläufers* after the end of the war). Since his mandate had been issued by Providence, each and all the Germans—the new Nazi-ruling class and its subjects—did not have to feel guilty about using force and murdering the millions of the impure, nonbelieving subraces, including the six million Jews. They did not because of several major historical precedents that involved massive religious wars: the First Council of Nicaea in AD 325 in which both Emperor Constantine and Pope Sylvester declared that "henceforth, violence and war will be resumed in the defense of Christianity and its intention to create a Christian *Universitas*," then the Crusades, and then the Thirty Year's War (1618–1648, with its eight million casualties). The use of absolute power had been sanctified by Providence and was therefore just and moral. In this sense, Rosenberg's *Myth of the Nineteenth Century* clearly reminds us of the Divine influence upon Adolf Hitler's attempt to live up to the demands of the mandate by Providence.

At this point, I feel that we need to answer the following question: If Providence really expresses the care exercised by the Almighty God over the universe and his foresight and care for each and all its humans at present and in the future, aren't we logically and morally justified to ask whether the most dehumanizing effects of Vatican's century-old accusation of Jews having murdered Jesus Christ did or did not add to the resolve by the *SS-Einsatztruppen* to proceed with the murder of millions of Jews? May we also ask whether the catastrophe of the Holocaust could or could not possibly have been part and parcel of Hitler's mandate from (the Christian) Providence? Last but not least, how should we view the Holy See's policy to laud rather than to condemn Hitler's decision to battle godless communism in the attempt to "save Western civilization" (and its Christian churches)?

From what I have learned of the incredible savagery on the eastern front, many of the *Waffen-SS* officers and soldiers who were killed fighting the Red Army had been dying—in spite of Himmler's continuous attempts to eradicate God from the brains of his *Waffen-SS*—with the name of the God of the Christians on their lips. But uttering the name of God does not necessarily mean that all of them had been unwilling to murder Jews. Actually, reading through the files of several of the *KZ Kommandeure*, we discovered that most of them had been practicing Christians. I also recall to have never seen any Christian-faith priests present at the Germans' mass hanging of Serbs who were presumed to be communists or partisans. Neither has the author noticed in postwar photo documentaries about the killing of Jews and Slavs, any priests of any faith anywhere on the killing grounds. But I do recall seeing photographs of Hitler celebrating *Weihnachten* (Christmas). Neither were there ever any Christian-faith priests assigned to provide religious services in any of the *KZs*, present to ease the suffering and to administer the last rites to the prisoners about to be killed or to see to it that the Nazi guards would exempt rabbis from being gassed.

Even after the publication of the encyclical "Burning Worry" by Pope Pius XI, there remained a total absence of official bishops and archbishops from each and all the Nazis' concentration camps and killing fields, because even though Hitler had signed the *Konkordat* treaty with the Vatican and had been invoking the *Vorsehung*, Hitler's own ideological priorities remained predominant: "There was to be no law but Hitler and ultimately no God but Hitler. The long-term plan was to de-Christianize Germany after the final victory." Even though Hitler had executed Pater Dietrich Bonhoeffer and more than two thousand German and Polish Catholic and Protestant priests and bishops had been imprisoned in Dachau, the church-ordained benediction of Hitler's troops invading the USSR, combined with the rather passive attitude of Pope Pius XII, makes the author suspect that the ranking Christian churchmen, terrified about the atrocities in the Spanish Civil War, had no choice but to remain passive bystanders, equivalents of the many millions of German Christian *Mitläufers*.

With the destruction of the original chosen people, the Old Testament and its embodiment of human ethics and morality would thus become redundant, replaced, as willed by Providence by a set of new guiding principles that are derived from the character of the racial purity of the German people and embodied into both the ancient Germanic tribal kinship-based common law and the basic credos and dogmas of the Christian faith. The structure of this new thousand-year state would be not the horizontal togetherness of all humankind that is deemed to be equal but as a vertically structured *Universitas*, a worldwide-enforced union of all people, countries, and states that will be run by the *Herrenmensch*—Germans. It is to be headed at its center in Berlin by generations of pure-German-blood *Führers* who would wield absolute secular and spiritual power in Adolf Hitler's *Universitas*.

Viewing as feasible this interpretation of the philosophy of the Nazi ideology as a moral act that had been sanctioned by the Christian God, the tragedy of the Holocaust takes on an explicitly religious connotation elevating Hitler's *NSDAP* ideology well above and beyond secular, earthly political power considerations. Moving it up onto the realm of the mythical, of the spiritual, of faith, it qualifies as a religion for those millions of Germans who *believed* Hitler and his National Socialism. However, unlike the other theistic religions, whose credos emphasize the attainment of peace among mankind since God had created all humans equal and equally loving, the credo of National Socialism as it emanates from Providence is viewed as a permanent state of war—a heavenly mandate by which the master race will engage in continuous war until it attains absolute universal power, one that is guaranteed to last at least for one thousand years. Hitler's principal wartime slogan in seeking to justify the invasion of the USSR demonstrates this religious commitment as mandated by the *Vorsehung*: "Our task is to save Western civilization—and its Christian religion—from the threat of Stalin's godless Bolshevik empire." Let us recall at this point that Cardinal Innitzer, of Vienna, had personally given his benediction to the Nazi troops that were about to invade the USSR.

On the one hand, each of the definitions of *Providence* refers to God as the "Almighty Creator who has the foresight to care for and to direct people to do the good." On the other hand, here we have Adolf Hitler with his claim to have received from Providence the absolute mandate to create his pure Aryan *Reich*, even if it meant enslaving the whole world, in fact ordaining the destruction of the Jewish community and religion. We also know from history that unlike civil wars, religious wars are sanctioned by the respective gods, which means that they are not viewed as sin or war crime. But we cannot logically have it both ways. Since we postulate that Providence, as our Creator, holds absolute power over humans, we cannot at the same time expect Providence to consent to share any of it with us.

So, we are left with two opposite conclusions: either Hitler must have lied about his "mandate from Providence", or Providence itself is but a product of revelation, not of proven fact. As Christians we are raised to believe in Providence and God's promise to care equally for all human beings. In Hitler's mandate from Providence, he claimed that Providence would care for the "racially purified Aryan Germans" more than for any other humans: the *Herrenrasse* versus the *Untermenschen,* a delusion that he had derived from the Providence's revelation. As a former corporal, he apparently was not intelligent enough to ask Providence to provide the resources that would enable him and his *Reich* to conquer the world, to eradicate the sub-races, and to secure for the *Herrenmensch*-Germans an empire that would be guaranteed to last for one thousand years. The author feels compelled at this moment to point out that the German word for "delusion" is *Wahn.* Hitler's mind-boggling ambitious undertaking has since been referred to as *Größenwahn* (delusions of grandeur), a more permanent crisis-state of mind than its equivalent in English.

How do social psychologists view each and the historically manifested forms of behaviour of the Nazi-Germans, especially their determinants? Could they not have been triggered by a feeling of deprecation, of a lack of appreciation, or of not being loved—each and all of which generate an acute inferiority complex that would eventually lead to yet another war that would have to be won as the means to secure respect for the German nation? The feeling of its inferiority on the international scene may have been the effect of watching the British create their empire and elevate their English to the ranking universal language in commerce, in finance, and in the worldwide propagation of the British form of government as the oldest parliamentary democracy? Just as Latin had been the principal language in the pre-modern era, English has also become the principal language in worldwide communication, including the propagation of the uniqueness of British culture; while German remained a local national language (in spite of the remarkable achievement especially in philosophy and the natural sciences)? I recall several occasions in which my Nazi-German military superiors, most of whom spoke only German, kept on insisting that German was destined to become the new universal language in Hitler's *Eintausendjähriges Reich*.[4]

---

[4] The issue of the linkage between the ideology of Hitler's National Socialism and Christianity hasbeen discussed by several authors, with special attention to Martin Bormann's attempt to de-Christianize especially the members of the NSDAP, of the *Allgemeine-SS* and of the *Waffen-SS,* as an urgent public policy matter in a setting in which Hitler himself had repeatedly invoked *Vorsehung* in his quest to create his *Eintausendjähriges Reich*. George L. Mosse's treatise, *Nazi Culture* (New York: Gosset and Dunlop, 1966, pp. 236-60). But none have proceeded to inquire into Hitler's attempt to shift the allegiance of the Third Reich Germans from (their Christian) God, to himself by ordering the "Final Solution", Hitler's plan to replace, by force if necessary, "G-d's Chosen People', the Jews, with the Providence-destined master race of the Germans.

Conclusion
Specific Experiences and Concerns

Concluding, why have I decided to submit this very detailed description of that part of my life during which many of Hitler's *Reichsdeutsch Waffen-SS* officers and NCOs had forced upon me (then only seventeen years old) and my brother to wear their *Waffen-SS* uniform and causing both of us continuous mistreatment and grief, even though we had never belonged to an ethnic German community and had never been citizens of the Third Reich? The answer is, last year, I had suddenly undergone an operation for colon cancer. Should the cancer had already started spreading in my body, my life expectancy was expected to be reduced to at most two years, adding an acute sense of urgency that reminded me of the feeling of urgency when I decided to bring Julius Viel to court. I simply had to leave a written account about my life, especially after Hitler's military march into the *Bánát* and its immediate and long-run effect upon my life with all the mistreatments that the *Reichsdeutsch Waffen-SS* superiors are known to have forced upon their *Volksdeutsch* and *non-Volksdeutsch* subordinates, including my brother and my person. Here's a list of the most important considerations:

- The spiritual and intellectual burden of having been forced into the *Waffen-SS*, causing me throughout my long life to be branded a "former member of a criminal military organization."

- The shame, the disgrace, and the feeling of guilt that arose from my failure to intervene in Julius Viel's murder of his seven Jewish prisoners.

- Starting with my seventeenth birthday, the complete loss, during my three-year agony in the *Waffen-SS*, of the freedom to choose what to study and thereby to secure for myself the highest possible level of education and membership in the profession of my choice.

- Witnessing the even more tragic fate of my peace-loving brother, André, who had also been drafted against his will and whose life, not even twenty-two years old, ended by being murdered.

- My real-life written account should also be considered a confession, a report on some of the war-induced atrocities that had been committed by several high-ranking *Waffen-SS* staff officers. Whether the tortured death of my brother at the hands of Tito's partisans or by the *SS-Feldgendarmerie*, I can only point to the then chief recruitment officer, the *Waffen-SS Obergruppenführer* (General) Gottlob Berger, as both the instigator and the executor of the forced recruitment of the *Volksdeutschen* and therefore personally responsible for the war crime for the slaughter of more than two hundred thousand of them, none of whom had been citizens of the Third Reich, as well as for being indirectly responsible for the Nazis' war crimes against the local population in Serbia, Montenegro, and Bosnia-Herzegovina. Any and all of the Hitler regime's war crimes that were committed during the course of the Second World War stood in direct contradiction to the then already existing international agreements on the laws of war (also known as the Geneva Conferences).

In his book *Geschichte der Waffen-SS* (*History of the Waffen-SS*), Edition Droste, 1967, page 13, George H. Stein elaborates on Hitler's refusal to honor those agreements:

> However, Himmler preferred securing the necessary re-enforcements from Volksdeutschen living in Serbia by declaring that area inhabited by the Volksdeutschen was henceforth to be viewed as constituting part of the sovereign area of the Third Reich, while also re-invoking the Kaiserliche Tiroler Landesverordnung von 1872 [the Imperial Austria-Hungary National Decree of 1872], thereby claiming to have provided a legal basis for the introduction of general mobilization of the Volksdeutschen in that area.

With my specialization in international politics, I must take issue with Himmler's misuse of the meaning of *sovereignty* and the subsequent forced recruitment of foreign citizens. *Sovereignty* refers to a national area in which most of the inhabitants are citizens of that nation, citizens recognized as such by their own nation as well as by other nations. The *Volksdeutschen* then living in the area of the *Bánát* (that had remained under German occupation during 1941 to late 1944) had not been citizens of the Third Reich. Moreover, contrary to Hitler's promise in 1943, neither were they declared citizens of the Third Reich after the massive recruitment had started. Tito's own communist government revoked the Yugoslav citizenship of the ethnic Germans only in 1948, clearly implying that Himmler's manipulation of the law had been illegal. As a matter of fact, neither were the *Volksdeutsche* refugees who had escaped to West Germany accorded immediate citizenship. Even though recognized as *Deutsche*, they first had to fulfill the residence requirement. We should also note that the same provision applied to the *Volksdeutsche Waffen-SS* soldiers who had survived the war and had been allowed to resettle in West

Germany. Clearly, I am justified to conclude that drafting my brother and me constituted an illegal act, a war crime as per the Geneva Agreement of 1899, for not only had we been members of the Hungarian community, but also because we were drafted against our will (at the threat of being shot).

- The recruitment of teenagers less than eighteen years old was prohibited.

- The almost routinely dehumanizing treatment (e.g., the very often uttered debasing invectives like "complete idiots," "hole heads," "bacon eaters," "*Schweinehund*" [pig dog]) upon the recruits during the drills, as well as on the front, coupled with the continuous attempts to enforce the Nazis' racial ideology as expressed by the terms *subraces*, with the intention to induce the *volksdeutsch* recruits to proceed with the massive killings especially of the Jews, the Slavs, and the Gypsies, without feeling any remorse or shame.

- Even though Hitler had forbidden sexual intercourse with non-German women—reflecting the Nazis' laws on *Rassenschande* (racial disgrace)—there were many documented cases of outright rapes in the occupied territories, of forcing women to do slave labor, and in the case of senior staff officers, of using especially Slavic women as concubines.

To all these accounts of illegal forms of behavior on the part of Adolf Hitler's military, I also wish to add one more, a very private one, concerning my own person: I was not yet sixteen years old when the Third Reich troops invaded the Balkans, commenced the carving off to Hungary the northern province of *Vojvodina*, and proceeded with the forced recruitment of the local *Volksdeutschen* into the *Waffen-SS*. As a sixteen-year-old adolescent, I was a God-believing, ranking pupil and student with great dreams about human love and compassion, about justice and human rights, and about respect for one's elders. I had also been a virgin male, resolved that I would share my love and my sexuality with a virgin female, thereby committing myself to the lifelong sanctity of marriage. Then the Nazis drafted me against my will and carted me off up to Unna, in Germany's state of Westphalia, for training in signals.

Four weeks into our formation, we were granted a weekend pass into the town. Before leaving, we were ordered by the senior NCO, the really fervent Nazi *Waffen-SS Stabscharführer Mertens* (sergeant major), to open the left-hand side of our tunic and to look for a small pocket in its inside left corner, which we did. He then opened a large box and took out a handful of small see-through packages. Looking at us, he explained, "*Diese sind Preservative. Ich gebe zwei jedem von Euch. Ihr mußt sie gebrauchen, den der Führer braucht Soldaten. Ihr sollt keine Probleme haben, den die deutschen Frauen warten auf Euch. Ihr seid the Auslese, die Waffen-SS. Am Montag werde ich die Preservative selbst einzeln einsammeln, gebraucht.*" (These are condoms. Each of you will receive two of them. You must use them because the *Führer* needs soldiers. The German women are waiting for you since you are the elite, the pure Aryans, the *Waffen-SS*. Monday morning, I myself will examine them, hopefully used.)

As barely a seventeen-year-old whose mother had died in 1930, I had never before heard this kind of shameful, irreverent, insulting, vile reference to women, in this case, the women in question being German mothers, wives, fiancées, sisters, aunts, and grandmothers. But I had to hide my shock for fear of being labeled a *Wehrzersetzer* (underminers of the will to fight). I was also afraid because we were *ordered* to engage in *Geschlechtsverkehr* (sexual intercourse) and to use the condoms. What if I disobeyed the order? What would be the punishment? Luckily, one of the *volksdeutsch* recruits, a married man, had the answer: "*Das Ding mit Seifenwassen füllen!*" (Just fill that thing with soapy water!)

I must also note the practice during the area occupied by the Third Reich, of the German military command setup, all along well behind the various fronts, mobile *Puffe* (military slang for "whorehouses"), whose "residents" were at first exclusively German—following Hitler's decrees concerning sexual intercourse: "*Rassenschande wird begangen wenn ein deutscher Soldat mit einer Nicht-Deutschen Geschlechtsverkehr betreibt.*" (Racial disgrace occurs when a German soldier engages in sexual activity with a non-German female.)

During the summer of 1943, outside of Sarajevo, I witnessed several times rows of soldiers who had just returned from the front, after having gone through delicing, lining up and waiting for their turn— some of them already with their trousers down—to be served by what I had heard were only *five* women. To me, still a *Jungmann,* it was a tragedy and travesty, but I had to continue keeping my mouth shut. But it seemed odd to me that those prostitutes were German, *Herrenfrauen* (master race women) who were being used as sex slaves.

Using these *Herrenfrauen* as prostitutes was making no sense to me, an ideological contradiction, because at the same time, Hitler was talking many times about the dignity of women as members and devotees of the *NSDAP*, as upholders of women's virtues, and as performing the glorious task of procreating children for the future of the *Vaterland.* He even went on to create the golden cross of motherhood, personally honoring women who had given birth to at least five children. I sadly recall two instances in which two mothers happily contributed five children to Hitler's war effort, but with a very tragic ending: One was the wife of Hitler's propaganda minister, Goebbels, who poisoned all five children before committing suicide. The other was the wife of the *volksdeutsch* colonel, Dr. Reith, whose husband was eventually hanged for war crimes by the Tito government, leaving his family destitute.

The following are my concluding reflections about Julius Viel's murder, sentence, and the question. Following the process of natural justice, what should be the appropriate punishment to a former *Waffen-SS* officer who had wantonly killed seven Jewish *KZ* prisoners, if justice is to prevail? One of revenge or one of restitution?

Almost at the end of the final phase of my life, I now wish to inform the readers that I had written nine months ago letters to Germany's chancellor and to her three most senior ministers, letters in which I submitted the following requests:

- Order the appropriate federal department to find out, in fact, what had happened at the end of the war to my brother, André. Was he really tortured to death by Tito's partisans? Or was he hanged or shot, for going AWOL, by the *Waffen-SS* military police? Discover where his remains were buried, and arrange for a financial contribution to his monument. Each and all these in return for the war crime by the then *Waffen-SS Obergruppenführer* Gottlob Berger having ordered my brother's forced recruitment into the *Waffen-SS*.

- Arrange a financial settlement for my own illegal forced recruitment as only a seventeen-year-old for the three years of war, the one year as British POW, as well as a special remuneration for losing my senior teaching post at Concordia University, accused, following my public statement about Julius Viel, of having been a *Waffen-SS* war criminal. Special apology, preferably from Dr. Maas, the minister for justice, for my forced recruitment, the racial-hatred-induced dehumanizing treatment of my person, and the ten years of my life that were lost, owing to the grossly illegal power acts by the Third Reich.

- In an ideal world, *all* still living presumed war criminals— of both the victorious and the defeated powers—ought to be brought before the respective war crimes tribunals. Regretfully, thinking back to the United States' release of many top-level Nazis and top-ranking *Waffen-SS* generals years before serving their war crimes time in prison, present-day power politics has rendered this ideal impossible to achieve. Each and every one of the individuals whose names appear on page 1 and have never been tried for their war crimes and have since then died are Heinrich Himmler, Gottlob Berger, Sepp Janko, Lapp Sepp, Franz Reith, Jakob Awender, and Georg Spiller. Since the International Criminal Court will most unlikely be willing to bring to trial dead individuals, I take the liberty to submit the following proposal to Chancellor Merkel:

- During one of the formal sittings of the *Bundeshaus*, Dr. Maas, the Minister of Justice, would ask for a moment (a minute?) of silence and would then proceed to express— on behalf of Germany's *Bundestag, Bundeshaus,* and the citizens of Germany—his sorrow and regret for the murder of more than three hundred thousand *Volksdeutsche* (and non-*Volksdeutsche* like my brother) who had been forced into the *Waffen-SS*. He would then proceed to warn the remaining old Nazis and the neo-Nazis, that the "good Germans," by far the majority of citizens and represented by the entire *Bundeshaus* and *Bundesrat*, would see to it that in spite of many war criminals never having been tried, the catastrophe of the Hitler-regime would never again be allowed to re-occur.

Very much to my regret, not even one of the following German *Bundesministers* had bothered even to acknowledge receipt of my pleading *Abschiedsbrief* (good-bye letter), reminding me of the unpleasant, arrogant, haughty, and rude behaviour of their Nazi predecessors: the chancellor,

Madame Angela merkel; Sigmar Gabriel, minister for the Economy and Energy, head of the *SPD*; Dr. Thomas de Mazière, minister of the Interior; Dr. Frank-Walter Steinmeier, External Affairs minister; Dr. Heiko Maas, minister for Justice and Protection of Consumers.

The author has just learnt that Dr. Frank-Walter Steinmeier had just been elected the new president of the *Bundesrepublik,* effective as of March 19, 2017, thus being elevated from the world of powerpolitics, up to the level of absolute morality and humanitarian commitment. The author will expect Dr. Steinmeiner to instruct Dr. Heiko Maas, minister for Justice, to express in the *Bundeshaus* his sorrow and regret for the murder of three hundred thousand *Volksdeutsche* (and non-*Volksdeutsche* like my brother) who had been forced to join the *Waffen-SS*.

Following my reasoning, moral considerations, and the principles of natural justice concerning restitution payments instead of revenge, may I submit my demand for my and my brother's illegal, forced recruitment into Hitler's *Wafen-SS*:

André (Bandi) Lallier: 3-year forced recruitment and captivity + dehumanizing treatment +his murder at the age of only twenty-two + not able to live s full, productive happy life:

€100,000+€100,000+€200,000+30x€20,000=€600,000 = **€1,000,000**

Adalbert (Béla) Lallier: only 17-years old forcefully recruited for 3-years plus one year POW captivity +dehumanizing treatment + 4-year prevention of intellectual development + 50-year stigma as a "former *Waffen-SS* man" + forced to leave his teaching post three years before his final retirement + labelled "liar and traitor" at the war crimes court in Ravensburg:

€200,000 + €100,000 + €100,000 + €200,000 + €120,000 = **€720,000.**

Bibliography

German:

BundesarchivPersonalunterlagen, 1867–1945, located in Freiburg, Germany

WAStBundesarchiv, located in Berlin, Germany

English:

Axis History website

Fieldgray website

Holocaust Memorial Museum, Washington, DC The Jerusalem Bible, Doubleday, 1966

John P. Moore, *Führerliste der Waffen-SS*, Portland, OR

Rabbi ShmuleyBoteach, *Was the Holocaust Punishment for Sin?* (13 Sivan 5773, May 23, 2013)

My own contacts with surviving veterans and non-German researchers of KIAs and their burial sites.

Appendix 1
The Massive Postwar Amnesia of the Waffen-SS about the Holocaust: Did They Know?

The following three quotes from the archives of the Nuremberg Trials (the Nizkor Project, Twenty-Third Day, Wednesday, 19 December, 1945, part 7 of 8) may provide an answer to this question:

The origin of the Waffen S.S. goes back to the decree of 17th March 1933, establishing the *"Stabswache"* [staff guard] with the original strength of 120 men. Only volunteers are accepted. Out of this group developed the later-named *"S.S. Verfügungstruppe"* [S.S. Emergency Force], the *"Totenkopfverbände"* [Death Head Units], and the *"Leibstandarte S.S. Adolf Hitler"* [Hitler's Personal Bodyguard Unit]. In the course of the war these groups grew into divisions. It comes completely under military laws and regulations, but remains a unit of the N.S.D.A.P. politically.

The fundamental principle of selection was what Himmler called that of Blood and Elite . . . only Nordic blood can be considered. Not only did Himmler intend to build up an elite which would be able to take over Europe, but he indoctrinated that elite with hatred for all "inferior"—to use his word—races.

Obedience is unconditionally demanded. It arises from the conviction that the National Socialist ideology must reign. He who possesses it and passionately supports it, submits himself voluntarily to the compulsion of obedience. Therefore, the S.S. man is prepared to carry out blindly every order which comes from the Führer or is given by one of his superiors, even if demands the greatest sacrifice of himself . . . as expressed in the Oath of Fealty to Adolf Hitler.

In my own experience during the war (September 1942 to May 8, 1945), even those who had been drafted against their will—and were not even any more pure-Aryan types—but nevertheless did partake on the ceremony of the Oath of Fealty, were totally bound by unconditional obedience, whether witnessing a war crime (the hanging of civilians), obeying any and all commands (like turning the faces away when passing by a concentration camp), or being ordered to engage in sexual intercourse, for the *Führer.*

In this sense, we also need to recall the three different categories in postwar trials of accused war criminals, as follows:

- *Hauptschuldige* (capital crimes): Highest-ranking members of the *NSDAP* and its organizations including the *Allgemeine-SS, Gestapo, SD,* the *OKW,* and the *Waffen-SS;* commanders of the *concentration* camps.

- *Mitschuldige* (accessory to war crimes, executors of orders from the top): Viewed as active participants who did not refuse those orders even though they could or should have.

- *Mitläufer* (fellow travelers who remained passive supporters or witnesses but were hoping to derive benefits from joining as members). Evidently, absolute obedience from the top down implied that the orders that come from the very top are absolutely binding and must be immediately executed at the threat of being shot or hanged (in the *NSDAP* and its organizations, for *Ungehorsam* [disobedience]; in the *Wehrmacht* and the *Waffen-SS*, for *Wehrzersetzung* [corroding the will to fight]).

In this sense, each and all the *Wehrmacht* and *Waffen-SS* generals (*Gruppenführers* and *Obergruppenführers*) who had ordered the executions of civilians (including Jewish) should have been tried and executed, but that did not happen. Instead, among the almost one hundred *Waffen-SS* generals, only sixteen were hanged, of whom only two had been active field commanders, while all the others had been HSSPF commanders of police and *Einsatzgruppen* units who had been involved mainly in the Holocaust. Two others, Eicke and Phelps, had been linked to concentration camps but were KIA as commanders of their *Waffen-SS* divisions.

Of the sixty-eight *Höhere SS und Polizeiführer* (chiefs of the *NSDAP, SS*, and police formations) that have been listen in *Wikipedia*, sixty-five had been *Gruppenführers* or *Obergruppenführers*, as well as members of the *NSDAP, Allgemeine-SS, and Waffen-SS*. Sixty of them had been engaged in massive murders of civilians, both Jewish and non-Jewish. It may be also interesting to note that an unusually high percentage (for a military unit) of these highest-ranking officers had obtained doctorates in jurisprudence. Of the sixty that had been tried as *Hauptschuldige*, ten were hanged, ten committed suicide, five were KIA or murdered, twenty-seven were imprisoned but were let go early, four had died from illnesses or accidents during the war, five were freed for "lack of evidence," two had "disappeared," and the remaining two were never tried because they had changed their identity after the end of the war. All of them have since died.

In reference to the question whether the officers and soldiers of the *Waffen-SS knew* about the concentration camps and the Holocaust, we must distinguish between those who had spent the entire war at the various front lines from those who had actually been ordered for duty, full-time or part-time, in the various concentration camps. From the various archives in Germany, I have discovered that there had been close to fifty-seven thousand officers in the *Waffen-SS*, the largest number of *Reichsdeutsche* by far, all of whom had had their *Waffen-SS* numbers, and around 70 percent of whom had also been members of the *NSDAP*, with much higher frequency in the ranks of staff officers (some going back to 1929). Of this total, going by their military records, 191 had been posted at the concentration camps for periods longer than one year, while fifty-three had been there throughout the whole war. Their records also show that nineteen were hanged, seven had committed suicide, and thirty-five had been doctors of medicine, of whom most were never tried for war crimes even though most of them had very low *Waffen-SS* numbers as well as equally low (early registration) *NSDAP* membership numbers.

Most of the postings to concentration camps during mid-1943 and 1944 were officers with severe wounds from the eastern front, incapable of front duty. However, toward the end of the war, requests for being sent back to the front increased in frequency at the staff officer and senior commanders level, presumably in their attempt to cover up their having served in concentration camps. It must also note here that several doctors of medicine who had been posted to concentration camps proceeded to conduct terrible experiments on their prisoners, usually resulting in their deaths (see the file of Dr. Mengele, the ultimate war criminal but, regretfully, not the only one who had managed to escape to South America).

With regard to the *Waffen-SS* as a criminal organization whose members were declared as war criminals, who must have known about the concentration camps and were involved in the killing of millions of prisoners, we must distinguish between the highest-ranking commanders and the lowest ranks, or simply, the *Waffen-SS* men).

All the *Obergruppenführer* and *Gruppenführer*, whether commanders of entire armies or just of individual divisions, were usually in direct contact with Heinrich Himmler. They may be presumed to have been fully informed about the KZs and their conditions, since literally all of them had participated in Himmler's speech to the *SS-Gruppenführers* at Posen on October 4, 1943. However, descending to the lowest level, the NCOs and the *Waffen-SS* men, especially those on the various fronts, they may be assumed to have known very little, except for those who had been ordered to report for duty with the SIPO, Gestapo, SD, or the *Einsatzgruppen*.

This explains why myself and my group of six had quietly turned our faces to the left after being ordered to do just that, even though, except for rumors, we had never heard of a *KZ,* and neither had we ever seen one. Even the rumors had initially suggested that the Jews had been sent to places of protective custody. After the war, the German denazification trials declared most of the very low-ranking *Waffen-SS* men as *Mitläufer,* letting them go home (myself included).

Given the authoritarian, rigid *Waffen-SS* system of command and instant obedience, my first reaction to Julius Viel's killing the seven Jewish prisoners in the antitank ditch was to presume that he had been ordered to do it, since he was still only a junior officer. However, after decades of study of the method of recruitment of new volunteers and of their initial training, military as well as ideological, I've arrived at the conclusion that Julius Viel must have been thoroughly indoctrinated during his posting at the *KZ Dachau* to detest and even hate the Jews, having been turned into a master over their lives, as well as over their deaths, a particularly terrible example of a totally successful Nazi ideological indoctrination that left him unable to reflect upon his intention and to recognize that what he was about to do was murder, plain and simple.

So what is the answer to the question whether Hitler's ideological elite troops, the *Waffen-SS*, the officers, the NCOs, and the almost one million "volunteers" knew about the existence of the concentration camps (the *KZs*) and the horrors of the Final Solution? Each and all the *Waffen-SS* generals present on October 4, 1943, at Himmler's conference at Posen knew. Since most of them were *Kommandeure* of their respective *Waffen-SS* divisions or heads of the regional *HSSPFs* (centralized police and security centers) commanded by Hitler's personal appointees, most of their senior staff officers also knew, some of whom were known to have been visiting the most destructive *KZs*. The practice of sending hundreds of badly wounded officers to serve in concentration camps added additional evidence that a large percentage of middle-rank officers also knew, as well as their most trusted senior NCOs.

As regards the hundreds of thousands of (simple) *Waffen-SS* men, their personal knowledge of the existence of *KZs* depended on where they were in combat. If on the *Ostfront*, rumors would circulate but would not be discussed, mainly out of fear. Additional rumors would have been brought back from furloughs but would also never be discussed. In my own case, before being drafted, I had heard of the disappearance of Jews from the *Bánát* and the *Bácska*'s protective custody somewhere in Germany. I had heard nothing while with the *Prinz Eugen* until on my journey to the officers' school in *Leitmeritz*. We were ordered to turn our faces to the left, having at that moment no idea why. However, the officer who gave us that command must have known, as did presumably his fellow senior officers. Then on the fateful days of March 18 and March 19, suddenly all of us knew. So did the highest *Waffen-SS Kommandeur* in Prague, who had instructed our school commander to send a squad to the *KZ Theresienstadt*.

With these reflections, we are left with a despairing final question: If most of the highest-ranking *Waffen-SS* officers and a large proportion of medium-level officers *knew* of the existence of Nazi concentration camps, how come they remained passive and therefore had failed to abide by the commitment to "being an officer means being a gentleman"? Was it only the Oath of Fealty to Adolf Hitler? Or was it the consequence of their Nazi-ideology-induced hatred of the *Untermenschen*, especially the Jews—hatred whose origins might have originated with the Vatican's claim, as derived from Peter's gospel, that "the Jews were responsible for the death of Christ"?

Appendix 2
Quo Vadis, the Jewish People of Israel and in the Diaspora?

As revealed by the Jewish version of Providence, the Jews are G-d's chosen people, empowered to care for all humankind in their quest for survival. Reviewing the evidence for success, we note the following:

- Twenty-seven percent of Nobel Prize winners are Jewish persons, even though Jews make up only 0.0002 percent of the human population, thereby attesting to their relatively much higher level of intelligence.

- Seventeen percent of the most important inventions have originated in Jewish minds and know-how, attesting to their relatively higher level of imagination and desire to experiment.

- In Canada and in the United States, the continuous selection of Jewish-origin Supreme Court justices has enabled our society to benefit from their brilliant legal minds and contributions to the highest possible level of natural justice.

- Literally in all modern Western-style governments (including the USSR and present-day Russia), Jewish minds have been called upon to serve as chief advisers of presidents and of key ministries.

- At present, of the 1,500 billionaires worldwide, more than three hundred are accounted for by individuals of Jewish origin, including several score in the United States as well as in Russia.

- In capitalist, socialist, and communist ideologies, statespersons of Jewish origin have been at the forefront in their quest to better the lot of humankind, from Marx and Trotsky, to Herzl and Weizmann, to Morgenthau and Kissinger.

In spite of these extraordinary contributions to their good life as promised by Providence, the Jewish people have had to endure the agony of hundreds of years of racial discrimination, political suppression, pogrom, and worst of all, the Holocaust, with anti-Semitism even in Christian countries still rampant, especially concerning the survival of the state of Israel and the increasing numbers of Holocaust deniers spreading their lies.

As non-Jews who believe in Providence's mandate to the Jewish people, who aver the State of Israel's right to exist and who recognize the Jewish persons' enormous contributions in all fields of human endeavor, we shall forever mourn the six million Holocaust victims who were murdered by Hitler's self-appointed pure Aryan German master race, recalling that Hitler had falsely and dishonestly averred that the Christian version of Providence had mandated him to replace, by killing if necessary, G-d's own chosen people and to replace them with his own *Eintausendjähriges Reich*. We shall never cease mourning because the verdict of "forever guilty" will remain firmly embedded in the consciences of all humans, in particular those of the Germans (we hope). While mourning, we shall turn to our fellow Jewish citizens and welcome them as fully equal, grateful for their contributions and their incessant quest to comply fully with the mandate of their Providence.

Appendix 3
Additional Postwar Data on Top-Level Nazis

- Hitler's Nazi *Gauleiters* (regional party leaders). German Nazi era statistics provide the following account as to what had happened after the war to Hitler's former top regional Nazi administrators who had been accountable directly to him. Of the forty-four who were still alive just before the war ended, thirteen committed suicide by end of May 1945, eight were executed after trials by various courts of the allies, one died in Soviet captivity, three died in jail, eight went missing, and the remaining ten were never tried and were living in West Germany as free men and have since died.

- Referring to war crimes, a more important statistic concerns the officers in the *Gestapo*, *SD*, *RSiHa*, *Einsatzgruppen*, *Dirlewanger*—most of whom had also been cross-listed as officers in the *Waffen-SS*—and their fates after the end of the war. The list includes the names of many *Waffen-SS* generals and staff officers, confirming that senior *Waffen-SS* officers were informed about the massive executions of Jews and non-Jewish prisoners and of the existence of concentration camps. It also shows the names and numbers of those who were executed after the postwar trials. The pertinent lists are included below for study and reflection.

- The perfect accuracy of the listings of all these names is not guaranteed, many of the Waffen-SS files having been destroyed during the retreat from the USSR and at the end of the war, in particular, the final ranks, the dates of KIAs, and the burial sites.

Appendix 4
Additional Personal Information:

- **What inspired you to write UNFORGIVEN?** My dehumanizing experiences during World War Two and their consequences: Even though not citizens of the Third Reich, my brother and I had been drafted against our will into the Waffen-SS, thus forcing me to witness many of their war crimes, especially the murder of seven Jewish prisoners just outside of the Nazi-concentration camp Theresienstadt. For five decades my conscience was plagued with guilt and shame until I decided the look for their killer and bring him to justice.

- **Summarize your book in three sentences**: (a) Starting with my childhood, describing how my brother and I were drafted against our will into the *Waffen-SS*, and, not being German, what race-linked insults we had to endure; (b) after a brief description of the war (1942-44) description of Lieutenant Julius Viel's seven acts of murder, its Nazi-inspired motives and consequences; (c) Having survived the war and then while trying to do my personal best to help Holocaust survivors and their children cope with the catastrophe and start a new and promising life in Canada, researching for many years the question of the guilt of Nazi-Germany and of the appropriate punishment for their murder of six million Jewish victims.

- **What is the overall theme of the book?** Confirmation, using a particularly savage example, that the Holocaust had indeed happened. Unlike most of the six million Jewish victims whose moments of death remain unknown, the story in this book is unique in that it accounts for the names of each of the Jewish victims, of how they were driven to the anti-tank ditch, the hour in which they were murdered, the exact manner in which they were killed, and the transport of their bodies to the ovens. The authenticity of the tragedy as described in the book derives from the author's (forced) presence at the ditch, of his agony when witnessing the murder but being unable to put a stop to it, and after the war, from his many years of guilt and shame. It is also unique in that the story is revealed by one who had been an INSIDER within the Nazi-system, of its totalitarian command structure, ideological reasoning, absolute obedience, the binding nature or the (personal) Oath to Adolf Hitler, and, towards the end of the war, of massive hangings and shootings of Nazi-soldiers who had gone AWOL.

It is also unique in that its author —after the war highly educated in renowned "Western" universities (McGill, Columbia, Sorbonne/ASSASS, L.S.E.) — spent his lifetime studying the linkage between colonial conquests through war by most powerful countries and the question whether, as WINNERS they have ever been punished for their involvement in many war crimes? Also asking, in specific reference to Hitler's Third Reich of "pure Aryans, whether its "guilt" for murdering six million Jews has been appropriately punished, however long it might take and for how long? Would their punishment reflect the ancient Judaic "...eye for an eye..." of would it be sufficient to impose upon the Germans a "retribution", i.e. years of monetary compensation? So far, the total amount paid amounts almost to one hundred billion "restitution" dollars and is viewed as "implementing the course of natural justice". However, since 100 billion dollars divided by six million Jews gives us only 16,666 dollars for each Holocaust victim, in my eyes we're speaking of just a pittance. In my view as social scientist, the lifetime earning capacity of each Jewish should have been accepted as the minimum amount, for the principle of natural justice to have been invoked. See my calculation below.

• **Where does the action in this book take place?** Most of it describes events in Europe since the beginning of World War Two: the author's place of birth, his forced recruitment and military training in Germany, then the course of the war mainly in the Balkans and the Eastern Front, followed by the officers' school, the murder of the seven Jews, then the author's work at the International Refugee Organization in Vienna and his subsequent emigration. After settling down in Canada's Province of Québec. Then, from August 1955 to June 1958, honours degree in economics and political at McGill, M.A. in economics and graduate diploma in Soviet studies, in New York city, followed eight years later, with a *doctoraten sciences éonomiques* at the Sorbonne-ASSASS, and concluding with post-doctoral studies at the London School of Economics and Political Science. As professor I also acted for years as consultant to governments, to private banking, and as visiting professor at other universities, ending with a two-year contract at Sripatum University in Bangkok, to create an undergraduate business programme in the English language. Included in my business travels were in 1996 and 1997, solemn visits to the former concentration camp in Theresienstadt (Teresin), recalling the murder and praying for the souls of the victims. Finally, in 1999 I made the decision to have Julius Viel brought before the German war crimes court, in which I participated on two occasions as the principal witness.

• Who are the main characters and why are they important to the story (my auto-biography)? The very essence of the story involves one particular Holocaust tragedy at which I was a witness: Julius Viel, *Waffen-SS* lieutenant, murdered seven Jewish KZ-prisoners in a setting that had been ordered by the entire top-level Nazis in their quest to destroy the Jewish people. Except for the death of my mother (I was only five years old), there were major tragedies during my adolescence, my father's mother, a disciplinarian, having raised me and my brother. My forced recruitment into the Waffen-SS made me face hordes of Reich-German self-declared

"Master-Race" types, and endure for three years their attempts to indoctrinate me, unsuccessfully, because witnessing Viel's war crime I knew instantly and instinctively that is was WRONG! Among my *Waffen-SS* uniform wearing Nazi-superiors several were really evil racists (Colonel Schmidhuber, Sergeant Eichholz); a few were friendly (Giermann, Obst, Barocka), while the others seemed mere supportersand keeping quiet. After the war, finally free to make choices as a man, many individuals were involved in my return to "normal life: General Woods at the I.R.O; Father Dr. Sekyra, Benedictine Abbott in Vienna; U.S. Major "Brown", in Bamberg. After my arrival in Canada, the following professors were instrumental in my intellectual formation: Dean Solin, of McGill; Drs. Kenen, Hart, Florinsky, at Columbia; Dr. Luc Bourcier de Carbon, at Sorbonne/ ASSASS; Dr. Wiles, at L.S.E. Years later involving Julius Viel, Steven Rambam, Rabbi Poupko, Steven Korda, and the trial: Judge Dr. Winkler, Prosecutor Dr. Schrimm, defense attorney Dr. Pfliegner; two adversarial German journalists: Frau Friedrichsen and Herr Roos.

• Why do you think the book will appeal to the readers? This book represents a complete revision of the first edition, I Swear to you, Adolf Hitler, Fealty and Obedience – Sin and Retribution 2. The average German had become emotionally indifferent to the tragedy of the Holocaust and its Nazi perpetrators, grandfathers and fathers of the present generation, thus rendering the title unattractive. In Canada and the United States the first few Jewish readers warned me instantly that the State of Israel does not permit Jewish Israelis to murder Nazi war criminals who were being tried in German war crimes courts, an attitude that reflect Israel's respect for post-war jurisprudence concerning such matters: Revenge" was out, "Restitution" was in, thus disallowing my first editions key tenet: "... an eye for an eye" .... Indigo-Chapters blocked my first edition from its shelves, diminishing sales to zero. Several of my concerned Jewish friends thereupon advised me to rewrite to story along the lines of a personalized biography, thus leaving out completely the fiction part of the first edition, but retaining the acts of the murder, the eventual court proceeding, and the final-scene judgement. And by adding not only my personal description of the tragedy but also my reflections concerning the question of "just punishment", thinking that they might interest many readers.

Thus advised I proceeded with the rewrite, with emphasis on the Nazi-Germans misdeeds and war crimes, results of their crazed "Master-Race" ideology induced quest to murder millions of the "sub-races" [*Untermenschen*], Adolf Hitler having claimed that he was fulfilling the mandate by "Providence". Drafting me against his will, they forced him through the processes of Nazi-style militarization and indoctrination, thus making him a witness of their war crimes, one from "within", one who would eventually break the Oath of Fealty, and would talk.

Chapters Three to Five are crucial in the author's portrayal of the "death match', the murder and the author's immediate recognition that a terrible WRONG had been committed, the school commander's decision not to charge Julius Viel with murder, and, after the end of the war, the author's decision to help Holocaust survivors to convert the tragedy of the Holocaust into a positive, life-creating quest for re-birth and survival. During the trial, the author was repeatedly referred to as "traitor" and "liar" fathers–attesting to the presence of neo-Nazis at the trial–thereby enticing the author to provide believable evidence as well as to encourage him to intellectualize about the question of "the guilt of an entire nation and the course of natural justice".

- **How is your book relevant in today's society?** Contemporary international agreements, including the United Nations Charter of Human Rights, have replaced the ancient legal system of "... an eye for an eye ...", and has replaced it by a system of jurisdiction that puts moral emphasis upon "restitution", financial compensation for damages suffered. Recalling that the several revenge-seeking articles of the Treaty of Versailles may have triggered the rise of Nazi-Germany, the application of "restitution" in the context of reparation payments "to Israel by West Germany for the murder of six million Jews was making much more logical and real-political sense than the hanging of additional hundreds of the surviving ranking former Nazis. Deciding upon RESTITUTION as the preferred answer to the question of how to punish West Germany for the war crimes—especially the Holocaust—of its predecessor, Nazi-Germany, created the impression that the exigencies of the process of natural justice had been met. But it left open the issue of just how many dollars of restitution payments would it take in order to conclude that "justice had been fully accomplished"? Germany is still paying, in a world in which neo-Nazism has re-emerged, Holocaust-deniers are increasing in numbers, the Holocaust has passed into history, and Israel has become dependent on German reparation payments (implying that the Jewish community and Israel may have forgiven the Germans, even though, possibly, not forgotten).

• **What makes your book different from other books like it?** Actually, there are no books "like it". It reveals the account of an author who had been forced into Hitler's army, of goings on within Nazi-Germany, who had witnesses Julius Viel's war crime, and bothered by his conscience, decided to bring Julius Viel to court, an act that labelled him a "traitor". There have been many stories by and about Holocaust victims, those who had perished as well as some of those who had survived. Most of these involve masses of Jewish persons whose names and times of death have disappeared amongst the six million victims. The author's story is person-specific: the march to the anti-tank ditch, their death song, their names, the seconds in which they were shot and how they died, their being carted away to the crematoria. Followed by the author's discussion of the motives and of the officer-school commander's decision not to subject Julius Viel to a court-martial. None of the many other Holocaust books have raised the question of "just punishment" of the Nazi-perpetrators: should it be REVENGE or RESTITUTION, of how to compel the Nazi-killers' heirs in post-war Germany to pay over time that quantity of dollars that would do full justice to the six million victims. The author's purpose is not only to describe the Nazi-Germans' evil deeds, but also to explore the manner in which the decision for the "Final Solution" had been taken by Adolf Hitler's claim that the mandate had come directly from *Vorsehung* presumably of the Christians).

• **Can you provide instances that are of particular significance?**
(a) the main emphasis rests upon the act of killing the seven Jewish victims, described second by second within a five-minute time span, with the forever image of the *Herrenmensch*-killer standing on the top of the ditch, shooting dead the *Untermensch*-Jews standing at the bottom of the ditch; (b) the *Herenmensch*-mania of several of my *Waffen-SS* superiors who threw at me racially-induced insults like *Untermensch* [sub-human], *Vollidiot*[complete idiot], *Lochkopf*[hole head], and *Zigeuner* [gypsy]; (c) the officer-school-commander's verdict not to subject Julius Viel to a court-martial: What happened two days ago cannot any more be undone or rectified. In total war many more and much graver problems need to be faced. Winning this war will absolve us of any responsibility, for anything. Should we lose this war, presumably all of us will be dead. There will be no official inquiry into this event, neither will the named officer be subjected to a trial. Following our Oath of Fealty to Adolf Hitler, I order all of you in the *Waffen-SS* henceforth and forever to remain silent unto your deaths; (d) At the end of the trial, Chief Judge Dr.Winkler's verdict: I declare the accused, Julius Viel, guilty of the wanton murder of seven Jewish prisoners, with the sentence of twelve years in prison.

Dear readers, please note: The author had been expecting a sentence of "life in prison" for Julius Viel, asa punishment that reflects the author's perception of what constitutes the process of natural justice.

Appendix 5
Waffen-SS Officers in the S.D., RSiHA, HSSPF, Gestapo, Einsatzgruppen, VOMI, RFSS, Dirlewanger, Jagdverbände

Namens List A:

Ahrendt Adolf Ostuf 11. 5.10 Löbau216 423 III. Rgt. Dirlewanger 04.45 † 4.46 Ostuf 20.Waffen-Gren.Div 06.44

Ahrens August Ostuf 18.12.93 ? 337 321Chef,Bandenbekämpf1.45

Alexander Heinbert Ustuf 6.11.21 Grube Marga 316 685 Begl.Btl. RFSS 2.45

Altgayer Branimir Stubaf 8.11.97 Przekopana 459 556 Hauptamt VOMI 10.44 v. Alvensleben Ludolf Gruf 17. 3.01 Halle 177 000 HSSPF Elbe 7.44 Oberf Chef Adj. RFSS 11.38

Amerlaan Antonius Ustuf 3. 7.10 Poerwakarta? Rgt. Dirlewanger 5.44

Anderlik Anton Ostuf 9.12.12 Grödig 420 700 32.SS-Frw.Gr.Div 2.45 43 Abt.IVA B868 8.44

Arlt Fritz Ostuf. 13.04.12 Nledersdorf 82 165 IVa, I.WGR1.45 HSSPF Nord 3.43

Arnold Josef Hstuf 28.01.96 Weißkirchen/Ban? HSSPF Italien 2.43 HSSPF Serbien11.44

Names List B:

Bach Kurt Ostuf 16.1217 Homburg 286 659 SS-Pi.Sch 2.45 HSSPF Ungarn 11.44 v.demBach-Zelewski Erich Ogruf 1.03.99 Lanenburg 9 831 Kdr.XIV. SS-Armeekorps 3.45

Bandenkampfverband 10.44

Bachl Eduard Oberf 13.10.99 Neustadt 651 IVa, HSSPF Ruß Nord 6.44 Oa West 1.39

Bahrke Ludwg Ustuf 12. 8.22?? Sturm-Brig Dirlewanger 12.44 † 12.44

Baku Raimund Ustuf 1.12.13 Kronstadt/Rum 401 607 HSSPF Ungarn 8.44

Balzer Karl Hstuf 30.12.01 Bildstock/Saar 391 871 HSSPF Oslo 11.44 TWF, Inf.Rgt.10 4.43

Baranowsky Heinz Ustuf 22. 2.10 Guben 186 856 HSSPF Süd-Ost 4.45 † 20. 4.45

Bareuther Adolf Hstuf 24.11.02 Asch 336 907 HSSPF Italien 3.45 † 1945 de la Lieux

Barteleit Wolf Ostuf 08. 1.13 Gerdauen 72 852 SS-RSiHa 1.45 † 26.10.92TFN Nachr.Abt 10 4.43

Bartram Günther Hstuf 15. 3.09 Neumünster 13 925 HSSPF Nord 1.44 v.

Bassewitz-Behr Georg Gruf 21. 3.00 Lützow 35 466 HSSPF Nordsee 2.44 Brigadef HSSPF Dnjetropetrovsk 10.42

Bastians Hans Ostuf 2.11.94? 2 363 Führer Begleit Kdo 6.40 † 14. 6.40

Bauer Heinrich Ustuf 16. 1.21 München 466 598 Belg.Btl.z.b.V.RFSS 2.45

Bauer Dr. Leopold Ustuf 3.5.15 Jena? Pers. Stab RFSS

BauerbachPeter Ostuf29. 3.02? 48 485 HSSPF Ost 1.44 1.44

Baumert Paul Staf 20. 5.04 Breslau 137 317 Pers. Stab RFSS 4.44 6.44 Oscha ? 2./Flak Abt. 2 5.40

Bauser Franz Ostuf 28.9.06 Wehingen 4 657 Adj.Rgt.Dirlewanger 4.44 Ustuf SS-Hauptamt 4.43

Beermann Helmut Hstuf16. 7.11 Clausthal 19 236 Begl.Kdo.d.Führers 1.45 † 3. 6.99

Behrendt Werner Ustuf 20. 2.13 Berlin ? HSSPF Adri.Küste 7.44

Belz Ernst Stubaf 31. 5.92 Unterbürden ?Begl.Kdo.d.Führers 1.45

Bender Fritz Ustuf 4.12.14 Nürnberg265 169Kommandostab RFSS 11.44

Bender Horst Oberf 24. 2.05 Lyck/Ostpr. 122 746 III,Pers.Stab RFSS 11.44

Bennewitz Karl Ustuf 1.11.11 Ladenbrug 100 50 HSSPF Rußl.Süd 9.43

Berg Gustav Hstuf 6. 9.14 Königsberg 326 126Pers. Stab RFSS 3.45

Berger Joachim Ostuf 1. 9.20 Schönheide 364 173Begleit.Btl.RFSS 11.44

Berke Edmund Ustuf 7. 9.11 Lipine 176 523 HSSPF West 10.44

Bernard Hermann Ostuf 26. 8.97 München 150 63 Brig. Dirlewanger 10.44 †25.10.44Chef,7./Art.Rgt 3.43

Bernard Willi Ostuf 5. 6.11 Berlin 421 924 Kommandostab RFSS 11.44

Berns Gerhard Hstuf 2. 3.03 Hannover 6 727 SS-RSiHA Norwegen 4.42 † 26. 4. 42 Tellevaag

Bernsmann Wilhelm Ustuf 1.4.06 Holsterhausen 33807SS-RSiHA4.44

Beyrich Oskar Ostuf 7.3.90 Kahndorf 449 563Begl.Btl.RFSS 7.41

Biedermann Gottfried Hstuf 26.10.07 Villach13947 Strafvollzugslager-SS 8,44 Rttf 7/Sta"Deutshland" 10.34

Bierter Rolf Hstuf 14. 7.13 Elberfeld 163 222 HSSPF Nord 6.44 Ustuf 4./Kav.Rgt 2 4.40

Binder Gustav Hstuf 2. 1.11 Nördlingen 218024 HSSPF Adria.Küste2.45 IVa, Art.Rgt.8 9.43

Binder Helmuth Ostuf 5.12.17 Gmünd a.D. 404 762 HSSPF Serbien 1.45

Blessau Werner Hstuf 18. 5.18Beeskow290 636 Sonderkdo.Dirlewang 8.43 Strm 8/LSSAH 1.40

Blessmann Rudolf Uscha 5.10.10 ?17 632 Brig. Dirlewanger 3.45

Degradiert † 9.4.91 Ustuf Vet.Kp.20 12.44

Blum Heinrich Hstuf 12.5.17 Niedersaulheim286 835 HSSPF Triest 6.44 Ostuf IVa, Begl.Btl RFSS 4.42

BodammerWaldemar Ostuf 4.10.03 Stuttgart 31 15 SS. Erg.Amt 1.45 Ustuf Rgt. Dirlewanger 2.43

Bödecker Heinrich Ostubaf 14. 2.87 Zwickau 47 193 SS-Hauptamt 1.45 StubafBrig Dirlewanger 12.44

Bomeier Dr. Gerd Stubaf 15.12.11 Hamburg 93 031 HSSPF Ost 6.44 † 13. 8.44 b. Tarnow IVb, Po.Inf.Rgt.2 4.42

Bonness Otto Brigadef 4. 4.89 Salzdahlum 21 294 HSSPFItalien 1.45 Oberf HSPPF Italien 6.44

BoseckKarl-Heinz Ustuf ? ?Pers. Stab RFSS10.44

Böttcher Helmut Staf 24.4.07 ? 323 036 SSPF Radom 1.45 † 12. 6.50

Böttger Kurt Ustuf 6.10.16 Schleberoda 313 041 HSSPF Warthe3.44

Brandes Willi Ustuf 7.5.07 Hildesheim ? Begl.Btl.RFSS 1.45 11.SS-Fw. Pz.Gr.Div 3.44

Brandt Erich Ostuf 14.11.11 Grevesmühlen 353102 Brig.Dirlewanger 11.44 SS-Hauptamt 11.43

Brandt Rudolf Staf 2.6.09Frankfurt/Oder129 771 Adj.Pers.StabR11.44 † 2. 6.1948 Landsberg

Brauch Karl Ostuf 22. 9.09 Wien 460 407 HSSPF Ost 7.44 IVa, SS-Flak AuERgt/ 4.44

Braun Rudolf Ostuf 22. 6.13 Meran 426 255HSSPF Italien 4.44 UstufSS-Bekl.Werk Dachau 7.42

Braunschweig Franz Ostuf 26.5.97 Insterburg2 973 SS-Pz.Aufkl..Abt10 HSSPF Rum Süd 8.43

Breh Albert Schütze 22. 4.12 Kempten33 882Reg. Dirlewanger10,44 Degradiert Ostuf 3.SS-Pz.Div 11.41

Bredow Wilhelm Ostuf 30.12.14 Bremen 270 857 SS-Kdo Obersalzberg11.44 Ustuf 3.42 9.43

Breinig Helmut Hstuf 6..7.12Volklingen273 102 Flak-Abt/KdoStabRFSS 1.45 Ustuf KommandostabRFSS 9.41

Breitfeldt Fritz Stubaf 10.1.13 Marienwerder 154730 Pers.Stab RFSS 11.44 11.44

Breuer Konrad Oberf 26. 3.91 Manfort 268 868SS-WVHA 11.44 Staf HSSPF Rußl.Mitte 10.43

Brücher Dr.Heinz Ustuf 14. 1.15 Darmstad?Pers. Stab RFSS 2.44

Brück Dr. Walter Ostubaf 4. 2.00 Düsseldorf 204 77 HSSPF Nordwest 1.45 Ostuf Ic, 2.SS-Inf.Brig 6.42

Bruckmoser Siegfried Ostuf 4.2.21 Mauerkirchen 452 426 Pers. Stab RFSS 11.44

Buchmann Erich Staf 23. 5.96 Berlin 5 118 Kdr. BrigDirlewanger 1.45 Stubaf Kdr.1/Inf.Rgt 6 1.41

Buchner Hans Stubaf 22.8.01 München1 156Hauptamt SS-Gericht 9.44 HSSPF Ost 1.42 HstufRgt."Deutschland" 1.35

Budde Adolf Hstuf 12. 9.12 Hameln 232 63 Pers. Stab RFSS 3.45

Bufe Helmut Schütze 5.8.15 ? 175151 StrafvollzugslagerSSuPol 9.44 Degradiert ‡ 09.44? Ustuf

Buff Walter Ustuf 2.1.20 Halle/Sa ? Reichsjugendführer 12.44 SS.-Pz. Gr.AuE.Btl1 11.44

Bühnemann Werner Ostubaf 9.8.07 Stendal 393 271 Komandostab RFSS 2.45 Stubaf Ia Chef Bandenkampf 4.44

Bünger HansUstuf 28. 7.08 Haan 144 264 Rgt.Dirlewanger 10.44

Bürckel Josef Ogruf 30. 3.95 ? 289 23 Stab RFSS 9.44 † 28. 9.44

BürgerErhard Hstuf 7.3.97 Warnsdorf ? HSSPF Adr.Küstenl.11.44

BürgerKarl-HeinzOberf 16. 2.04 Güstrow 151 563 SS-PHa 1.43 Ostubaf HSSPF Rusßl Süd 10.41

Burkhardt Karl Ostubaf 17. 7.00 Schmalkalden52 909 HSSPF Italien 4.44

Burmeyer Rudolf Ustuf 10.01.22 Detmold 451 9528./Pz.GR.35 6.44 † 25. 6.44 Begleit Btl. RFSS 11.42

Busse Raimund Hstuf 11.6.11 Bielefeld2 37 155 HSSPF Nord 1.45

Bußmann August Ustuf 2..12.15 ? ? Begl.Kdo.d.Führers 6.44

Butterwegge August Ustuf 20.4.06 Paderborn 183 498HSSPF Rußl Süd 9.43

Names List C:

Callesen Hans Hstuf 24. 2.11 Flensburg 421 623 18.SS-.Pz.Gr.Div 12. Ustuf HSSPF Heeresgr. Süd 7.41

Christiansen Willi Stubaf 10. 4.08 Hamburg 14611X.Waffen-Geb.Korps 10.44 ‡ 2.45 Budapest Hstuf Kdr.Begl.Btl RFSS 11.41-1.43

Conrad Gerhard Ustuf 11 3.20 ? 387 721 Pers. Stab RFSS6.44 v. Craushaar Harry Brigadef 10.7.91 Lobau 347145 SS-RSiHA 11.43 Staf SS-RSiHA 9.39

Creutz Rudolf Oberf 6.11.96 Triest 77815 Hauptamt R.K.F.6.44 Hstuf SS-Hauptamt 11.36

Names List D:

Daluege Kurt ObstGruf15. 9.97 Kreuzbur 1 119 Chef. Ordn.Pol. 3.45 † 20.10.46

Darges Fritz Ostubaf 8. 2.13 Düsselberg72 222Kdr.Pz.Rgt. 2 4.45 Stubaf Adjutant Hitlers 1.44

Darré Walter Ogruf 14. 7.95 Belgrauo/Ar 248 251Pers.Stab RFSS 1.45 (Hitler's Minister of Agriculture)

Desmitnieks Herberts Ustuf 24. 6.20 ? ? HSSPF Ostland 6.44

Deutschmann Rudolf Hstuf 27.12.07 Pirmasens 56 83 Pers.Stab RFSS 6.44

Diebitsch Karl Staf 3.1.99 Hannover141 999 HSSPF Italien 6.44 Kdr.Art. Rgt.54 11.43

DiedrichEmil Hstuf 29. 3.14 Occalitz 169 1944 SS.Kdo.Obersalzberg 6.44 † 17. 3.85

Diener Walter Hstuf 26. 5.17 Pröhl 367 337 Kdr.II./Pz.GR.49 3.44 †14.3.44 Wesenberg Ustuf 1/Begl.tl RFSS 11.41

Dillersberger Walter Stubaf 17.2.04 Kufstein 323 771 Hauptamt SS-Gericht 11.43 Ustuf HSSPF Nordwest 4.41

Dirr Adolf Hstuf 24. 2.07 München 54 958Führer Begleit Kdo. 4.44 † 7.1.98

DittjenWilhelm Stubaf 6. 9.94 Wehnen 28 023 IVa, Oa, Südost Breslau 4.45 SSPF Rußl. Süd 4.42

Dittmar Walter Ustuf 6.7.16 ? 265 403 Pers. Stab RFSS 11.38

Doose Heinrich Ustuf 1. 7.12Kiel 257 590Führer Begleit Kdo 1..45 I.SS-Pnze Korps 11.44

Dransfeld Dr.Heinz Ustuf 24. 6.10 Hirls 487 737 Brig. Dirlewanger 3.45 SS-FHA 4.44

Dreßler Arno Stubaf 22.7.94 Weimar 5 945 HSSPF Adria.Küstl. 8.44 II.SS-Pz.Korps 6.44

Droese Hans Ostuf 22. 3.07 Strehla182 542 HSSPF Ungarn 8.44

Dröschel Wilhelm Stubaf 3.5.08 Köln 130 211 III,b.HSSPFRußl Süd10.44 Ostuf Hauptamt SS-Gericht 7.41

Dumpinieks Arvids Ustuf 24.9.21 ? ? HSSPF Ostland 6.44

Dunckern Anton Brigadef 29. 6.05 München 3 526 HSSPF Westmark 11.44

Duplitzer Emil Ostuf 12. 4.17 Istanbul 287 805SS-RSiHA 11.41

Dürring Herbert Ustuf 28.12.23 Hannover 472 331 Kommandostab RFSS 3.44

Names List E:

v. Ebenstein Karl Ogruf 14. 1.94 Halle/Saale 1 386 HSSPF Süd 9.44

† 10. 2.79

Eckert Helmut Ostuf ? ? 311 430 Kommandostab RFSS 9.41

Eckstein Dr.August Hstuf 30.12.05 Laudenbach 200 118 Kommandostab RFSS 4.44 Ustuf Kommandostab RFSS 1.42

Edling Karl Ostuf 25.12.19 Griefstedt 285 441 HSSPF Ost 1.45

Eger Josef Ustuf 9.1.17 Fröllersdorf 321 827 Begl.BtlRFSSz.b.V. 1.45 † 16.2.45

Egersdorff Hans-Georg Staf 3.11.89 Kie 390 310 Hauptamt VOMI 1.43 Staf Kdr. Nachschub 3 11.41

Egger Kurt Ustuf 28. 1.18 Graz 381 549 SS-RSiHA 9.43

Eggert Dr.Hans Ostuf 28.12.09 ?141 831 SS-Strafvollzug Danzig1.43.

Ehlers Ewald Stubaf 3. 1.10 Lelm 309 721 Kdr.III./Pz.GR.5 1.45 † 28. 4.45 Hstuf Brigade Dirlewanger 9.44

Eichmann Adolf Ustuf 19. 3.06 Solingen 45 326 SonderstabRFSS 11.44 † 6. 4.61 Tel Aviv

v.Elfenau Johann-Eugen Oberf 18.8.97 Hausen 450 700 HSSPFtalien 1.45 † 1980

Engel Josef Ustuf 2. 3.12 Neuenkirchen 180 189Begl.Btl.z.b.V.RFSS 2.45 4./Pz.Gr.AuE.Btl.5 9.44

Engelhardt Karl Ustuf 8. 6.0? ? 275 779 . HSSPF Rußland Süd 9.43

Ennenbach Josef Ustuf 30. 9.05 Duisburg 53 744 Pers.Stab RFSS 12.44

Ernst Dr. Leo Hstuf degrad30.9.07 Ingolstadt 124 389 Chef.10./Oz.GR.6 10.44 Ostubaf Haupt Amt SS-Gericht 6.44 Stubaf Kdr.Strafvollzugslager d.SS 11.42 Stubaf Chef,9.Pz.GR.261,41

Ernst Siegfried Hstuf 22. 8.16 Liegnitz 354 129 KommandostabRFSS 11.43

Ernst Peter Ostuf 26.9.98 Großgai/Banat ? HSSPF Italien 12.44 7.SS-Frw. Geb.Div. 7.43

Esser Walter Hstuf 18.11.13 Odenkirchen 162 660 Chef,2./Flak-Abt.16 4.44 3./Begl.Btl.RFSS 8.41

Ewald Hans Ustuf 21.11.06 Pforzheim 49 600 Begl.Btl.z.b.V.RFSS 2.45 Oscha 11./Pz.G 11.43

Exner Erwin Ustuf 22. 9.13 Oberaltstadt 305 182 HSSPF Nordwest 3.45 † 7. 3.45 Ustuf SS-Pz.Aufkl.AusbAbt1 11.44

Names List F:

Fälschlein Martin Stubaf 14. 5.14.Münche 142 084 Pers. Stab RFSS10.44 Ostuf Adj.I./LSSAH 7.41

Fassing Walter Ostuf 30. 8.11 Pforzheim 233 183 HSSPF Serbien 1.44

Feiertag Heinz Ostuf 20.12.14 Herne 71 322 SS-Hauptamt 3.45 Hscha Sonderko.Dirlewanger 7.43 Mann LSSAH 10.34

Fent Josef Hstuf 5. 1.12 ? ?4 847 Insp.K.L. 1.42 † 18.1.42 Nachschub 3 8.41

Fichtner Karl Hstuf 29. 3.06 Wesermünde8 741 HSSPF Italien 11.44

Fiedler Richard Hstuf 24. 4.08 Berlin 337 769 HSSPF Montenegro 6.44

4.SS-Pol.Div.11.43

Fischer Friedrich Ustuf 16. 6.0? ? ? Kommandostab RFSS 1,42

Fitzner Dr.Helmut Ostubaf 5.12.00 Laurahütte 185 026 Pers.Stab RFSS 1.45

Flir Dr. Erich Stubaf 5. 3.05 Innsbruck 279 582. HSSPF Ungarn 8.44

Förster Dr. Norman Ostuf 25.1.13 Döbeln 420 788 SS-Sonderkommando 10.42 † 11.10.42

Frank Dr.Bernhard Ostubaf 15.7..07? 105 013 Kdr.SS Obersalzberg 2.45 Hstuf Kdr.I.Leg."Nederland" 3.42

Frank Karl-Hermann Ogruf 24.1.98 Karlsbad 310 466 HSPPF Böhmen- † 22. 5.46 Prag Mähren 1.45

Franke Dr. Otto Ostubaf 10.5.04 Bad Harzburg 460 773 HSSPF Ukraine † 19. 8.44 6.44

Franke Werner Ostuf 29.10.14 Zeitz 60 232 HSSPF Serbien 4.44 † 14. 7.44 . b. Ruma

Franz Kurt Ustuf 17.1.14 ? 316 909 HSSPF Ost 6.43

Freytag Erich Hstuf 15. 5.13 Aue 172 239 HSSPF Ost 1.44

Frick Gernot Hstuf 26. 4.18 Waidhofen 309 585 SS-RSiHA 4.44

Fricke Helmut Stubaf 19. 8.09 Zwickau 221 122 HSSPFRußland N 8.44

FriederikDr.Walter Hstuf 18.4.11Wien-Percht. 296 873HSSPF Ost 11.43 Ustuf SS-Lazarett Prag 1.42

Friedrich Andreas Ostuf 8. 9.,14 ? SS-Jagdverband Süd 3.45 Oscha Begl. Btl.RFSS 6.44

Frimmersdorf Hermann Ostubaf 4.3.03 Berlin 29 023 GefängGleiwitz 5.45 † 5. 6.46Ostubaf Kdr.Frw.GR.78 2.45

Fröhlich Walter Ostuf 24.12.16 Breslau 10 774 Begl.Btl.RFSS 4.43

NAMESLIST G:

Gaerte Felix Ustuf 2. 6.18 Birnbaum 312 719 SS-RSiHA 10.44

Gaida Hermann Ustuf 2.1.20 Mährisch-Trübau 466 617 Stabsp.d.W-SS 12.44 Ustuf SS RSiHA 9.43 Unforgiven

Gall Ferdinand Ostuf 20. 3.19 Knittelfeld 316 994 BeglBtl.z.n.V.RFSS 2.45 Ustuf 6./Pz.GR. 7.43

Gallinat Franz Ustuf 2. 8.21 Groß-Schillehlen 365 508 SS-RSiHA 9.44 Ustuf IVa,I./Pol.Inf.Rgt.3 2.43 Ustuf 5./LSSAH 7.41

Gallion Richard Ostuf 8.11.12 Stuttgart 148 940 25.Waffen-Gr.Div 1.45 Ostuf HSSPF Rußland-Süd 4.43

Gegenwarth Ernst Ustuf 4. 5.14. Grünewört 55 361 K.L. Lublin 7.44 † 2. 8.44 Warschau Oscha 17/Sta."Deutschland" 10.38

Gerber Siegfried Ustuf 24.3.22 Lübeck 466 619 SS-Ärztl. Akademie 6.44 Rttf. 2./Begl.Btl.RFSS 3.42

Gernert Alexander Ostuf 10.2.12 Hildburghausen 199 583 SS-FHA/Gren. Rgt HSSPF Ost 11.43 . z. b.V. 3.45

Gerstmann Ernst Ustuf 9.10.13 ? SS-RSiHA 8.44

Gesche Bruno Oscha Degrad. 5.11.05 Berlin 1 093 Brig.Dirlewanger 1.45 Ostubaf Führerbegl.Kommando 8.42 Stubaf Führerbegl.Kommando 4.42

Gevant Erhard Hstuf 25.11.17 ?Brig. Dirlewanger 3,45 27.SS-Fw.Gr.Div. 2.45

Gillner Karl Hstuf 26. 9.01 Zadel 421 660 Kommandostab RFSS 4.44

Gläsmann Heinz Ustuf 22.12.21 Wiese 467 043 NO,Aufkl.Abt.17 9.43 Fu NZ, Begl.Btl.RFS 7.41

Glende Franz Ostuf 27.2.06 Frankfurt/M 107 024 SS-RSiHA 10.44 SS-WVHA 4.44

Globocnik Odilo Gruf 21.4.04 Triest 292 776 HSSPF Triest 2.45 Brigadef. Pers.Stab RFSS 11.39 † 21. 5.45 Freitod

Gneist Hermann degrad. Schütze 13. 4.08 ?349 291Rgt. Dirlewanger 1.45 Ostuf Flak-Abt.KommStab RFS 5.44

Göecke Wilhelm Ostubaf 12. 2.98 Schwelm 21529 HSSPF Adria.Küste 10.44 † 22.10.44 Fontana Kdr.K.L.Kauen 6.44 Kdr. III./Inf.Rgt.6 6.41

Golda Stefan Ostuf 22.12.17 Konin 378 432 Strafvollz.Lag.SS&Pl.11.44 Strm. 9./LSSAH 9.41 r

Götte Walter Ustuf 19. 7.13 Steinbach 163 463 Pers.Stab RFSS 4.44

Göttl Karl Ustuf 6.3.11Kreka/Kroat. SS-Sonderkomm.Berlin 4.45 † 4.45

Gottstein Rainer Ostubaf 10. 8.10 Reichenberg 219 699 Kdr.Sipo u.SD † 13.2.45 TökBudapest 2.45

Götze Horst Ustuf 14.10.20 Hamburg ?SS-RSiHA 9.43 Strm VII./LSSAH 11.42

Graff Gustav Hstuf 30.8.04 Mannheim 382 470 Kommandostab RFSS 11.43

Gramatke Kurt Hstuf 10. 4.09 3 260 Chef,1./Btl.Dirlewanger 5.43 † 30. 5.43

Granner Richard Ostuf 1.10.13 Wien 300 099 HSSPF Ostland 1.45 Ustuf. HSSPF Rußland Süd 6.43

Gratz Josef Ustuf 10. 7.22 Saarbrücken 456 007 SS-RSiHA 3.44 Strm. 2./Inf.Rgt.4 11.41

Grawitz Dr. Ernst Ogruf 8. 6.99 Berlin-Charlottbg 27 483 Reichsarzt-‡ 25.04.45 Berlin(Rassenauslese)SS&Polizei 6.44

Gruf Kommandostab RFSR 1.42

Grevemeier Willbrand Stubaf 18.11.04 Norden 401 372 NO,HSSPF Ost 12.44

Grieseböck Karl-Gerd Hstuf 22. 4.12 Vallendar 230289 Begl.Kdo.d.Führers 4.45 ‡ 4.45 Berlin Begl.Kdo.d.Führer 11.44

Grumbach Karl Ustuf 13. 3.19 ? Hauptamt VOMI 1.44 Strm. 7.SS-Frw. Geb.Div 4.43

Guglhör Michael Hstuf 13. 3.97 ? 1 012 ivA, Sturm-Brig.RFSS 7.43 †10. 9.43 Ostuf Begl.Btl RFSS 5.42

Gunne Roland Hstuf 11.12.13 Agnethelm/Rum 456 012 SS-RSiHA 7.44 ‡ 1.45 Bukarest

Guth Wilhelm Ustuf 6. 3.22 Wien ? ? SS-RSiHA 6.44 Rttf. SS-Sonderverband z.b.V. 3.43

Names List H:

Haas Jakob Ustuf 15. 1.02 St.Nikolaus Banat 477 564 SS-Jagdverbände 1.45 6.SS-Geb.Div 9.44

Haase Willy Stubaf 17.5.06 Berlin 1 07 714 Waffen-SS-Gr.Div .10.44 HSSPF Ost 9.42

Häfner Alfred Ustuf 30.12.20 Steinbach404 539 2/Begl.Btl RFSS2.45 ‡ 2.45

Hahn Franz Stubaf 10.9.10 Kamperbruch55 572 Ia,28.SS-Frw.Gr.Div 2.45 Adj.Btl.Dirlewanger 9.43-12.43"

Haiber Eugen Ustuf 30. 7.14 ? 113 802 Brig.Dirlewanger 1.45

Hakenberg v.Gaasbeck Alfred Ustuf 15. 4.20 Hilversum SS-Jagdverbände 1.45 SS-Hauptamt 10. 6.42 Strm. 1./Pz.GR.10 7.41

Hallmann Otto Ostuf 15.1.10 Sächs.Regen 451 427 SS-Jagdverbänd 1.41 SS-Hauptamt 11.44

Hart Hermann Brigadef 30. 9.94 Halle/Saale 21 342 SsuPF Kauen 10.43

Hartmann Anton Hstuf 31. 3.08 Bad Tölz 1 226 SS-WVHA 6.44 Ostuf. HSSPF Rußland Süd 4.42

Hartmann Ernst Brigadef 10. 5.97 Wuppertal 275 542 HSSPF Pripjet 8.44 Oberf HSSPF Rußland Mitte 7.43 † 3.45 Karlovy Vary

Heckmeyer Karl Ostuf 30. 5.04 Augsburg 208 797 HSSPF Nord 11.43

Heidelberg Ernst Stubaf 1. 5.08 Beuthen 209649 Chef,4.Rgt.Dirlewanger 7.44 Nachschub.Kdtr.Rußland.Süd 5.42

Heigl Josef Ostubaf 10. 3.98 Larsbach 1 641 VI,HSSPF Main 12.44 Hauptamt O.P. 6.44

Heil Hermann Ostuf 12. 1.16 ? 230 034 SS-Verband Druschina (SD) 8.43 † 20. 8.43 Smolensk

Heimann Karl Hstuf 15. 5.91 Breslau 22 219 HSSPF Nord 6.44

Heinen Dr. Otto Ostuf 28. 7.09 München 141 994 StraflagerSSu.Pol. 11.42

Heinisch Hermann Ostuf 16. 5.08 ? 18 370 SS-RSiHA 8.43 † .41 Norwegen (degrad.12.39) 4./T.I.R.1 1.39

Heisterhagen Karl Ustuf 5. 2.99 Aurick 88 564 HSSPF Nord 2.45

Helmbrecht Karl-Ernst Ustuf 27. 3.24 Eberswalde 412 708 NO, Begl.Btl. RFSS 12.44

Hempel Willy Stubaf 3.12.07 Hamburg 207 519 Kdr. Nachschub.13 11.44

Hstuf Kommandostab RFS 4.42

Hendriks Gerhard Johann Ostuf 18.2.17 Arnheim 423 670 HSSPF den Haag 9.44 Ustuf 5.SS-Pz.Div. 8.42

Henne Willy Staf 12.7.07 Grab 110 868 Org. Todt 6.44 Stubaf SS-RSiHA 11.39

Herf EberhardBrigadef 20. 3.87 Krefeld 411970 Ia Chef Bandenkampfverband 7.43

Herz Walter Ustuf 3. 9.01 Ilversgehofen 99 405 . HSSPF Ost 1.44 † 8. 1.81

Herzig Helmut Stubaf7. 6.12 Berlin-Charlott. 257 982Adj.XII.SS-Armeekorps 3.45 Hstuf Adj. HSSPF Rußland Mitte4.44

Hesse Robert Ostuf 29. 3.08 Biela 333 407 Wi.Btl.31 10.44 HSSPF Rußland-Süd 1.43

Heydrich Reinhardt Ogruf 7. 3.04Halle/Saale 10 121 Reichsprotektor B-M 5.42 Staf Leiter,Sicherheitsdienst-SS 7.32 † 4. 6.42 Prag("Leiter" in his 28th (!!) year)

Heise Karl Stubaf 31.7.09 Heidenburg 224 694VI, HSSPF Elbe12.44 Hauptamt O.P. 6

Himmler Heinrich RFSS 7.10.00 ?168Reichsführer-SS6.44 † 23. 5.45

Hintze Kurt Brigadef 8.10.01 Fehrbellin 252 066 HSSPF Riga 11.44 † 13.11.44 Kattowitz

Hippmann Hans Ostuf 20. 2.12 St.Joachimstal 328 970 SS u.Pol.Gericht Belgrad 6.44 23.SS-Frw.Pz.Gr.Div. 1.44

Höcken Richard Ostuf 5.11.12 Berlin-Friedenau 317 563SS-RSiHA 10.44

Hocker Siegfried Hstuf 2.12.16 Coburg 279 032 HSSPF Nordwest 1.44

Hoffmeister Richard Hstuf 22. 6.09 Crottorf 421828 Komm.StabRFSS 4.45

Hoffmeyer Willi Ostuf 28.12.13 Woltem93 050Abt.IbKomm.Stab RFSS 1.45 Kommandostab RFSS 4.42

Höfle Hermann Ogruf 12. 9.98 Augsburg 463 095 HSSPF Slowakei 9.44

Hoffmann Otto Ogruf 16. 3.96 Innsbruck (!) 7 464 HSSPF Südwest 7.44

Hölzel Georg Ostuf 13.11.19 Ingolstadt 431 100 HSSPF Oslo 1.45 Rttf 0./PzGr.3 3.41

HondelinkDr.Henri Stubaf 15.12.92 ? ? b. SSPF Niederlande 8.44 Hstuf Frw.Leg. Nederland 4.42

Honscheidt Karl Ostuf 26. 2.03 ? 107 482 HSSPF Ungarn 12.44 ‡ 2.45 Budapest

Horn Heinrich Hstuf 11. 6.99 Schleswig 264 768 Führer Begleitkdo.11.43

Horn Heinz-Hermann Ustuf 28. 6.10 Gießen 20 829 RSiHA 4.43

Hoyer Hermann-Otto Ostuf 25. 1.93 Bremen 107 407 Pers.Stab RFSS 12.44

Hübscher Gerhard Ostuf 18. 8.16 Wien 297 209 HSSPF Griechenland 6.44 Uscha 4./Pz.GR.4 8.41

Hurter Franz Stubaf 27.11.10 München 132 277 HSSPF Nord 8.44 Hstuf Adj. Inf.Rgt.7 7.41

Husen Hans Ustuf 21. 9.15 Hannover ? 6./Pz.Rgt.3. 7.43 † 11.43 Charkow Hscha Begl.Kdo.d.Führers 1.43

NAMES LIST I:

Ihl Erwin Ostuf 15. 2.20 Hermannstadt 466 660 Begl.Btl.RFSS 11.44 II./Pz.GR.36. 6.44

Ilschner Walter Ustuf 3.6.09 Oberfrohna/Sa 166 496 HSSPF Adriat.K.12.44 IVa,24.W-Geb.Div 8.44

Imhof Julius Ostuf 3. 9.00 Ulm 111 696 24.W-Geb.Div. 8.44 . HSSPF RußlandS 6.44

Ingruber Egyd Ostuf 14. 4.20 Mittersill 317 056 HSSPF Alpenland 1.45 Chef,1./Rgt.Dirlewanger. 2.43

NAMEN LIST J:

Jacht Karl Ostubaf 20.12.92 Münster 59 446 Dienstst.Heißmeyer 1.44 HSSPF Rußland Süd 11.42

Jäckel Ernst Stubaf 2. 9.92 Görlitz35 029 Pers.StabRFSS (Ahnenerbe) 7.44 Hstuf SS-RuSHA 11.38

Jäger Dr. Willy Ostuf 22. 3.02 Landau 185 044 HSSPF Adriat.K. 1.45 K.L. Dachau 11.43

Janssens Carolas Ostuf 18. 9.01 Antwerpen ? HSSPF Adriat.Küste. 7.44 HSSPF Ost 3.43

Jeckeln Friedrich Ogruf 2. 2.95 Hornberg 4 367 Kdr. V.SS-Geb.Korps 3.45 11.42 Riga HSSPF Ostland 11.42v.

Jena Leo Gruf 8. 7.76 Biebrich 277 326 ?Pers.Stab RFSS 11.44 Stubaf SS-Hauptamt 11.36

Jensen Börries Hstuf 14.11.17 Moskau 138255 SS-FunkschutzBtl. 1.43 Ustuf Begl.Btl.RFSS 1.42 Ustuf 01O Kommandostab RFSS 7.41b

Jentsch Georg Hstuf 11.8.08 Zittau 11 803 SS-Pz.Gr.AuE.Btl.5 11.43 Ustuf SS-RSiHA 4.40

Johannik Wilhelm Ustuf 10.5.14 Bad-Fischau 303 932 SS-RSiHA 4.45 SS-WVHA 4.44

Junge Wilhelm Ostuf 26. 6.18 Obernjessa 286 486 Kommandostab RFSS 10.43 Ustuf Pol.Inf.Rgt.1 6.42

Jungkunz Otto Oberf 23. 7.92 Würzburg 21 765 HSSPF Italien 6.44 † 9.6.45 Hstuf Kdr.SS-Kraftf.Ers.Abt 7.40 .

Just Rudolf Ustuf 9.12.07 Eydtkau 72 774 b. HSSPF Rußland Süd 2.44

NAMENS LIST K:

Kaaserer Richard Stubaf 21. 8.96 Trient 9 774 HSSPF Nord 8.44 † 5.42 Belgrade Hstuf Kdr.I./Geb.JR.14 5.42

Kahl Reinhold Hstuf 12. 3.16 Antonstahl 292 492 Begl.Btl.RFSS 4.45 Ostuf II./Pz.GR.35 6.44

Kähler Friedrich Ostuf 16. 2.21 Fürth 413 594 Pz.GR.19 6.44 † 30. 6.44 Ustuf Sonderkommando K 7.42

Kaiser Karl Hstuf 18. 4.93 Basel/Schw 103 810 SS-Bewährungsabt 3.33 Kdr.II./Geb.JR.13 11.43

Kaminski Bronislav Brigadef ? ? Kdr.29.W-Gr.Div (Rona) 8.44 † 4.10.44

Kaminsky Otto Ustuf 17.12.20 Rowe Hauptamt VOMI 10.44 Strm 4./Pz.GR.9 7.41 v.

Kampitz Jörgen Ogruf 11. 8.91 Aurich 292 714 (?!) HSSPF Italien 7.44 Oberef Stab RFSS 3.38

Karduck Gottfried Hstuf 27. 8.11 ? 237 790 HSSPF Ungarn 7.44

Karklin Voldemars Ustuf 16. 3.20 HSSPF Ostland 6.44

Karnap Hans Hstuf 1.10.97 ? 314 223 Rgt. Dirlewanger 11.44

Katz Dr. Adolf Brigadef 9. 3.99 Hannover 3 199 Pers. Stab. RFSS 1.45 † 7. 5.80 Stubaf Kdr1./Art.Reg.3 5.40

Katzmann Fritz Gruf 6. 5.06 Langerdreer 3 063 HSSPF Weichsel 7.44

Kauder Emil Ustuf 12. 2.24 Neu Pasua Kr .495 944 Hauptamt VOMI 10.44 Jäger 6.SS-Geb.Div 8.42

Kegel Bruno Stubaf 18.11.07 24 504 Pers. Stab RFSS 9.41 † 12. 9.41 Unfall

Kehrl Hans Brigadef 8. 9.00 Brandenburg 276 899 Stab RFSS 1.44

Kircher Dr. Werner Ostubaf 4.10.06 Halle/Sa 245 540 IVb, SS-RSiHA 6.44 Stubaf Sani Abt 5 6.42

Klein Götz Ostuf 12 9.10 Leipzig 94 255 HSSPF Ostland 4.43 SS-WVHA 11.41

Kleinfelder Fritz Ostuf 14.10.07 Schönaich 58 544 HSSPF Ostland 11.43

Kloth Albert Staf 3. 1.05 Altlagen 34 424 Pers. Stab RDSS 6.44

Kluge Rudolf Ustuf 18. 3.07 Rinkerode 24 656 TFK 7.44 † 8. 7.44 Budziszowice Oscha HSSPF Lublin 9.41

Knaack Heinz Hstuf 7. 4.11 Stralsunc Wi.Btl.20 8.43 † 4. 8. 43. SS-RSiHA 8.42

Knöringer Fritz Hstuf 25. 6.00 Waiblingen 110 941 Brig.Dirlewanger 2.45

Knörr Wilhelm Ostuf 22. 3.15 Primasens 303 430 HSSPF Polen 6.44

Knudsen Aksel Hstuf 7.5.00 Fole/Denm. 427 372 SS-RuSHA 3.44 Ostuf HSSPF Rußland S. 1.44

Köhle Walter Hstuf 19. 3.12 Gebelsberg 367 733 17.SS-Pz.Gr.Div. 4.45 ‡ 5.45 Tirol HSSPF Warschau 11.43

Koppe Wilhelm Ogruf 15. 6.96 Hildesheim 25 955 HSSPF Ost 9.44

Körber August Hstuf 24.1.05 Edesheim 5 887 Pers.Steab RFSS7.42

Korn Helmut Ustuf 27. 6.15 Berlin-Span. 251 373 HSSPF Fulda Werra 7.44 †4.45 Wien Rttf 2./Sta. Deutschland 3.35

Kornbeck Paul Ustuf 9. 9.11 HSSPF Ost 1.43

Korreng August Brigadef 1. 5.78 Trier 29625 Pol.Präs.Düsseldorf 2.45 † 7. 6.45 FreitodOberf SD Hauptamt 3.45

KossikDr.Karl Ostuf 4. 7.16 Kichdrauf 339 938 SS-RSiHA 9.44

Kosubek Paul Ostuf 9. 9.11 Königshötte 455 148 HSSPF Ost 4.44 Uscha Pz.Jg.Abt.4 7.41

Kräntzle Carl Ustuf 23. 6.10 München 83 641 TFK,Amt II/SS-RSiHA 1.45

Krätzer Theodor Ostuf 30.10.14 Nürnberg 276 344 Brig. Dirlewanger 2.45 K.L. Auschwitz 4.42 Ustuf IVa,II./Pz.GR3 3.39

Kraus Franz Stubaf 27. 9.03 München 16 299L.H.W.L. Breslau 6.44 HSSPF Rußland M.12.42

Kreipe Kurt Ustuf 7. 4.08 Kassel 47 778 SS-RSiHA 1.44

Kripsch Josef Ostuf 15.12.12 Wien 337 377 Pz.GR.4 3.45 † 3.45 RSiHA 1.42

Kronester Heinrich Ostuf 15. 9.07 Erlangen 32 921 Rgt. Dirlewanger 2.45 IVa,7.SS-Frw.Geb.Div 4. 43

Krotoff Serge Ostuf 11.10.11 Tananarive 33.Waffen-Gr.Div. 9.44 † 8. 5.45 SD Paris 1.44

Krüger Friedrich Wilhelm Ogruf 8. 5.94 Straßburg 6 123 Kdr.V.SS-Geb. Korps †5.45Freitod Kdr. SS6th Gebirgsdiv 6.43. 6.44 HSSPF Ost 1.43 HSSPF 3.43

Krüger Walter Ogruf 27. 2.90 Straßburg 266 184 Kdr.VI.SS-F.Armeek 4.45 † 20. 5.45 Kurland Freitod Brigadef 4.45Kdr.2.SS-Pol.Div 7.43

Krünes Karl Ustuf Bennisch Begl.Btl. RFSS 3.45

Küllenberg Ernst Ustuf 11. 2.09 Begl.Gtl. RFSS 4.45

Kunikowsky Eberhard Ustuf 25.12.22 Chef,Bewährungskomp.39.43

Kunrad Franz Ustuf 20. 9.21 Salzburg 472 334 SS-RSiHA 1.44 Schütze 18./LSSAH 7.41

Kunz Dr.Helmut Stubaf 26. 9.10 Ettlingen 284 787 SS-RSiHA 7.44 Hstuf V.SS-Geb.Korps 7.43

Kutschera Franz Brigadef 22. 4.04 Oberwaltersdorf19 659 HSSPF Warschau † 1. 2.44 Warschau 1.44

Names List L:

Lacher Walter Hstuf 19. 1.11 ? HSSPF Ost 11.43

Lange Erich Stubaf 10.10.88 Zwickau 117 088SS-WVHA 6.44 Hstuf Kommandostab RFSS 1.42

Larsen Otto Ustuf 4.10.08 Douxberge 466 696 SS-RSiHA 9.44 Oscha 1.SS-Inf.Brig 1.43

Lassig Rudolf Stubaf 22. 3.04 Daichingen 107 190 SS-RSiHA 6.44

Laus Gerhard Hstuf 2 2.13Orlasschacht 292 479 Pers.Stab RFSS 11.44

Laux Helmuth Ostuf 10. 6.16 Donaueschingen 401 257 Nachr.Abt 501 10.44 Ustuf Kdo. Stab RFSS 7.41

Lentz Georg Ostuf 7. 3.17 ? 365 754 HSSPF Schw.Meer 4.44 Strm 6./LSSAH 1.41

Lewandowski Helmut Ustuf 1. 6.06 Liegnitz 197 021 Rgt. Dirlewanger 7.44 SS-Hauptamt 1.44

Liebhart Samuel Ustuf 10. 3.21 Schorsten 466 701SS-RSiHA 7.44 † 11.44 Strm 12./LSSAH 1.41

Liebmann Werner Stubaf 20. 9.22 Bienrode 2 786 NO,HSSPF Denmark 11.44 Chef Meldewesen 6.44

Löblich Otto Ustuf 17. 1.99 ? 8 730 HSSPF Rußland Süd 9.43 10./T.I.R.T. 5.40

Lochmüller Rudolf Hstuf 2. 4.89 Berlin 62 704 Chef, 2./Pi.Btl.29 1.45 HSSPF Rußland Süd9.43

Loh Hans Ostubaf 15. 3.02 Friedrichshain 241 014 HSSPF Nordsee 10.44 Kdr.Nach.Abt. 501 3.44

Looss Helmut Ostubaf 31. 5.10 86 617 1c,16.SS-Pz.Gr.Div 7.44 Einsatzgruppe B 4.44

Loots Hermann Ustuf 24.10.22 Burlage 408 398 HSSPF Spree 1.44

Lorenz Werner Ogruf 2.10.91 Grünhof 6 636 Chef, Hauptamt VOMI † 26.1.77 6.44

Loritz Hans Oberf 21.12.95 Augsburg 4 165 HSSPF Nord 6.44 † 1.46

Lucas Franz Stubaf 12.12.01 Stahnsdorf 46 676 Pers. Stab RFSS 6.44

LudwigDr.S tefan Stubaf 21. 7.10 Nürnberg 307 630 HSSPF Italien 10.44

Lünenschloß OttoOstuf 21. 3.93 Elberfeld 421 410 HSSPF Warthe 2.44v.

Lütgendorff-Gyllenstorn Erhardt Hstuf 13.11.12 Steyn SS-RSiHA 11.44 Ostuf Geb.JR.13 1.44

Lützelberger Erich Ustuf 26.11.20 Pers. Stab RFSS 3.45

Names List M:

Macher Heinz Stubaf 21.12.19 Chemnitz 311 752 Pers.Stab RFSS 3.44

Macher Karl Hstuf 18.11.11 Wien 353 500 3.SS-Pz.Div. 1.45 Ostuf SS-RSiHA 4.42

Maeter Theodor Hstuf 9.9.12 Berlin 323 856Stb.Kp.Pz.GR.35 3.45 Ostuf Begl.Btl.RFSS 8.42

Magill Franz Ostubaf 22. 8.00 Kleist 132 620 Kdr.Nachschub14 10.44 10.44 Stubaf Brig. Dirlewanger 1.43

Mai Dr. Wilhelm Ostuf 22.11.12 Pirmasens 309 456 Pers. Stab RFSS 8.44

Maier Franz Ustuf 7. 1.13 69 554HSSPF Italien 5.44 de la Lieux

Maldups Eriks Ustuf 23. 1.20 HSSPFOst 8.44

Maninger Wilhelm Ostuf 4.6.02 Recklinghausen 201 569 HSSPF Ost 8.44

Marabin Karl Hstuf 24.7.13 Würzburg 67 906 Chef Meldew. 1.44 Ostuf NO, Hauptamt VOMI 1.42

Marquardsen Heinz Ostuf 5. 7.14 Pinneberg 277 117 Brig. Dirlewanger 11.44 SS-WVHA 1.44

Marquardt Hans Hstuf 19. 4.17 353 087 Kdr.III./Pz.GR.35 7.44† 1.7.44 Begl. Btl.RFSS 1.44 Ustuf 6./LSSAH 1.41

Marquardt Karl Ostuf 6. 7.20 Krangen 319 115 SS-Inf.Ers.Btl.Ost 8.43 Ustuf OO,Kdo.Stab RFSS 7.41

Märtens Emil Ustuf 3.1.20 319 092 SS-Strafvollzuglag.9.44

Martin Dr. Benno Ogruf 12. 2.93 Kaiserslautern 187 117 HSSPF Main 8.44

Martin Gerhard Usttuf 1. 1.14 Mediasch/Rum 495 897 Hauptamt VOMI 10.44

Martin Karl Ustuf 21.11.20 Feistritz/Kä 496 364 Straflag.d.SS&Pol. 1.45

Martini Werner Ustuf 15.11.96 Eisenach 35 086 TFK,Pers.StabRFSS 4.45 † 4.45 Marx Wolfgang Ustuf 29.10.20 Berlin 465 740 Rgt. Dirlewanger 8.44 Strm 2.SS-Pz.Div. 5.40

Matthäus Dr. Wilhelm Stubaf 3. 7.89 Duisburg 391 971 SS-RuSHA 11.43 Komm StabRFSS 1.42

Matzelle Dr. Julius Ustuf 17.8.11 Chicago/US 487 745 SS-RSiHA 4.44 SS-FHA 4.44

Maurer Kurt Stubaf 19. 7.09 490 356 Komm.StabRFSS 8.44

Mayer Adalbert Ustuf 4. 1.14 Pelmonostor Rgt. Dirlewanger 2.45 6./Art. Rgt.13 8.44

Mayer Karl Hstuf 7. 8.09 Wien 296 501 HSSPF Nordwest 1.44 † 31. 5.61

Mayer-MaderAndreas Ostubaf 25.10.91 Schlaggenwald 475 802 Dirlewan 5.44 † 2. 5.44

Mayrl Georg Hstuf 9.6.09 Raubling 77 599 HSSPF Ost 1.44

Mazuw Emil Ogruf 21. 9.00 Essen 2 556 HSSPF Ostsee 7.44

Meinhardt Günther Ostuf 12. 4.14 206 768 b. HSSPF Rußl.Mitte 1.43

Meißner Siegfied Ostuf 0. 1.15 Neuthal 184 418 Kartenst.11 Pz.Gr 3.44. † 9. 3.44 HSSPF Rußl.Mitte 11.42 Unforgiven

Menges Wilhelm Hstuf 28. 7.04 Grossenlinden106 433 Pers.Stab RFSS 4.44 † 12. 4.58 Ustuf SS-Nchr.Zeugamt 8.41

Menschel Hans Ostuf 6.7.16 Mühlheim/Ruhr429 619 Pers.Stab RFSS 2.45 Chef,1.Pol.Inf.Rgt2 4.43

Meyer-Ernst Dr. Georg Ostubaf 1.12.98 Marburg/Lahn 139 885 HSSPF Serbien 6.44

Meyer Hans Ustuf 4. 4.21 Magdeburg Pers.Stab RFSS 5.44 † 31. 5.44 SS-J.Sch.Klagenf. 5.44

MeyerJohannes Ustuf 12. 6.08 Kiel 280 206 SS-RSiHA 4.44

MeyerKurt-Heinz Ustuf 24.10.17 Trubenhausen 268 018 Rgt.Dirlewanger 2.45 † 24. 2.45 Ustuf Geb.JR.14 1.43 Uscha 12./LSSAH 7.41

Meyer Walter Hstuf 21.7.00 Straßburg 8 461 HSSPF Nordwe 11.41 Kdr. Wi.Btl.11 2.44

Mickeleit Hans Hstuf 19. 3.98 Hamburg 37 237 HSSPF Ost 10.44

MilkayDr.Arnold Stubaf 21. 3.07 276 798 Rgt. Direlwanger 2.45 Chef,2./ Sani.Abt.4 4.43

Miosga Helmut Ustuf 14. 9.09 Warthenau 452 016 Rgt.Dirlewanger 2.45 13./Geb/JR.13 1.43

MöbusHans Ostuf 10. 5.14SS-RSiHA 9.44

MöbusWilhelm Hstuf 14.8.89 Giesendorf 458 932 HSSPF Riga 7.44 † 2. 7.44 SS-RuSHA 4.44

Moder Paul Stubaf 1.10.96 Neheim 11 716 Kdr.I.Art.Rgt.32.42 † 8. 2.42 HSSPF Warschau 11.39

Mülle Fritz Hstuf 27. 9.15 Leipzig 313 935 SS-RSiHA1.43 1./Po.Inf.Rgt.3 11.41

Mrugowsky Dr.Joachim Oberf 15. 8.0 Ratheno25 811 D.St.Reichsarzt-SS. OstubafKomm.Stab RFSS 1.42 6.44

Müller Frank Ostuf 27.12.11 Chemnitz 277 223 Strafvollz.L.Danzig11.42

Möller Franz Staf 29. 4.90 277 284 Pers.Stab RFSS 6.44

Müller Friedrich-Karl Hstuf 17. 2.02 Karlsruhe 21 201 HSSPF Serbien 1.44

Müller Martin Hstuf 7. 3.05Leitmertitz327 741 NO SSPF BerlinWest 2.45

MüllerHorst Stubaf 20.12.99 Gunslach 43 395.HSSPF Nordost 11.44

Mürmann Friedhelm Ustuf 26. 6.21Sterkrade 468 195 b. HSSPF Ost 6.44 † 20. .8.44

Names List N:

Nagler Walter Stubaf 16. 9.98 Walsrode 118 884 Kdr.SS-Kav.Rgt. 1.45 Kommandostab RFSS 1.42

Nehrling Harald Ostuf 19. 3.10 Erfurt 211 317 2./Flak-Abt.17 6.44 Kommandostab RFSS 4.44

NeuweilerFriedrich Hstuf 21. 2.03 Stuttgart5 377 Rgt. Dirlewanger 3.45

Niebel Walter Ustuf 2.11.12 Stuttgart 401 385 HSSPF Nord 6.44

Niemann Johann Ustuf 4.8.13 Völler270 601 Sonderkdo.Sobibor 8.43

† 14. 8.43

Nierhaus AnatolOstuf 16.4.08 Moskau55 088 NO, Pz.GR.8 12.44 †1.45 SondereinsatzKdo.R.Sü 1.43

NockenmannDr.Hans Ustuf 16.11.03 Aachen 264 225OO, III./Pz.GR.4 8.41 -RSiHA 12.38

Nöster Dr.FritzOstuf 4.10.13 Linz 405 437 HSSPF Italien 11.44

Names List O:

Oberg Karl Ogruf 27. 1.97 Hamburg 3 075 HSSPF Frankreich 8.44 † 3. 6.65 Head of Gestapo in France

OehlerArthur Ustuf 17.12.11Sotterbach 223 094HSSPF Rußl Mitte 2.44

Ohlsen Hans Hstuf 17. 1.00 Rudolfstadt 81 117 .HSSPF Rußl Mitte10.42

Ohm Willy Hstuf 28. 7.12 Kiel 65 966 SS-Jagdverbände 6.42 † 13. 6.87

Oresic Slavko Ustuf 24.12.19 Pavlovac Straf-Kp./Pi.Btl.13 3.44

Ott Johann Ustuf 14. 4.95 Vogldorf.Sud Rgt. Dirlewanger 1.45 SS-RuSHA 11.43

Names List P:

Paul Wilhelm Hstuf 18. 8.08 Stuttgart 1 572 HSSPD RußlandSüd 6.44

Peiper Jochen Staf 30. 1.15 Berlin 132 496 Kdr.Pz.Rgt.1 4.45 † 14. 7.76 Traves Ustuf Adj. RFSS 4.38

Pemsel Ludwig Hstuf 31. 1.13 172 002 KommandostabRFSS 1.45

Pennigner Ludwig Hstuf 4.10.13 Traunstein25 360 Chef, 7./Pz.GR.6 10.44 HSSPF RußlandSüd11.43

Pernar Franko Ustuf 17.11.10 Hauptamt VOMI 1.45

Petero (Peters) Gerhard Stubaf 22. 4.07 Rotterdam 372 322HSSPF Adriat. Küste 4.45

Petersen Karl Ostuf 14.6.12 Langenfelde 146 747 Begl.Komm.d.Führers1.45 Ustuf Kraftf.Kp./Pz.Rgt.1 6.44

Petersen Walter Ostuf 12. 4.09 Berlin Hauptamt VOMI 9.44

Petrusch Alfred Ustuf 30. 5.03 Königsberg 29 428 Reg. Dirlewanger 7.44

Pfarre Bernhard Ostuf 27.11.14 86 875Chef,2./Pz.Jg.Abt.3 9.41 † 24. 9.41 SS-RSiHA3 0.38

Pfensig Hans Hstuf 12.12.06 Hamburg 50 358 SS.Bewährungsabt 6.44 Ustuf 9./T.I.R..3 2.42

PhelpsDr. Reinhard Ostuf 16. 2.17 Waltendorf 467 463 Feldkdo.StabRFSS 1.45 IVb,III./Geb.JR.13 12.44

Pilz Gustav Stubaf 17. 6.93 Stuttgart 264 123 Pers.Stab RFSS 6.44 6.44

Pint Otto Ostuf 28. 2.12 Graz 302 442 SS-RSiHA 10.44 I C.SS-Kav.Div. 8.44

Plaul Wolfgang Hstuf 13. 4.00 Freiburg a.S. 59 933 Sonderkom.Dirlew. 4.44

Ploetz Hans Achim Ustuf 5.3.11Berlin 275 271 10./Pz.GR.6 7.44 † 3. 8.44 b. Stawiska Stubaf Degradiert? Einsatzgr.A/Sipo 2.42

Plötner Dr. Kurt Hstuf 19.10.05 Hermsdorf 221 871 Pers.Stab RFSS 11.44 SS-Lazarett Minsk 1.43

Poeck Hans Hstuf 2.12.07 Königsberg 29 433 Rgt. Dirlewanger 3.45

Pohl Oswald Ogruf 30. 6.92 Duisburg 147 614 Chef, SS-WVHA 2.45 † 7. 6.51 Landsberg Staf Chef,AbtIV,Stab RFSS 2.34

Pohl Dr. Werner Stubaf 12. 7.08 Kassel 93 789 HSSPF Fulda-Werra 12.44 Hauptamt O.P. 6.44

Polack Siegfried Ustuf 31. 7.99 Sommerfeld 25 720 Chef,2./Rgt. Dirlewang.4.44 † 12.44

Pönisch Helmut Ustuf 28. 6.21 Geringswalde 476 202 NO,i./Pz.Rgt 7.44 Funker Komm.Stab RFSS 6.41

Portugall Kurt Hstuf 23. 9.09 Essen 42 670 Chef,3./Flak-Abt 8 12.44 Ustuf Komm.Stab RFSS 9.41

Präfcke Karl Stubaf 7. 7.11 Neustrelitz 234 960 StbQttr.31.SS-FrwGrDiv 1 7 Kdr.Btl.Dirlewanger 5.43 7.44

Prietzel Kurt Staf 29. 4.97 Langwaltersdorf 276 744 HSSPF Nord 6.44 Hstuf IVa,Nachr.AbtSS-VT 9.37

Proschwitzer Albrechts Ustuf 31. 8.14 339 954 IVb,Begl.Btl RFSS 6.42 † 12.6.42 Komm.Stab RFSS 1.42

Prützmann Hans Ogruf 31. 8.01 Tolkomit 3 002 HSSPF Nordost 11.44 † 30. 6.45

Pultar Traugott Ostuf 18. 4.90 29 261 Rgt. Dirlewanger 7.43

Puppel Alfred Hstuf 14. 8.11 Schulitz 213 431 IVa.Aufkl.Abt.2 6.44 HSSPF Ost 11.43

Names List R:

Raab August Hstuf 2. 4.85 Ober-Rosbach 382 526 PersStab RFSS 4.42

Raddatz Karl Ostuf 31. 1.02 Weidenau 16 040 b. HSSPF West 10.44 † 1988 1.SS-Pz.Div 4.43

Rath Ferdinand Stubaf 30.10.97 Köln-Hohenberg 10 470 HSSPF Italien 6.44 Hstuf Schlächt.Kp.Wi.Btl2 1.42

Rattehuber Ernst Gruf 30. 4.97 Oberhaching 52 877 Stab RFSS 2.45 Stubaf Stab RFSS 4.34

Raubold Dr. Heinz Ostuf 25. 5.07 Berlin 219 106 Hauptamt SS-Gericht 1.45 Ustuf SS-u.Pol.Gericht Riga 4.44

Raulien Fritz Stubaf 29. 3.01 Waldau/Könbg. 263 719 HSSPF Danzig 12.44 SS-Hauptamt 8.43

Rausch Heinz Ustuf 16. 8.15 Dresden Brig. Dirlewanger 4.45 ‡ 4.45 Cottbus

Rauter Hans-Albin Ogruf 4. 2.95 Klagenfurt 262 958 HSSP Nordwest 9.44 † 25. 3.49 Oberf SS-Hauptamt 4.36

Redieß Wilhelm Ogruf 10.10.00 Heinsberg 2 839 HSSPF Nord 1.45 Suicide Norway ?

Reich Michael Ustuf 3. 4.09 Zipser-Bela Hauptamt VOMI 9.44 SS-J.Sch. Tölz 8.44

Reichel Werner Ustuf 4. 9.19 Niederlauterstein 284 794 HSSPF Italien 12.44 † 15. 3.45

Reichenberger Herbert Ostuf 19.10.14 München 93 39 Pers.Stab RFSS 1.45

Reichenfart Heinz Ogruf 26.12.03 Gnesen 56 634 Kdr. XVIII.SS-Armeekorps † 7. 5.79 Brigadef 2.45 HSSPF Warthe 4.44

Reiner Willy Hstuf 7. 3.95 , XII.SS-Armeekorps10.44 Ostuf Rgt. Dirlewanger 5.43

Reuther Wolfram Hstuf 1. 4.12 Köln 243 396HSSPF Denmark 6.43 Ostuf IVb,II./Inf.RgtNordland 9.41

Rhinow Alfred Ustuf 16 4.11 Küdow 272 4592. SS-Pz.Div. 1.45 † 3.45 Raab SS-RSiHA 11.44

Rochter Dr Walther Stubaf 12.10.02 Wien 309 061 SS-RSiHA 10.44 Hstuf Feldlazarett 5 1.42

Riegler Heinz Stubaf 9. 5.10 Hirschschlag 58 092 Sonderkdo Dirlewanger † 22. 4.44 Hautpamt VOMI 7.43 12.44

Ries Ludwig Ostuf 16. 3.07 Amberg 5 714 IVa,HSSPFItalien10.44

Rindfleisch Dr.Heinrich Ostuf 3. 3.16Straßburg 289 832 Begl.Btl.RFSS 2.45 K.L. Lublin 1.44

Rist Paul Stubaf 6. 3.91 Frankfurt/M 92 212 HSSPF Rhein- Kdr.Nachr. Abt15 6.44 Westmark.45

Ritter Alfons Ostuf 4. 5.14 Sesel 83 222 HSSPF Ost 11.43

Ritter Bruno Ustuf 26. 1.09 Kaiserlautern 9 707 10. SS-Pz.Div 4.45

Roch Heinz Oberf 17. 1.05 Essen 2 883 HSSPF Krim 5.44 Ostuf 3.SS-Pz. Div 9.41 † 1945 Norwegen

Rockmann WernerOstuf 17. 9.14 Liebertwolkwitz 474 3754./Begl.Btl. RFSS1 1.44 † 9. 1.45 Ustuf II./Pz/GR.35 6.44

Rode Ernst Brigadef 9. 8.94 Wüstenwalterdorf 401 399 SSBanenkampf- Osrubaf Ia Kdo Stab RFSS 2.44 Verband 11.44

RohneTheodor Ostuf 25. 9.10 Leipzig 210 339 HSSPF Polen 1.45

Rosche Alois Stubaf 8. 3.08 Haselünne 219 135 SS-GHO 9.44 Ostuf Komm.Stab RFSS 1.42

Rösener Erwin Ogruf 2. 2.02 Schwerte 3 575 HSSPF Alpenland 9.44 † 31. 8.46 (4. 9.46) Belgrad

Rosenquist Heinz Ustuf 18. 9.02 Hamburg 234 978 HSSPF Serbien 8.44

Rösigner Ludwig Stubaf 28. 9.95 Kaiserslautern 276 173 SPPF Södwest 12.44 SS-PHA 6.44

Roßbach Paul Ostuf 19.12.07 Plauen 47 025 Rgt. Dirlewanger 2.45 ‡ 2.45 Frw.Leg.Nederland 11.41

Rubbert Karl Ostuf 14.8.85 Sonnenberg 246 909 b.HSSPF Rußland Süd 1.43

Rudolph Georg Ustuf 25. 1.13 Lübeck 118 998 Kdo.Stab RFSS 8.44

Rüger Werner Ustuf 24. 7.17 Krummhübel 270 839 Begl.Kdo.Führers 11.44 † 4.45 Strm 7./LSSAH 4.37

Ruh Hans Hstuf 8. 3.97 Kisbecskerek 457 771 HSSPF Serbien 4.43

Rührig Andreas Ustuf 24. 9.14 Heidendorf 351 717 Hauptamt VOMI 8.43

Ruland Karl Ustuf 23. 4.08 Bensberg 291 026 SS-Pz.Gr.AuE.Btl 18 Kommando-Stab SS 9.41 8.43

Runge Werner Hstuf 22.12.06 Schwerin 264 287 Hauptamt VOMI 1.43

Names List S:

Sacharov Paul Hstuf 21.12.02 Reval 400 679 Kdo.Stab RFSS 1.45 Ustuf Kdo.Stab RFSS 4.43

Salchow Dr.Otto Oberf 15. 1.74 Krien/Anklam 353 116 HSSPF Spree 6.44 Ostubaf SS-Sanitätsamt 4.40

Sansoni Richard Staf 7.1.02 Eisleben 261 907 Chef, Amt VIII./SS-RSiHA 11.44 Stubaf Kdr.Nachr.Abt.3 7.41v.

Sarközy Alois Ostuf 14. 7.18 464 124 HSSPF Serbien 11.44 Strm 8.SS-Kav. Div 11.42

Sattler Karl Ostubaf 6.10.91 Lippstadt 19 474 SS-PHA 6.44 HSSPF Rußl. Mitte 1.44

Schädle Franz Stubaf 19.11.06 2 609 Kdr.Begl Kdo.d.Führers 4.45 † 1. 5.45 Selbstmord

Schäfer Dr.Ernst Stubaf 14. 3.10 Köln 138 803 Kommand. Pers.Stab RFSS 9.42

Schafer Karl Brigadef 17. 6.9 Görlitz 20 865 HSSPF Dnjetro- Oberf HSSPF 9.42 Dnjetropetrovsk 7.43 † 23.10.43 b. Pjatichatka HSSPF RußlandSüd 9.42

Schäftlmeyer Hans Ostuf 18. 6.10 Stuttgart 244 253 Rgt.Dirlewanger11.44

Schairer Erwin Ostuf 15. 2.19 Eßlingen 319 653 Begl Btl RFSS 1.45

Scharf Gerhard Ostuf 15.12.09 Halle/Saale 40 511 Kdo.Stab.RFSS 8.43 Oscha 1./Flak-Abt. "Ost"3.42

Scharr Walter Hstuf 7.12.03 Zeitz 70 114 HSSP Rusland Süd 6.44

Scheffler Willi Ustuf 14. 8.11 Königsberg 113 401 RSiHA 8.43

Scheibe Helmut Ostuf 8. 4.04 Offenbach 264 599HSSPF Italien 11.44 Ustuf SS-WVHA 11.41

Schellenberg Walter Brigadef 16. 1.10 Saarbrücken 124 817 Chef Amt VI,SS-RSiHA 12. 39 †31. 3.52 SD-Hauptamt1.35

Schellin Erich Staf 16.10.92 Falkenburg 13 208 HSSPF Ost 6.44 † 21. 3.78

Schenck Dr. Ernst Stubaf 3. 8.04 Marburg/Lahn 353 139 Begl.Kdo. Führer4.45 † 21.12.98 SS-WVHA8.44

Schenk Dr Erich Stubaf 9. 8.13 Tübingen 352 996 Sani.Abt.9 2.45 Ostuf Kdo.Stab RFSS 1.42

Schenkenhofer 9.9.09 Stuttgart 3 882 HSPPF Italien10.44

Scherner Julian Hstuf 10. 2.10 Taxenbach 39 495 Rgt.Dirlewanger 4.45 Oberf Degradiert SS-Hauptamt 8.44

Schiebel Kurt Ostuf 14.10.10 Wittenberg 464 414 SS-RSiHA 11.44 Uscha Nachschub 4 10.42

Schimana Walter Gruf 12. 3.98 Troppau 337 756 HSSPF Griechl.7.44 Brigadef Kdr.14.W.Gr.Div 7.43 † 12. 9.48 Salzburg Freitod

Schlapeit Bernhard Hstuf 20. 3.05 Nemonien 9 09 2.Kosaken Kav.Div11.44 HSSPF Ost 1.44

Schlauderer Matthias Ostuf 2.11.01 Gailsbach 24 146 HSSPF Ost 8.44

Schlegel Dr.Heinz Stubaf 5. 7.12 Neuruppin 318 473 IVb,Pz.GR.2410.44 Hstuf Kdo.Stab RFSS 1.42

Schlotmann Ernst Ostuf 1. 9.13 Moers 26 550 Begl.Kdo.Führers 4.44 Mann LSAH 5.33

Schmauser Heinrich Ogruf 18.1.90 Hof 3 559 HSSPFNiedSchlei10.44 † 31.12.45 (?)

Schmid Karl Ostuf 7.12.09 München 1 703 I.SS-Pz.Korps 1.45 "alter Kämpfer"? SS-Kdo.Oberesalzberg 6.44

Schmidt EugenEmil Ostuf 2. 1.11 Hauptamt VOMI 8.44

Schmidt Franz Ustuf 2. 3.04 Langewiese 321 603 Rgt.Dirlewanger 10.44 Rttf.6.SS-Geb.Div 1.44

Schmidt Werner Hstuf 25. 4.96 Solingen 414 935 SSWaffenrenDiv 1.44 Ustuf HSPPF Kaukasus 1.43

Schmincke Rudolf Stubaf 26. 4.94 Braunschweig 422 238HSPPF Ost 3.44 † 27. 3.44 Krakau

Schmitt Walter Ogruf 13. 1.79 Hamburg 28 737 Pers.Stab RFSS 6.44

Schmitz Karl Stubaf 2. 6.10 Püm/Eifel 94 445 KG Prutzmann 4.44 Hstuf HSSPF Rußl.Süd 1.43

Schmuckerschlag FritzOscha 13. 1.11 276 077 BrigDirlewanger12.44 Ostuf Inf. Regt. 4 6.41 degradiert 12.44

SchnäbeleCarl Ostubaf 20. 1.96 276 32Stab RFSS 10.42 † 10.42

Schneider Ludwig Hstuf 28.11.93 Schäßburg/Siebenb.HSSPF Serbien11.44

Schneidt Kurt Ostuf 18. 3.09 Hamburg 15 766 16./Pz.GR.38 4.45 4.45 Oscha Btl. Dirlewanger 2.43

Schneier Willy Hstuf 12. 2.12 Neustadt 71 143 Ostturk.Waf.Verb.. Rft. Dirlewanger 10.44 Werfer-Bttr.500 6.44

Schnell Otto Hstuf 19. 9.02 Bad Neustadt 161 369 RgtDirlevang11.44 SS.-Hauptamt 6.43

Schnitt Dr.Kurt Ostuf 22. 8.09 Berlin 139 000 SS-RSiHA 9.44 Ustuf 2,SS-Pz.Div. 9.41

Schode Viktor Ustuf 23.1.15 Punevescy Strafvollzugslager d.W-SS 11.44 SS-Sanitätsamt 3.41

Scholz Herbert Ostuf 12.1.1 Zirlau 311 071 Rgt. Dirlewanger 2.45 SSKraftf. AuE.Rgt 1.45

Schön Ludwig Hstuf 27. 1.11 76 690 HSSPF Ost 4.44

Schönfellner Hubert Ustuf 15.12.12 4./Pz.Rgt.1 12,43 † 29.12.43 Zhitomir HSSPF Ost 11.42

Schramm Kurt Ostuf 13. 5.11 Berlin 235 491 Pz.GR.2 5.43.HSSPF Kaukasien 1.43

Schreiner Max Ustuf 21. 6.99 Eßlingen Rgt. Dirlewanger 9.44 † 6. 9.44 Warschau Rgt. Dirlewanger 6.43 12.2.22 Magdeburg 392 347 OO.Feldkdo. RFSS

Schreuder Dr.Jan Hstuf 31. 5.98 Reeuwyk/Nl 393 396 Rgt.Dirlewanger 4.44

Schröder Hans Ustuf 14/Inf.Reg Nordland 7.41 Schütze. 2.45

Schröder Walter Ustuf 25.1.23 Redekin 490 330Begl.Btl.RFSS8.44 SS-J. Sch.Tölz 6.44

Schröter Walter Ustuf 17.1.1 Hamburg 117 333 Hauptamt VOMI Strm 5./LSSAH 9.39 7.41

Schubert Rudolf Ustuf 19.11.13 Gelsenkirchen115 437 RgtDirlew. 2.45. ‡ 2.45

Schuler Heinz Hstuf 29. 7.00 Ludwigshafen 244 109 HSSPF Rußlal 6.43

SshullerDr.Andreas Stubaf 22.11.13 Petersberg/Rum 310 483 Kdo. Stab RFSS 6.44

Schulz Werner Ustuf 28.10.13 Westensee 367 288 2./Nachr. Abt. 2./Nachr. Abt.106 4.44 Hscha SS-RSiHA 4.42

Schulze Otto Ustuf 4.1.23 Ebergötzen 496 526 Begl. Btl. RFS 12.44

Schulze Richard Ostubaf 22.10.14 Berlin-Spandau264 059 Kdr.II/Pz GR . 25 12.44 Stubaf Pers.Adj.Hitlers 10.42

Schumacher Ernst Schtz. 7. 8.08 Hattingen 276 527 Strafvollzug. Lager SS 4.44 Ustuf degradiert3./Geb.JR.13 6.43

Schüßler Josef Ostuf 3.5.10 Hamm 26 296 HSSPF Nord west 11.44 TWL Den Haag 4.41

Schuster Karl Staf 6. 7.95 Stuttgart 6 236 NO, HSSPF Weichsel 10.44 Stubaf HSSPF Rußl.Mitte 8.42

Schtrumpf Dr.Rudolf Ostuf 30. 7.09 Frankfurt/M 400 035 Pers.Stab RFSS AmtA 3.44 Uscha 11./Pz.GR.9 9.39

Schütz Erwin Ostuf 11.11.16 11./Rgt.Dirlewanger 4.45 ‡ 4.45

Schütz Markus Ostuf 14. 6.14 HA VOMI 1.45 Ustuf Frw.7.SS-Frw.Geb. Div. 1.43

Schütz Peter Ustuf 5. 9.11 Nürnberg 161 060 Pers Stab RFSS 1.43

Schwägermann Günther Hstuf 24. 7.15 Uelzen 312 231 Begleit. Kdo.d.Führers .4.45 Ostuf Chef, 10./Pol.Inf.Rgt.1 6.42

Schwaiger Hans Stubaf 28. 7.01 Ulm 23 449 SS-Kdo Obersalzb.1.45 Hstuf Chef, 14./Pz.GR.3 8.42

SchwarzGottfried Ustuf 3. 5.13 HSSPF Ost 6 † 19. 6.44 Italien

Schwarz Gotthilf Hstuf 18. 3.08 Tuttlingen 9 272 HSSPFNor Ostuf 4. SS-Pol.Div 11.41 4.44

Schwarzäugl Hans Ostuf 25. 1.03 Triest 130 125.HSSPFNord 4.43

Schweiger German Ustuf 8. 4.11 München 109 835 HSSPF Italien 11.44

SchweigerSebastian Ustuf 2. 3.20 Bay.Gmain 455 151 1./Pz.Rgt12 HSSPF Rußl.Süd 1.43

Seidel Hans Hstuf 16. 4.94 Rothenkirchen 266 183 HSSPF Nord 12.44 IVa, Art.Rgt.2 6.42

Seidensticker Herman Hstuf 1. 6.12 Hamburg 194 452 HSSPF Italien Ostuf VIa, 29.W-Gr.Div 10.44 1.45

SeifertDr.Herbert Ostuf 26. 3.07 Schwarzengrund 171 262 SSWHA KrakauHSSP1.43 Amt A V 2.45

Sesemann Karl Stubaf 28.12.09 Mühlhausen 143 242 HSSPF Ukraine 6.44

Sieben Hans Hstuf 17. 7.12 Bottrop 76 597. HSSPF † 1945 IVa,III./SS.Pz.Korps 12.43 Ostland 3.45

Sieber Hans Ostuf 22. 4.16 Hamroth/Ungarn423715Haupt- † 23. 8.44. Ustuf 8./Inf.Rgt.7 4.42 amt VOMI 8.44

Siebert Joachim Hstuf 6.12.04 Wiesbaden 78 948 HSSP † 6.11.44 SkutariAlbanien 4.44

Sieling Heinz-Paul Ostuf 2. 5.14 Berlin 266 271 Rgt. „Dirlewanger 6.44 Degradiert Schtz SS-Bewähr.Abt 1.44 Ostuf Chef,3./Inf.Rgt.8 4.42

SnidarsicBorislav Ustuf 16. 6.21 Zagreb SS-RSiH 11.44 9./Geb.JR.27 11.43

Solleder Erich Stubaf 6. 3.12 Schw.Gmünd 110 191. HSSPF Ungarn 10.44 Hstuf 4, Art.Rgt.2 5.40

Sommer Heinz Ostuf 1.10.05 Berlin 464 413. HSSPF Italien 11.44 † 4.45 Italien Ustuf SS-Kraftf.AuEAbt 8,43

Spacil Josef Staf 3. 1.07 München 6 797 RSiHAS- Ostubaf Va KG Prutzmann 2.44 1.45

Spieker August Ostuf 13. 1.06 Mengede 426 267 HSSPF IVa, H.W.L.Danzig 11.43 Adriat.KüsL 9.44

SpindlerWernerOstuf 4.5.11Magdeburg 160 021 Pers. StabRFSS 10.44

Sprang Paul Hstuf 20. 3.14 Königsberg 5 437HSSPF Ost1.44 Ostuf TWL Reval 1.42

Staib Karl Ustu f 12. 1.01 Auenstein Rgt. Dirlewanger 8.44

Staudt Eitel Hstuf5. 6.98 36 599 Frw.Leg.Nieder Kdo. Stab RFSS 1.41 lande 2.43 10.44

Steinhoff Hermann Ostuf 16. 6.06 Angerstein 350 242 Kdo.Stab RFSS 6.44

Stelzer Hugo Stubaf 15. 9.01 Uelzen 77 074Hauptamt O.P6.44.

Steurer Friedrich Ostuf 10. 5.14 Kehl 65 278 HSSPF Adria.KüsL HSSPF Rußland 4.43 4.44

Stiebeler Richard Stubaf 8. 2.91 Sandau 71 434 SS-Kraftf.AuE.Rgt HSSPF Ost 8.44 10.44

Stöhr Fritz Ustuf 27.12.15 Freiburg/Br 429 640 Hauptamt VOMI 10.44

Stolle Richard Ustuf 1.11.11 Posen 2 782 R.u.S.Fhr.in SS-FHA Stoweno 9.42 Ungarn 10.44 Rudolf Herbert Hstuf 11. 4.01 Wollstein 16 489 SS-Brigade. Dirlewanger 11.43 †Dünaburg 15.11.43 DSS-Hauptamt 6.43

Strater Kurt Ostuf 16.10.0 Rheydt 461 893 . HSSPF Serbien 11.44

Strebl Walter Ustuf 1.8.20 FreilassingPers.Stab RFSS 1.44

Streit Bernhard Ostuf 6.10.13 Gablonz 369 540 TFK Haupt-amt VOMI 7.43

Streit Hermann (A-SS) Ostuf 29.10.10 Düsseldor 13 455SS-RSiHA Oscha 1./LSSAH 5.38 9.42

Stroop Jürgen Gruf 26. 9.99 Detmold 44 611 HS Ostuf OO,III./T.I.R.3 7.41 Rhein-Westmark 11.44† 12. 7.52 Warschau hanged

Stuck Hans Ostuf 2. 9.09 Danzig 60 270 Pz.GR.5 HSSPF Rußl.Mitte 4.434.44

Names List T:

Tauber Siegfried Ogruf 11.12.80Brallentin 23 128 Pers. † 13. 2 SS.Schule Wewelsburg 6.44 Pers.Stab RFSS 6.44

Täubner Max Schtz 22.5.10 Neulußheim 112 659Straf-degradiertlager d.SsuPol10.43 UstufTFK,Kdo.Stab RFSS9.41

Telesko Gustav Ostuf 6.10.07```Pantschowa HSSPFTrieste 1.45 Apotheker,SanAbt. 6.43

Teschnere Otto Hstuf 14. 4.00 Schweidnitz 108 027 .HSSPF Chef, Fernmeldew 4.4 Süd-Ost 12.44 Ustuf Nachr, Abt.5 2.44

Teufel Christian Ustuf 16.11.20 Bondorf .Stab RFSS 7.41

Thaler Alois Stubaf 28.11.09 Bruneck 347 172 HSSPF † 2. 5.45 Hstuf Chef. 12 ./Inf.Rgt.7 3.42Italien10.44

Theml Hartwig Ostuf 30. 6.16 Weipert 304 832 SS- Oblt. OKH 11.44 SiHA 12.44 Oblt OKH v. Thermann Dr. Edmund Staf 6. 3.84 Köln 100320Haupt-amt VOMI 6.44

DE LA LIEUX

Thorbeck Otto Stubaf 26. 8.12 Brieg 216 334 Haupt- . HSSPF KAukasus 1.43 amt SS-Gericht 11.44

Thull Dr. Hermann Hstuf 7. 2.09 Saarbrücken 275 819 Kdo Stab RFSS` 4.42

Tiefenbacher Josef Staf 13. 8.01 München 276 849 Pers. Stab RFSS 6.44

Timm Karl Hstuf 4.10.06 Naugard 12 213 SS- Ostuf Hauptamt VOMI 4.43 Hauptamt 6.44 Hauptamt 6.44

Tögel Walter Ustuf 21. 2.24FlakAbt KdoStabRFSS 9.43

Tolweth Fritz Ostuf 18.9.14 Betschkerek HSSPF Serbien 11.44

Tomm Rudolf Hstuf 16. 9.05 Posen 33 685 Kom. Stab RFSS1.43

Trattenschegg Adalbert Ostuf 29. 5.05 St.GeorgenBrig. Dirlewanger 9.44 † 18. 3.45 Olarzew Nachsch. 13 11.43

Trautmann Hermann Ustuf 9.5.99 MünchenSS--Dolm.Sch 10.44.

Treusch Wilhelm Stubaf 24.1.05 Ebenbach 291 215 Pers. Stab RFSS 6.44 StabRFSS 6.44

Tschimpke Erich Oberf 11. 3.98 Breslau 40 065 HSSPF HSSPF Italien 4.44 Staf . Nachschub34.43

Turner Dr. Harald Ostuf 5. 4.18 Düsseldorf275143 Kom.Stab Pers.Stab RFSS 7,42RFSS11.44

Names List U:

Ullmann Otto Oberf21.9.99 Homburg276 658 Pers.Stab RFSS 6.44

Upenieks ArtursUstuf 29. 9.20 HSSPFOst Kom.Stab 6.44

Urbat René Ostuf 22. 2.07 Mühlhausen 92 293 WachKp Kom.Stab RFSS 11.43 Obersalzb 9.44

Appendix 6
Waffen-SS Officers Posted in Nazi Concentration Camps

List A: Abraham Dr. Karl Hstuf 2. 8.08 Untergeis 167 177 K.L. Sutthof 4.44 Ustuf K.L. Auschwitz 4.41

Albert Rolland Ostuf 21. 4.16 Schässburg/ 467 018 K.L. Auschwitz 1.45 Siebenbürgen

Alexnat Walter Ustuf 11. 1.20 ? ? 9.SS-Pz.Div. 3.44 † 21. 6.79 K.L. Niederhagen 4.43

Altfuldisch Johann Ostuf 11.11.11 **11 958** Marbach K.L. Mauthausen 6.44

Andresen Otto Stubaf 3.10.90 **18 865** Lauban Kdr.Pi.Bau.Btl 1 6.44 Pi.Btl.2 3.42 Hstuf **K.L.Sachsenhausen** 9.41

Arold August Hstuf 4. 8.83 74 999 Aschaffenburg SS-WVHA 4.42 Insp. **SS-K.L.** 7.44

Aumeier Hans Stubaf 20. 8.06 **2 700** Amberg SS-WVHA 11.44 K.L. Auschwitz 2.42

List B: **Waffen-SS Officers Posted in Nazi Concentration Camps**

Babor Dr. Karl Hstuf 23. 8.18 296 670 Wien IVb,I.Pz.GR.6 8.44 K.L. Groß-Rosen 11.41

Bachmayer Georg Hstuf 12. 5.13 69 535 Friedolfing K.L. Mauthausen 10.44 Ustuf K.L. Mauthausen 1.41

Baehr Paul Ostuf 19. 7.04 **25 731** Germersdorf Nachschub 10 1.44 Ustuf K.L. Sachsenhausen 11.41

Baer Richard Stubaf 9. 9.11 44 225 Floß/Obpf. **Kdr. K.L. Auschwitz** 10.44 Ostuf Chef, 1./T.I.R.1 9.41

Baranowski Hermann Oberf. 11. 6.84 24 009 ? Kdr. K.L.Sachsenhausen 2.40 † 5. 2.40

Barnewald Otto Stubaf 10. 1.96 **6469** Leipzig K.L. Buchenwald 2.42 Ostuf IVa,II.Staf."Germania2" 9.36

Baumgart Hans Ostuf 23. 4.05 143 890 Freiburg/Br. K.L. Dachau 11.44 SS.-WVHA 5.43

Baumgartner Ludwig Ostuf 8.11.09 257 276 Nersingen K.L. Flossenburg 11.41 Ustuf K.L.Flossenburg 4.40

Baumköther Heinz Hstuf 7. 2.12 278 430 Burgsteinfurt K.L. Mauthausen 11.43 Ustuf SS.WVHA 10.41

Bayer Johann Ustuf 12. 2.24 ? ? K.L. Auschwitz 6.44 ‡ 1.45

Beck Johann Hstuf 22. 7.88 **179** Nürnberg K.L. Mauthausen 6.44

Becker Josef Hstuf 16. 8.84 105 804 Feudenheim K.L. Dachau 1.42 Becker Wilhelm Ustuf 29. 4.87 ? Holzhausen K.L. Dachau 6.44

Beer Rudolf Ostuf 17. 2.11 322 278 Friedland 5. SS-Pz.Div 10.44 Ostuf K.L. Ravensbrück 11.41

Behrndt Harry Stubaf 12. 2.09 174 497 Rummelsburg Apoth.SaniAbt15 10.44 Hstuf Insp. K.L. 1.42

Benedict Hugo Ostuf 10. 1.98 174 559 Hamburg K.L. Neuengamme 4.44

Berger Dr. Arno Hstuf 29. 8.12 254 208 Stralsund IVb, Aufkl.Abt 17 2.45 Ustuf K.L Ravensbrück 2.45

Bergmaier Fritz Ustuf 23. 1.20 475 290 Erlangen K.L. Buchenwald 5.44 Strm Pz.GR3 7.41

Bertl Josef Ustuf 30. 8.14 160 972 München ? 1.45 Hscha K.L. Buchenwald 1.42

Bessert Artur Hstuf 4. 2.99 257 406 Moritzfelden K.L. Mauthausen 11.44 † Kowno 5 1.46

Beyer Wilhelm Ostuf 5. 4.94 292 029 Gröningen K.L. Auschwitz 4.44 Ustuf K.L. Dachau 11.42

Bischoff Fritz Hstuf 4. 8.96 ? Augsburg K.L. Buchenwald 6.44

Blancke Dr. Max Hstuf 4. 5.09 162 897 Heinsberg K.L. Oranienburg 4.42

Blaschke Dr. Otto Ostuf 24. 9.08 391 852 Obernith 1.SS-Pz.Div 11.42 Ostuf K.L. Mauthausen 1.42

Blei August Ostuf 26. 8.93 454 747 Hüsten K.L. Mauthausen 6.44

Boehme Ludwig Stubaf 21. 8.93 249 802 ? K.L. Auschwitz 10.44

Bömichen Karl Hstuf 31. 5.12 256 732 Rheine IVb Nachr.Abt 106 6.44 Hstuf K.L. Neuengamme 11.43 v. Bonin Engelbert Hstuf 13.12.92 205 878 Danzig K.L. Sitthof 11.44

Borell Gustav Ostuf 15. 4.98 244 456 Friedrichsthal K.L. Ravensbrück 1.42

Bosch Jakob Ostuf 2.11.91 **6959** Mörzheim K.L. Sachsenhausen 4.43

Brachtel Dr Rudolf Hstuf 22. 4.09 327 556 Gaya/Sud. 4.SS-Pol.Div. 1.44 Hstuf 2./San.Abt.9 7.43 Ustuf K.L. Dachau 4.42

Brandenburg Peter Ostuf 10.02.89 424 556 Hörde/Westf. K.L.Groß-Rosen 11.43 K.L. Groß-Rosen 6.42

Brauer Karl Ostuf 29. 9.93 203 635 Belgern/Elbe K.L. Groß-Rosen 11.43 Ustuf K.L. Groß-Rosen 11.42

Bräuning Edmund Hstuf 2. 7.05 66 975 Naumburg/Sa K.L. Ravensbrück 1.44

Brennels Otto Hstuf 3. 7.00 73 378 Landau/Pfalz IVa, Pz.Abt 11 4.45 † 10. 5.45 K.L. Flossenburg 3.41

Breitschneider Hans Ostuf 14.12.13 177 918 Werdau Hpt.San.LagerW-SS 6.43 Ustuf K.L. Buchenwald 1.42

Broßmann Otto Hstuf 1. 2.89 352 200 Brawin K.L. Auschwitz 11.43

Büngeler Heinz Ostuf 29. 3.13 94 968 Halle OO, Pz.GR.6 2.43 † 4. 3.43 Krassnyj Adj. K.L. Buchenwald 4.42

Burger Wilhelm Stubaf 19. 5.04 47 285 München SS-WVHA 6.44 Stubaf IVa, K.L.Auschwitz 1.43 Hstuf IVa, T.I.R.1 5.42

Busch Dr. Karl Hstuf 24.11.08 208 587 Gaukönigshofen IVb,III./Art.Reg.12 6.44 Ustuf K.L. Ravensbrück 11.41

List C: **Waffen-SS Officers Posted in Nazi Concentration Camps**

Campe Hermann Ostuf 8.11.10 49 126 Köbbelitz 10.SS-Pz.Div. 2.45 Ustuf K.L. Sachenhausen 9.41

Chlebus Karl Hstuf 30. 8.94 ? ? K.L.Sutthof 6.44

Christ Gotthilf Hstuf 10.12.18 ? ? K.L.Sachsenhausen 3.44

Conrad Hans Ostuf 9. 2.12 169 822 Küstrin IVa, I./Sani.Abt.10 4.44 Ustuf K.L. Auschwitz 1.42

Conrad Dr. Ladislaus Ostuf ? 411 908 ? 5. SS-Pz.Div. 4.43 Ustuf K.L. Mauthausen 11.41

Conradi Heinz Hstuf 14. 6.98 97 966 Wiesbaden 7.SS-Frw.Geb.Div. 11.43 † 4.45 Ostuf K.L. Mauthausen 4.42

LIST D: **Waffen-SS Officers Posted in Nazi Concentration Camps**

Dankhof Theo Ostuf 13. 8.15 Neesbach 144 303 11./Pz.Gr.Brig.51 8.44 Ustuf K.L. Neuengamme 4.41-4.43

Degelow Fritz Stubaf 25. 2.92 Gotha 178 978 K.L. Dachau 1.45 Hstuf VI.SS-Frw.Armkorps 2.44

Dembeck Bruno Ostuf 22.10.87 Marienwerder 230 247 K.L. Buchenwald 4.43 † 31.12.44 Greiz/Thür

Detmers Heinrich Ostuf 20. 4.19 Norden/Ostfries 309 930 1.SS-Inf.Brig 4.43 K.L. Dachau 4.42

Diembt Otto Ostuf 18. 3.07 Bad Flinsberg 189 176 K.L. Mittelbau 1.45 Ustuf SS-WVHA 5.43

Dienstbach Dr. Oskar Hstuf 30. 9.10 Usingen 101 741 IVb, Aufkl.Abt 1 4.43 K.L. Mauthausen 2.41

Dietrich Eugen Ostuf 15. 9.89 Ludwigshafen 262 643 K.L. Buchenwald 1.43 † 1948

Dillmann Herbert Ostuf 31.10.13 Dresden 270 728 Kaukas.Waffenverb. 2.45 K.L. Natzweiler 1.44

Ding (jetzt Schuler) Dr. Edwin Stubaf 19. 9.12 ? 280 163 K.L. Buchenwald 4.44 † 1945 Adj.Sani.Abt 3 5.40

Dittmann Dr. Alfred Ostuf 18.11.06 Neutech/Danz **11 090** IVb.III/PzGR 2 12.44 K.L. Mauthausen 6.44 K.L. Revensbrück 1.44

Drees Eduard Ostuf 29. 1.01 Eutin/Holst 214 402 K.L. Flossenburg 11.44

Dumbock Karl Ostuf 19. 4.06 ? 267 674 K.L. Buchenwald 1.42

Dumm Josef Ustuf 11. 8.08 Mainburg **23 050** Wi.Btl 13 4.43 K.L. Dachau 1.42

LIST E: Waffen-SS Officers Posted in Nazi Concentration Camps

Eckermann Werner Ostuf 18. 1.12 ? 68 543 K.L. Mauthausen 6.44 2./LSSAH 4.41

Ehle Paul Hstuf 22.10.97 Danzig/Ohra 153 968 K.L. Sutthof 5.44

Ehrenberger Raimund Stubaf 6. 8.93 Wien 308 257 IVb, Art.Abt 105 1.45 K.L. Auschwitz 6.41-2.43

Ehser Max Ostuf 24. 3.93 Eilenburg **9 785** K.L. Auschwitz 1.42 Ustuf K.L. Flossenburg 3.40

Eicheldörfer Johann Hstuf 20. 1.90 ? ? K.L. Dachau 6.44

Eisenhöfer Heinrich Ostuf 19. 2.93 Pirmasens 162 304 K.L. Mauthausen 1.44 Ustuf K.L. Mauthausen 1.42

Engelhardt Erich Ostuf 4. 5.93 ? 246 525 K.L. Mauthausen 1.44

Entreß Friedrich Hstuf 8.12.14 Posen 53 124 9. SS-Pz.Div. 2.45 Hstuf K.L. Auschwitz 11.43

Ernstberger Walter Ostuf 23. 8.13 Pforzheim 270 670 K.L. Groß Rosen 4.45 † 4.1945

Euler Emil Ostuf 15. 2.84 Odernheim 349 618 K.L. Mauthausen 6.44 † 13. 9.50 Polen

LIST F: **Waffen-SS Officers Posted in Nazi Concentration Camps**

Faschingbauer Karl Hstuf 21. 5.04 Fürth/Bayern 55 074 34.W-GrenDiv 2.45 K.L. Natzweiler 11.42

Faßbender Wilhelm Ustuf 8. 3.92 Köln 411 910 K.L. Flossenburg 11.41

Fent Josef Hstuf 5. 1.12 ? **4 847 Insp. K.L.** 1.42 † 18. 1.42

Filleböck Sylvester Ustuf 16. 6.96 Pfronten **25 250** K.L. Dachau 11.44

Finkenzeller Franz Ostuf 1. 8.13 Pfaffenhofen **15 185** K.L. Ravensbrück 11.41

Fischer Dr. Hans Ostuf 11.10.12 Nachrodt 228 469 SS-Wehrgeol.Btl 4.45 K.L. Buchenwald 1.44

Fischer Hugo Ustuf 16. 2.20 Bielefeld 381 746 3. SS-Pz.Div 11.44 K.L. Neuengamme 1.41-4.43

Flach Dr Karl Hstuf 5.11.01 Aschaffenburg 102 396 10.SS-Pz.Div 4.44 Ustuf K.L. Dachau 9.41

Foerschner Otto Stubaf 4.11.02 Dürrenzimmern 191 554 K.L. Buchenwald 6.44 Hstuf I./Pz.GR.10 6.41

Forster Heinrich Hstuf 14. 1.97 Langenaltheim **36 647** 14. W.Gren.Div. 12.44 K.L. Sachsenhausen 4.41

Frank Rudolf-Julius Hstuf 2. 8.97 ? ? K.L. Neuengamme 6.44

Frank Dr. Willy Hstuf 9. 2.03 Regensburg 289 643 3.SS-Pz.Div. 11.44 K.L. Auschwitz 6.44

Friesemann Heinrich Ostuf 18.10.14 Völlenerföhn 270 654 K.L. Sachsenhausen 4.45 ‡ 4.45

Freyer Otto Hstuf 9. 3.94 ? ? K.L. Neuengamme 8.44

Fritzsch Karl Hstuf 10. 7.03 Nassengrub **7 287** K.L. Auschwitz 4.41

Frohne Wilhelm Hstuf 24. 1.96 ? ? K.L. Buchenwald 6.44

Frowein D. Ernst Stubaf 25. 8.16 Iserlohn 411 912 SS.San.AuE.Btl 2.45 Ostuf K.L. Sachenshausen 11.42-4.44 ‡ 5.45

LIST G: Waffen-SS Officers Posted in Nazi Concentration Camps

Gaberle Dr. Alois Ustuf 30. 9.07 Öls-Löberney 363 185 K.L. Sachsenhausen 4.44

Ganniger Heinrich Ostuf 16. 7.08 Mannheim 102 470 K.L. Auschwitz 11.43

Ganz Anton Hstuf 6. 2.99 Kettershausen **34 572** K.L. Mauthausen 11.43

Garms Hellmut Ustuf 21. 4.05 Burg/Magdeb 136 554 K.L. Ravensbrück 11.44

Gehrig Heinz Stubaf 27.10.90 Laudenbach 250 066 K.L. Dachau 6.44 IVa,Inf.Reg.8 11.41

Gegenwarth Ernst Ustuf 4. 5.14 Grünewört 55 361 SD Lublin 7.44 † 2. 8.44 Warschau 17./Sta "Deutschland" 10.38

Geiger Hans Hstuf 7. 2.13 Liebenstein 142 033 K.L. Flossenburg 1.45 Ostuf Begl.Btl RFSS 10.42

Geiß Ludwig Ustuf 13. 4.86 Ellweiler **14 765** K.Z. Dachau 6.44

Gerber Gerhard Ostuf 5. 8.15 Straßburg 433 204 K.L. Auschwitz 1.45

Gerdes Magnus Ostuf 30. 8.87 Berlin 420 738 K.L. Groß-Rosen 4.42

Giesenhaus Wilhelm Ustuf 17. 4.11 ? 271 790 Apotheker K.L. Lublin 10.42 † 4. 1.43

Glatz Josef Ostuf 3. 5.11 Hodosch/Rum ? K.L. Mauthausen 11.44 Ustuf SS-WVHA 2.44

Glücks Richard Gruf 22. 4.89 Odenkirchen 58 706 SS-WVHA Chef Amts- Gruppe D 11.44 Brigadef Inspektion K.L. 4.41 † 10. 5.45 (suicide)

Goecke Wilhelm Ostubaf 12. 2.98 Schwelm **21 529** HSSPF Adria.Küste 10.44 Kdr. K.L. Kauen 6.44 † 22.10.44 Fontana Kdr. III./Inf.Rgt 6 6.41

Goedicke Fritz Hstuf 20.10.97 **? 11 012 Kdr.** K.L.Neuengamme 4.42 † 4. 2.44

Gossow Erich Ostuf 13. 3.03 Gruneberg 270 203 K.L.Sachsenhausen 11.44

Göth Amon Hstuf 11. 2.08 Wien **43 673** K.L. Lublin 4.44 † 13. 9.46

Gottstein Rainer Ostubaf 10. 8.10 Reichenberg 219 699 **Kdr.Sipo-SD** Budap 2.45 † 13. 2.45 Tök

Greunuß Dr. Werner Ustuf 20. 2.08 ? ? K.L. Buchenwald 1.45

Grollitsch Dr. Karl Ostuf 13.10.08 St.Veit/Glan 308 212 16.SS.Pz.Gr.Div 6.44 K.L. Dachau 6.43

Großmann Hermann Ostuf 21. 7.01 Petersdorf 150 923 K.L. Buchenwald 2.43

Groth Johannes Ostuf 21. 3.03 Neustettin 253 188 K.L. Dachau 4.45 ‡ 4.45 23.SSFrwKavDiv 2.44

Grünberg Georg Ostuf 10.10.06 ? **23 860** K.L. Dachau 4.44 Uscha 9./T.I.R.2 5.40

Grünewald Adam Ostuf 20.10.02 Frickenhausen 253 631 2./Pz.Jg.Abt 3 2.45 Kdr. K.L. Vught 6.43

Grüter Heinrich Ostuf 10. 1.87 Krefeld **40 945** K.L.Niederhagen 11.42

Güssow Hans Stubaf 19. 5.89 Seehausen 135 798 K.L. Sachsenhausen 6.44

Gust Erich Ostuf 7. 4.90 ? **54 444** K.L. Buchenwald 1.43

LIST H: **Waffen-SS Officers Posted in Nazi Concentration Camps**

Haas Adolf Stubaf 14.11.93 Siegen 28 943 SS-PzGrAuEBtl18 1.45 Kdt K.L. Bergen-Belsen 6.44

Hackmann Hermann Hstuf 11.11.13 Osnabrück 164 705 K.L. Buchenwald 6.44 7.SS-Frw.Geb.Div 8.43

Hafner Karl Ustuf 3. 5.93 Saarbrücken 292 038 K.L. Dachau 11.44

Harbaum August Ostuf 25. 3.13 Gütersloh **37 163** Adj. K.L.Sachsenhausen 2.45

Hartjenstein Friedrich Ostubaf 7. 3.05 Peine 327 350 Kdr. K.L. Natzweiler 11.44 † 20.10.54 Metz Stubaf Kdr. I./T.I.R.3 8.42

Hartmann Willibald Ustuf 25. 5.10 Großdorf 305 189 K.L. Herzogenbusch 11.44

Hassenbroeck Johannis Stubaf 11. 7.10 Halle 107 426 Kdr. K.L. Groß-Rosen 10.44 Hstuf Chef, 10./Inf.Rgt. 9 4.42

Hattler Dr. Josef Hstuf 26. 2.12 ? 142 037 IVb. Flak-Abt. 1 1.44 † 8. 1.44 K.L. Flossenburg 1.41

Heeß Otto Ostuf 17.10.97 Bretten/Ba 103 482 K.L. Mauthausen 6.44

Heidingsfelder Hans Ostuf 18. 2.02 Amberg 1 537 K.L. Mauthausen 4.44

Heidt Dr. Otto Hstuf 13. 7.97 Arnau/Sud **43 268** K.L. Sutthof 6.44

Heidrich Hermann Stubaf 23. 3.86 Oberstein **22 606 K.L. Sachsenhausen** 6.44

Heim Dr Aribert Hstuf 2. 6.14 Radkersberg 367 744 6. SS-Geb.Div. 4.44 Ustuf K.L. Buchenwald 7.41

Heimann Karl Ostuf 28. 3.93 Berlin 219 906 K.L.Sachsenhausen 4.44

Hellinger Dr. Martin Hstuf 17. 7.04 Pirna 134 328 K.L. Ravensbrück 11.44

Henkel Dr. Wilhelm Hstuf 14. 6.09 Odenhausen 244 628 11.SS-Frw.Pz.Gr. Div 8.43 K.L. Mauthausen 6.43

Hennings Dr. Rudolf Stubaf 2. 5.12 Düsseldorf 372 353 Zahnarzt, 3.SS-Pz. Div. 1.45 Hstuf K.L. Niederhagen 11.42

Heschl Dr. Erwin Hstuf 28.11.11 Graz 303 997 III./Pz.GR.10 3.44 Ustuf K.L. Mauthausen 1.41

Heß Otto Ustuf 17.10.97 ? ? K.L. Mauthausen 11.42

Heußler Paul Ostuf 13. 1.90 Rottweil **27 301** 4. Nachschub 22 1.45 ‡ 2.45 Budapest K.L. Sachsenhausen 4.44

Hieronimus Johann Ustuf 16. 5.11 Leer/Ostfries. 82 486 Pi.Kp.Frw.GR.87 4.45 † 16. 4/ 45. K.L. Mauthausen 9.42

Höcker Karl Ostuf 11.12.11 Engershausen 182 961 K.L. Lublin 6.44

Hofmann Franz Hstuf 5. 6.06 Hof/Saale **40 651** K.L. Auschwitz 4.44 † 1945

Höller Dr. Walter Hstuf 20.10.08 Windisch-Gorsten 295 116 IVb,III./ArtRgt3 5.44 K.L. Buchenwald 11.43

Holzmann Georg Hstuf 7. 5.87 Diespeck **7 661** K.L.Sachsenhausen 10.43

Hoppe Paul-Werner Stubaf 28. 2.10 Berlin 116 695 Kdr. K.L. Sutthof 5.44 † 7. 74

Hornung Leo Ustuf 29. 8.93 Salzheim 152 303 K.L. Dachau 11.44 ‡ 3.45

Horstmann Dr Rudolf Hstuf 12.10.13 Berlin 120 026 K.L.Sachsenhausen 11.44 8.SS-Kav.Div. 2.43

Hoven Waldemar Hstuf 10. 2.03 Freiburg/Br 244 594 K.L. Buchenwald 4.42 † 2. 6.48

Hüttig Hans Stubaf 5. 4.94 Dresden 127 673 **Kdr** K.L.Herzogenbusch 6.44

LIST I: **Waffen-SS Officers Posted in Nazi Concentration Camps**

Illig Eugen Ostuf 23.12.09 Ebersbach 67 972 IVb,Pz.Abt 18 4.45 K.L. Groß-Rosen 6.44

LIST J: Waffen-SS Officers Posted in Nazi Concentration Camps

Jäger Dr. Willy Ostuf 22. 3.02 Landau 185 044 HSSPF AdriaKüste 1.45 K.L. Dachau 11.43

Janßen Karl Ustuf 12.11.19 Rheydt ? 10./Pz.GR.5 7.43 † 30. 7.43 Stepanowka K.L. Sachsenhausen 4.42

Jarolin Josef Ostuf 6. 3.04 Rehpoint 238 596 K.L. Dachau 4.44 † 28. 5.46 Landsberg K.L. Dachau 4.42

Jobstl Dr. Rudolf Hstuf 25. 3.03 Steyr/ObDon 323 775 K.L.Sachsenhausen 4.43 Ustuf K.L.Sachsenhausen 4.41

Josten Heinrich Ostuf 11.12.93 Malmedy 92 316 K.L. Auschwitz 1.44 † 19.12.50 Krakau K.L. Auschwitz 7.44

Jung Georg Ustuf 11. 1.22 Lttfeld/Wf. 430 411 K.L. Dachau 11.43

LIST K: **Waffen-SS Officers Posted in Nazi Concentration Camps**

Kahr Dr. Karl Hstuf 11. 9.14 Fürstenfeld 382 463 K.L. Dachau 1.45

Kaindl Anton Staf 14. 7.02 München 241 248 Kdr.K.L.Sachsenhausen 1.45 †1951 Vorkuta Iva,3.SS-Pz.Div 1.42

Kappe Dr. Julius Hstuf 20.12.05 Litzum 367 748 Zahnarzt, AufkAbt8 2.43 Ostuf K.L. Neuengamme 1.41

Kather Dr. Erich Ustuf 18. 7.08 Hamburg ? K.L. Buchenwald 4.44

Kempe Kurt Ostuf 14. 6.13 ? 210 844 K.L. Buchenwald 1.45

Kenn Rudolf Ostuf 9.1014 Berlin 118 203 K.L. Buchenwald 1.45

Ketterl Josef Hstuf 22. 7.89 Straubing 156 607 K.L. Ravensbrück 6.44 SS-WVHA 1.41

Kitt Bruno Hstuf 9. 8.06 Heilsberg 246 756 K.L. Auschwitz 11.44

Klebeck Kurt Hstuf 6. 3.06 Berlin 129 556 K.L. Neuengamme 1.45

Klipp Kurt Ostuf 19. 9.07 Köln 293 197 K.L. Auschwitz 1.45

Knorr-Krehann Kamillo Hstuf 25. 3.99 Plumenau.Sud 341 397 K.L. Flossenburg 11.44

Kögel Max Ostubaf 16.10.95 ? 37 644 Kdr. K.L.Flossenburg 6.44 † 6.46

Kolb August Hstuf 15. 8.93 Rößleinsdorf 222 497 K.L. Oranienburg 4.43

Kollmar Theodor Ostuf 30. 4.11 Pforzheim 251 823 SS.St-Verw.Buchenwald 6.44

König Dr. Hans-Wilhelm Ustuf 13. 5.12 Stuttgart ? K.L. Auschwitz 4.44

Kramer Josef Hstuf 10.11.06 München 32 217 Kdr. K.L. Bergen 1.45 Kdr. K.L. Auschwitz 6.44 Ostuf Adj.K.L.Auschwitz 1.41 † 13.12.45

Krätzer Theodor Ostuf 30.10.14 Nürnberg 276 344 Brig. Dirlewanger 2.45 K.L. Auschwitz 4.42

Krebsbach Dr. Eduard Stubaf 8. 8.94 Bonn 106 821 K.L. Mauthausen 6.44 1./Sani.Abt 3 5.40

Kreibich Dr. Eduard Hstuf 16. 7.08 Bensen 335 385 K.L.Sachsenhausen 1.45

Kroemer Adolf Hstuf 19. 5.90 ? 119 440 .K.L. Auschwitz 11.42

Krone Heinrich Stubaf 2. 2.01 Lingen 270 465 SS-WVHA 1.45 Hstuf K.L. Buchenwald 11.42

Kühler Heinz Ostuf 25. 5.11 Essen 264 033 K.L. Auschwitz 1.44

Künstler Karl Ostubaf 12. 1.01 Zella/Mühlh 40 005 Kdr. Nachschub 7 10.44 ‡ **4.45 Kdr.K.L.Flossenburg 7.42**

Kurz Alois Ustuf 14 7.17 Saalfelden 382 378 K.L. Auschwitz 7.44 SS-Rekr. Debrica 7.42

<u>LIST L</u>: **Waffen-SS Officers Posted in Nazi Concentration Camps**

Lange Theodor Ostuf 28. 9.18 Essen 400 103 10.SS-Pz.Div. 7.44 ‡ 8.44 Adj. K.L. Auschwitz 1.44

Langermann Armand Hstuf 18. 5.85 Hadsinstädt 401 318 IVc,K.L. Auschwitz 7.41

Langleist Walter Stubaf 5. 8.93 Dresden **8 480 K.L. Dachau 6.44 † 1946**

Lau Hans Ostuf 17. 6.93 ? **10 997 K.L. Dachau 1.43 † 26. 3.43**

Lauer Hubert Stubaf 10. 1.97 Simmern 291 721 K.L.Sachsenhausen 6.44

Lautenschlager Wilhelm Hstuf 30.10.96 ? ? K.L. Natzweiler 6.44

Leipold Josef Ustuf 10.1.13 Altrohlau 344 830 K.L. Groß-Rosen 2.43 † 12. 2.43

Liebenschel Arthur Ostubaf 25.11.01 Posen-Stadt 39 254 Kdr.K.L. Lublin 6.44

Liebus Erwin Hstuf 24. 1.94 ? ? K.L. Mauthausen 6.44

Linde Dr. Herbert Ostuf 3. 7.07 Berlin 203 212 II./Pz.GR.35 1.45 † 30. 1.45 K.Z.Mauthausen 4.43-6.44

Ludolph Julius Ostuf 26. 3.93 Hamburg 114 013 K.L. Mauthausen 1.44

Lütkemeyer Albert Hstuf 17. 6.11 Wellingholzhausen 270 485 K.L.Neuengamme 4.44

Lutosch Gerhard Hstuf 8. 9.11 ? 216 574 VI,10.SS-Pz.Div 1.44 Ostuf K.L. Buchenwald 1.42

LIST M:

Maier Dr. Emil Ostuf 18.12.95 Freiburg/Br **32 185** K.L.Natzeiler 11.42

Mathesius Kurt Ostuf 19. 9.10 Ohra/Danzig 99 130 K.L. Sutthof 4.43

Matz Dr. Karl Ostubaf 21. 6.09 Kiel 291 210 31.SS-Fw.Gr.Div 1.45 Hstuf K.L.Mauthausen 4.40-5.42

Meimeth Dr. Alfred 11. 7.06 Frankfurt/M 400 015 Zahnarzt Pi.Btl13 7.43 K.L. Auschwitz 4.41

Meinck Karl Ostuf 13. 9.06 Schwerin 215 846 Werfer-Abt 102 6.44 K.L.Mauthausen 4.43

Melzer Martin Hstuf 16.11.01 Elchesheim 172 106 K.L. Lublin 7.44 ‡ 24. 7.44

Mengele Dr. Dr. Josef Hstuf 16. 3.11 ? 317 885 K.L. Auschwitz 1.44 † 2. 7.79

Merbach Hans Ostuf 10. 5.10 Gotha **3 387** K.L. Buchenwald 4.42 † 1945

Metzger Dr. Franz Hstuf 11. 7.11 Saarbrücken 376 736 3.SS-Pz.Div. 4.43 K.L. Groß-Rosen 4.42

Metzger Karl Hstuf 9.12.00 ? ? K.L. Dachau 6.44

Meyer Dr. Georg Ostuf 6. 9.17 Wien ? II.SS-Pz.Korps 1.44 K.L. Auschwitz 11.42

Meyer Traugott Hstuf 6.11.04 München **16 385** K.L. Ravensbrück 1.42 † 10.11.1947

Meyer Wilhelm Ustuf 11. 2.96 ? **41 722** K.L.Herzogenbusch 11.44

Michl Hermann Hstuf 23. 4.12 ? 71 076 K.L. Lublin 6.44 † 21. 6.44

Möckel Karl Ostubaf 9. 1.01 Klingenthal **908** K.L. Auschwitz 6.44

Möller Ernst Hstuf 5. 3.91 Isenbüttel 236 154 K.L.Sachsenhausen 1.45

Möser Hans Ostuf 7. 4.06 Darmstadt **9 555** K.L.Neuengamme 4.42

Müller Erich Ostuf 28.10.04 Graudenz **46 063** IVa, K.L. Lublin 3.44 K.L. Sutthof 4.43 † 19. 3.44

Müller Max Ostuf 19. 2.19 Friedrichshafen 382 504 5.SS-Pz. Div 10.44 K.L. Mauthausen 11.43

Müllmerstadt Dr. Helmut Hstuf 28. 4.13. Offenbach/M 245 841 II.SS-Pz-Korps 1.44 K.L. Dachau 11.41

Muthig Dr. Jullius Stubaf 9. 5.08 Aschaffenburg 104 518 SS-U.Sch.Laibach 11.44 Hstuf K.L. Dachau 4.42-8.42

LIST N: **Waffen-SS Officers Posted in Nazi Concentration Camps**

Norin Georg Stubaf 31. 8.09 Essen 226 546 K.L.Sachsenhausen 6.44

LIST O: **Waffen-SS Officers Posted in Nazi Concentration Camps**

Obermeier Alois Stubaf 10. 4.01 Landshut **1 885** K.L. Mauthausen 6.44

Otto Kurt Hstuf 7.11.10 ? **19 341** K.L. Auschwitz 1.43 † Suicide 1. 2.43 Chef, 14./Leg Nederland 4.42

LIST P: **Waffen-SS Officers Posted in Nazi Concentration Camps**

Palfner Gerhard Ustuf 26. 02.08 ? 205 909 K.L. Buchenwald 1.44

Pauly Max Ostubaf 1. 6.07 Wesselburen **5 448 Kdr.**K.L.Neuengamme 11.44 † 6.10.46 K.L. Sutthof 11.41

Petermann Helmut Ostuf 24. 4.12 Gersdorf **15 231** 7.SS-FrwGebDiv 4.44 Ustuf K.L. Ravensbrück 4.42

Peters Heinrich Ostuf 22. 8.90 Auenbüttel 139 396 K.L. Natzweiler 4.42

Petri Fritz Ostuf 18. 9.10 Sandhausen 100 760 SS.Sta.Oranienburg 4.45 K.L.Sachsenhausen 1.43 ‡ 4.45

Pfeiffer Dr. Arnold Ostuf 14. 3.12 Fraustadt 217 115 Zahnarzt, AufklAbt8 7.43 K.L.Mauthausen 11.42

Pfütze Bruno Ostuf 9. 7.12 Nerchau/Sa 81 491 K.L. Auschwitz 11.44 † Norwegen

Pinnow Willy Ostuf 14.11.98 ? **12 922** HSSPF Dänemark 9.44 K.L. Auschwitz 5.43

Pister Hermann Oberf 21. 2.85 Lübeck 29 892 Kdr.K.L.Buchenwald 1.45 † 1947

Plaettig Dr. Richard Hstuf 3. 5.09 Dortmund 136 785 K.L.Mauthausen 11.44

Plaza Dr. Heinrich Hstuf 10. 7.12 Hultschin 352 853 K.L.Sachenshausen 11.43

Pohle Walter Ostuf 6. 1.10 Obergrünberg 236 288 Jäger Btl 500 8.43 K.L. Buchenwald 11.40

Pütz Dr. Heinrich Hstuf 1. 9.08 Essen 237 817 K.L. Sutthof 10.44 1./Sani. Abt 3 11.42

LIST R: **Waffen-SS Officers Posted in Nazi Concentration Camps**

Ramsauer Siegbert Hstuf 19.10.19 Klagenfurt 301 007 K.L. Mauthausen 1.44 Ustuf Aufkl.Abt.8 9.41

Rascher Dr. Sigmund Hstuf 12. 2.09 München 347 142 K.L. Dachau 4.45 **† verhaftet, executed 26.4.45** SS.Hauptamt 11.43

Rautenberg Herbert Stubaf 19. 1.08 Berlin **2 297** K.L. Buchenwald 1.45 12.Inf.Regt.6 8.41

Reddig Richard Hstuf 27. 9.96 Siddau/Ostpr. **17 791** K.L. Sutthof 6.44

Redwitz Michael Hstuf 14. 8.00 Bayreuth 327 349 I. SS-Pz.Korps 2.45 K.L. Mauthausen 4.41

Reimer Guido Ostuf 31. 7.01 Rensperg/Sud 305 116 K.L.Buchenwald 4.43

Reinicke Otto Ustuf 1. 1.08 Steigra 156 653 K.L. Auschwitz 11.42

Reiß Paul Stubaf 12.10.88 Altgersdorf 260 562 K.L. Dachau 6.44 Nachsch/ Finnland 6.42

Rett Dr. Andreas Ostuf 20. 4.09 Ingolstadt 411 930 K.L. Auschwitz 11.41

Richter Dr. Hermann Ostuf 13. 8.15 Linz 340 076 K.L. Mauthausen 6.43

Rieck Willy Hstuf 3. 3.14 Jüterborg 63 900 IVa15.W-GrDiv 6.44 K.L. Auschwitz 1.41-6.43

Riemer Otto Ustuf 19. 5.97 Rastatt **13 599** K.L. Mauthausen 11.42 † 5.45 St. Pölten

Rieth Arthur Ustuf 14. 4.90 Pforzheim 233 111 K.L. Dachau 11.43

Rindfleisch Dr. Heinrich Ostuf 3. 3.16 Straßburg 289 832 Begl.Btl.FSSS 2.45 K.L. Lublin 1.44

Rink Otto Ustuf 15. 6.88 Brück/Mark 259 562 K.L. Flossenburg 1.44

Ritterbursch Fritz Hstuf 11. 1.94 Zschockau **9 107** K.L. Groß-Rosen 1.45

Rittingshaus Helmut Hstuf 25. 8.08 Dahlbruch 291 339 Apoth.SaniAbt20 12.44 K.L. Ravensbrück 11.42

Röderer Dr. Rudolf Ustuf 7.10.10 Karlsruhe 200 198 K.L.Sachsenhausen 6.41 LSSAH 11.39

Rödl Arthur Staf 13. 6.98 München 1 240 Kdr.SS-PzAuEBtl18 1.45 **Kdr.K.L.Groß-Rosen 7.42-10.44**

Röhde Dr. Werner Ostuf 11. 6.04 Marburg 283 486 K.L. Auschwitz 9.44 † 11.10.46

Rosenthal Rolf Ostuf 22. 1.11 ? **31 442** K.L. Ravensbrück 4.43

Roßner Emil Ostuf 2. 9.06 Hof/Saale **3 777** K.L.Sachsenhausen 4.43 † 25. 3.84

Rost Willy Ustuf 19. 9.02 Dresden 186 161 K.L. Natzweiler 4.44 † 25.10.92

Ruppert Wilhelm Ostuf 2. 2.05 Frankenthal **7 282** K.L. Lublin 11.43 K.L. Dachau 1.42

LIST S: **Waffen-SS Officers Posted in Nazi Concentration Camps**

Sauer Albert Stubaf 17. 8.98 Misdroy 19 180 Kdr. K.L. Riga 7.44

Schaaf Hans Ostuf 4. 1.06 Koblenz-Wall. 75 254 K.L. Dachau 1.45 IVa, Felders Btl 2 10.43

Schartinger Hans Ustuf 13. 7.05 Steyr 309 478 K.L.Mauthausen 1.45

Schemmel Alfred Hstuf 29. 7.05 Hermannstadt 430 416 27.SS-Pz.GrDiv 10.44 K.L. Auschwitz 1.43

Schiffler Otto Hstuf 16. 1.94 ? ? K.L. Groß-Rosen 6.44

Schindler Hans Ostuf 15. 6.07 Amstetten 300 975 K.L. Auschwitz 11.44

Schippel Helmut Ostuf 17. 9.13 Oberschlema 282 228 K.L. Auschwitz 11.44 SS-WVHA 12.43

Schimer Rudi Ostuf 10. 5.12 Klein-Jena **43 089** 20.W-Gr.Div 7.44 K.L. Flossenburg 1.43-4.44

Schlorf Dr. Joachim Hstuf 6. 2.08 Röbel/Meckl 68 519 SS-Wehrgeol.Btl 4.44 K.L. Neuengamme 1.42

Schlüter Friedrich Hstuf 12. 5.13 Essen 347 132 IVb, Felders Btl 18 6.44 K.L. Auschwitz 11.41

Schmidetzki Walter Ostuf 5. 1.13 Sohrau/O.S. 224 169 K.L. Auschwitz 6.44

Schmidt Emil Ustuf 11. 1.95 Falkenberg ? K.L. Dachau 11.44

Schmidt Hans Hstuf 25.12.99 Höxter 115 662 K.L. Buchenwald 4.44

Schmidt Heinrich Hstuf 27. 3.12 Altenburg **23 069** K.L. Dachau 11.44

Schmidt Dr. Karl Ustuf 15. 4.13 Riebelsdorf 350 471 K.L. Auschwitz 4.44

Schmitz Dr. Emil Ostuf 1. 7.14 Remscheid 162 492 K.L.Sachsenhausen 4.43

Schmutzler Kurt Hstuf 17.11.95 Elsterberg 153 980 K.L. Mauthausen 11.44

Schnabel Dr. Alfred Stubaf 11. 3..88 Wünschelburg 188 285 K.L.Sachsenhausen 7.44

Schneider Max Ostuf 5. 6.10 Freiburg/Br 262 531 15.Waffen-Gr.Div 4.44 K.L. Mauthausen 1.43

Schögl Paul Ostuf 20. 1.17 Feldkirchen/Kä 467 433 W-Gr.Rgt SS rum. 11.44 K.L.Sachsenhausen11.43

Schobert Max Stubaf 25.12.04 Würzburg **3 531** K.L. Buchenwald 11.44 I./ SS-TV "Oberbayern" 11.35

Schöpperle Karl Ostuf 23. 6.92 Triberg 100 510 K.L. Mauthausen 4.44

Schöttl Vincenz Ostuf 30. 6.05 Appersdorf **5 630** K.L. Dachau 1.45

Schrader Fritz Stubaf 16. 6.09 Essen 190 089 12.SS-Pz.Div 9.44 K.L.Flossenburg 6.42-4.44

Schrader Kurt Hstuf 21.10.11 Köslin 403 609 24.Waffen-Geb.Div 9.44 K.L.Ravensbrück 11.41- 6.44

Schröder Dr. Hermann Ostubaf 20.11.95 Bantorf 270 783 Kdr.SS-KTL 2.45 K.L. Buchenwald 1.40

Schuler (Ding) Erwin Stubaf 19. 9.12 Bitterfeld 280 163 K.L. Buchenwald 4.44 † 1945 Adj.Sani.Abt 3 5.40

Schulte Dr. Wilhelm Hstuf 27. 3.07 Eberfeld 236 174 19.W-Gr.Div 7.44 K.L.Auschwitz 11.41-6.44

Schulz Karl Ostuf 9. 9.02 Eberswalde 400 037 K.L. Mauthausen 6.44

Schury Otto Ustuf 4.11.92 ? **14 054** K.L.Sachsenhausen 11.44

Schüttauf Erich Ostuf 21. 2.87 Radebeul 172 513 K.L. Mauthausen 11.43 Ustuf K.L. Flossenburg 4.40

Schütz Walter Hstuf 24. 7.04 Coburg 104 277 K.L. Mauthausen 11.43

Schwald Anton Ostuf 13. 3.92 Ludwigsburg 284 525 K.L.Sachenshausen 4.41

Schwarz Albert Hstuf 28. 9.19 Schwarzenau **6 532** K.L. Buchenwald 4.44

Schwarz Heinrich Hstuf 16. 6.06 München **19 691** K.L. Auschwitz 4.43

Schwarzhuber Johann Ostuf 29. 8.04 Tutzing 142 388 K.L. Auschwitz 1.44

Schwela Siegfried Hstuf 3. 5.05 ? **33 754** K.L. Auschwitz 5.42 † verstorben 10. 5.42

Schwitters Rudolf Ostuf 13. 6.14 Leezdorf 270 562 SS.Rekr. DepKurmark11.44 K.L.Sachsenhausen 1.43

Seel Wilhelm Ostuf 2. 8.85 Aglasterhausen **4 672** K.L. Dachau 4.44

Seidler Fritz Hstuf 18. 7.07 Werdau/Sa 135 387 K.L. Mauthausen 11.43 Ostuf K.L. Auschwitz 11.40

Seifert Gustav Hstuf 11. 4.85 Neundorf 128 213 K.L. Neuengamme 1.45 Ustuf K.L. Mauthausen 10.40 † 3.45

Seitschek Dr. Robert Hstuf 29. 7.17 Wien 367 375 SS-San.E.Abt 1.45 Ustuf K.L.Mauthausen 5.41-4.42

Seitz Kurt Hstuf 9. 6.07 Karlsruhe **14 405** K.L.Herzogenbusch 11.43

Sell Max Ostuf 8. 1.93 Kiel **35 889** K.L. Sachenshausen 4.45 † 4.45

Siedler Johann Ostuf 27.12.94 Troppau 331 666 Nachschub 12 1.45 K.L. Buchenwald 6.41

Siegmann Wilhelm Ostuf 16. 8.98 Oebisfelde **49 125** K.L. Lublin 11.43 K.L. Auschwitz 11.41

Siggelkow Herbert Hstuf 17.11.06 Schleswig 222 606 K/L.Sachsenhausen 11.44

Sorge Hans-Hermann Hstuf 4. 4.12 Königsee/Th. 411 935 IVb,III./Pz.GR 38 6.44 K.L.Sachsenhausen 11.41

Sperling Herbert Stubaf 1. 1.14 Berlin-Spandau 83 427 Kdr.Wi.Btl3 3.45 K.L.Mauthausen 12.38-7.41

Stenger Franz Ostuf 8. 5.97Aschaffenburg 464 033 K.L. Auschwitz 6.44 † 23.11.49 Kattowitz

Stiller Edgar Ustuf 25. 1.04 Hermannseifen 298 149 K.L. Dachau 11.43

Stimweis Konrad Ustuf 17. 7.93 ? ? K.L. Dachau 1.45

Stocker Emil Hstuf 12. 3.02 Zürich **34 081** K.L. Auschwitz 1.43 Art.Reg.6 3.42

Stoltz August Ustuf 26.11.89 Karlsruhe 244 374 K.L. Dachau 11.43

Storch Henry Hstuf 7.11.10 Husum 268 218 ApothSanAbt16 4.45 K.L. Auschwitz 11.41- 4.43

Stötzler Wilhelm Hstuf 1.1093 Friedrichstadt 225 183 K.L. Kauen 7.44 K.L. Groß-Rosen 4.43

Strauß Xaver Hstuf 29. 5.10 Velburg 161 264 IVa,I./Inf.Rgt.8 11.42 K.L.Mauthausen 4.41

Streit Wilhelm Hstuf 2.10.96 ? ? .K.L. Natzweiler 6.44

Strese Gustav Ostuf 29.11.93 Linde/Greifenh. **27 669** K.L.Niederhagen 1.45 Ustuf K.L.Niederhagen11.42

Strippel Arnold Ostuf 2. 6.11 Unshausen 236 290 K.L.Herzogenbusch6.44 K.L. Lublin 1.42

Stumpf Wolfgang Ostuf 6. 8.10 Scheßlitz/Obfr **40 629** IVa, NachrAbt11 8.43 K.L. Dachau 1.42

Suhren Fritz Stubaf 10. 6.08 ? **14 682** K.L.Rvensbrück 6.44 Ostuf K.L.Sachsenhausen 9.41 † 12. 6.50

Suttrop Rudolf Ostuf 17. 7.11 Lünen/Horstmar 230 953 K.L. Dachau 11.43 Ustuf K.L. groß-Rosen 4.42

LIST T: **Waffen-SS Officers Posted in Nazi Concentration Camps**

Täger Heinrich Ostuf 23. 2.97 Lippstadt 249 766 K.L. Flossenburg 9.42 SS-Art.AuE.Rgt 1.42

Temes Anton Ostuf 8. 2.92 Trier 71 913 Abt.IVa, K.L.Lublin 7.44 ‡ 25. 7.44 Lublin SS-WVHA 11.42

Teuber Dr. Karl-Heinz Stubaf 26.12.07 Glogau 195 300S SS-J.Sch. Braunschweig 1.45 Hstuf K.L. Auschwitz 1.43-8.43

Thiele Heinrich Hstuf 12. 7.99 ? ? K.L. Auschwitz 6.44

Thilo Dr. Heinz Hstuf 8.10.11 Elberfeld 126 436 K.L. Auschwitz 11.44

Thomsen Reinhard Ostuf 7. 2.01 Eckenförde 146 483 SS-Kraftf.AuE.Rgt. 3.45 K.L. Auschwitz 11.43

Thumann Anton Ostuf 31.10.02 Pfaffenhofen **27 444** K.L. Lublin 11.43

Thunecke Friedrich Ustuf 17. 4.99 Magdeburg 132 746 K.L. Dachau 11.42

Totzauer Karl Ustuf 15. 6.09 Udritsch 383 925 K.L. Neuengamme 4.44

Treite Dr. Percival Ustuf 10. 9.11 Berlin 220 796 K.L. Ravensbrück 4.44

Trommer Richard Hstuf 16. 6.10 Münnerstadt 106 394 K.L. Neuengamme 6.43

Trzebinski Dr. Alfred Hstuf 29. 8.02 Jotruschin 133 574 K.L. Neuengamme 4.45 † 4.45

LIST U: **Waffen-SS Officers on Duty in Nazi Concentration Camps**

Ulbrich Karl Hstuf 16. 2.98 Freiwaldau **26 827** K.L. Groß-Rosen 11.44 Ustuf K.L. Buchenwald 4.40

LIST V: **Waffen-SS Officers on Duty in Nazi Concentration Camps**

Vetter Dr. Hellmut Hstuf 21. 3.10 Rastenburg 126 917 K.L. Gusen 1.44 Ustuf K.L. Dachau 11.41

Vieweg Bruno Hstuf 4. 6.89 Aue/Sa **4 050** Hauptamt VOMI 11.44 Ustuf K.L. Dachau 8.40

Vogler Wilhelm Hstuf 1. 3.06 Plauen **1 505 K.L. Bergen-Belsen 12.44** Nachsch.Kdtr Rußl. 4.43

Voigt Willy Ustuf 15. 5.91 Leipzig 420 727 SS-WVHA 4.42 K.L. Niederhagen 4.42

Volkmann Kurt Ostuf 13.11.11 Grimmen 215 329 K.L. Sutthof 1.45 Ustuf SS-WVHA 5.43

Völkner Karl Ostuf 26. 2.98 ? 160 325 K.L. Buchenwald 1.43

<u>LIST W</u>: **Waffen-SS Officers on Duty in Nazi Concentration Camps**

Wäckerle Hilmar Staf 24.11.99 Forchheim 9 729 Kdr.Pz.GR.10 7.41 Stubaf **Kdr. K.L. Dachau 3.33 † 2. 7.41** Rewa-Ruska

Wagner Hans Hstuf 24. 4.01 ? ? K.L.Sachsenhausen 6.44

Wagner Rudolf Hstuf 29. 6.13 ? 104 377 Stab, Pz.GR.53. 3.43 † 15. 3.43 K.L. Dachau 1.39 Wandrei Arnold Ostuf 8. 115 Melzelthin 348 911 12.SS-Pz.Div 11.44 K.L. Mauthausen 6.44 Rttf 9./LSSAH 1.41

Wedell Fritz Stubaf 22. 2.12 Groß Cutau 78 796 Kdr. Wi.Btl.66 6.44 Ostuf K.L.Buchenwald 11.38-4.41

Wegner Gustav Stubaf 16. 1.05 Groß Denkte 314 183 W-Gr.Regt/SSrum. 11.44 K.L. Sachsenhausen 6.44

Weigel Friedrich Hstuf 2. 7.12 Köln 102 687 Zahnarzt,K.L.Groß Rosen 8.44

Weiß Martin Ostubaf 3. 6.05 Werden 31 147 SS-WVHA 6.44 Stubaf K.L.Neuengamme 9.41

Weiter Eduard Ostubaf 18. 7.89 Eschwege 276 877 **Kdr.** K.L. Dachau 6.44 † 4.1945

Werner Bonifatius Ostuf 2. 6.91 Billafingen **22 052** Hauptamt VOMI 2.43 K.L. Dachau 3.40

Wessel Heinrich Ostuf 13. 4.04 Osterberg 201 020 K.L.Sachsenhausen 6.43 Ustuf K.L.Sachsenhausen 6.42

Wetzel Friedrich Hstuf 14. 6.09 Enzklösterle 67 959 K.L. Dachau 7.44 IVa, T.I.R.3 6.42

Weymann Hans Hstuf 18. 6.92 Berlin 57 002 SS-Gestüt Rude 8.44 K.L.Sachsenhausen 6.42

Wickenhäuser Friedrich Hstuf 30. 7.78 Heidelberg 55 359 K.L. Mauthausen 1.44 Ustuf K.L. Mauthausen 12.39

Wicker Heinrich Ustuf 30. 6.21 Gansbach 320 280 K.L. Dachau 1.45 ‡ 4.45

Wicklein Hermann Ostuf 14.12.11 ? 114 870 Adj.K.L.Flossenburg 11.43 Ustuf Adj.K.L.Ravensbrück 8.41

Wiedemann Karl-Helmut Ostuf 9. 4.06 Weilheim/Obb 92 975 K.L. Neuengamme 4.44

Wiegand Konrad Ustuf 28.10.10 Niederurff 52 809 K.L. Auschwitz 6.44

Winkler Jakob 24. 7.92 Zweibrücken **3 764** K.L. Mauthausen 11.43 Ustuf K.L. Mauthausen 10.39

Wirths Dr. Eduard Stubaf 4.09.09 Würzburg 3115 K.L. Auschwitz 10.44 † suicide 10.44 Hstuf 11.42

Wlach Josef Ostuf 19. 6.06 Osseg Apotheker 341 865 K.L. Dachau 11.44 Ustuf K.L. Dachau 11.43

Wolfarth Dr. Hans Ustuf 30. 8.03 Haildorf Zahnarzt 411 944 KradschBtl 3 1.45 K.L.Neuengamme 11.41

Wolter Dr. Waldemar Stubaf 19. 5.08 ? 104 540 K.L. Mauthausen 1.45

Worster Heinrich Hstuf 27.11.09 Osthofen 114 309 OstturkWaffVerband 1.45 K.L. Dachau 4.41-6.44

LIST Z: **Waffen-SS Officers on Duty in Nazi Concentration Camps**

Zepiska Herbert Hstuf ? ? 347 121 K.L. Flossenburg 6.41

Ziemßen Wilhelm Hstuf 21. 2.10 ? 232 939 Chef, 9./Pz.GR.3 9.43 † 30. 9.43 K. L. Auschwitz 11.42

Ziereis Franz Staf 13. 08.05 München 276 998 Kdr. K.L.Mauthausen 11.44 † 24. 5.45

Zill Egon Stubaf 23. 8.06 Plauen **535** Kdr. /Geb.JR.56 9.44 Kdr.II/Geb.JR.28 2.44 **Kdr.K.L.Flossenburg 10.42**

Zoller Viktor Hstuf 22. 6.11 Ravensburg 77 379 K.L. Auschwitz 1.44 Hstuf SS-Pz.Aufkl.Ers.Abt 10.43

Zutter Adolf Hstuf 10. 2.89 Zweibrücken 226 911 K.L. Mauthausen 3.44 Ostuf K.L. Mauthausen 4.41

Ranks of Waffen-SS officers:

Gruppenführer (Gruf)	Lieutenant General
Brigadeführer (Brif)	Major General
Oberführer (Oruf)	no U.S. equivalent
Standaternführer (Staf)	Colonel
Obersturmbannführer (Ostubaf)	Lieutenant Colonel
Sturmbannführer (Stubaf)	Major
Hauptsturmführer (Hstuf)	Captain
Obersturmführer (Ostuf)	First Lieutenant
Untesturmführer (Ustuf)	Second Lieutenant

Appendix 7
Gisela Friedichsen's Neo-Nazi Inspired Misrepresentations and Lies

As already mentioned earlier, my appearances and testimonials at the war crimes trial of Julius Viel in Ravensburg had been severely criticized but almost all of the reporters, each of whom in support of the accused defense, whose principal argument was that I had "invented the whole story in order to save myself from being expelled from Canada, for having lied aboutmy membership in the *Waffen-SS*, as well as having committed several war crimes. Gisela Friedrichsen, an acclaimed crimes-court reporter in Germany, proceeded to write for *DER SPIEGEL* three reports that were not only highly critical of the Chief Judge and the Chief Prosecutor, but, siding with the defense, also contained a number of misrepresentations and untruths concerning my person. My several letters for explanations that I had sent her have remained unanswered, as did my similar letters to *DER SPIEGEL*, reminding me of the haughty, master-race behaviour of their German-Nazi grandfathers. Here is a listing of several of Friedrichsen's accusations, misrepresentations, and untruths:

• Following the Nazi-recruiters' classifying me a *Volksdeutscher* during their forced recruitment against their will, of hundreds of thousands of ethnic Germans born in the then Yugoslavia, Friedrichsen proceeded, without ever approaching me - to refer to me as a *Donauschwabe* (postwar Germany's attempt to replace the racist, second-class *Volksdeutscher*, with a socially more acceptable term), without bothering to discover that I, half-French and child of a Hungarian mother and firmly ensconced in the Hungarian community, attending a Hungarian high-school, and speaking no German, had had absolutely nothing to do with the local German-speakers. Neither had she attempted to find out the means that the *Waffen-SS* recruiters had used to pull me out of the Hungarian community and force me into the "7th Volunteer *Waffen-SS* Division *Prinz Eugen* (I did eventually find out: My father had been an officer in the army of Austria-Hungary, reason enough for Adolf Hitler, originally an Austrian, to issue an order that was contravened the then existing Geneva-agreements on the conduct of war).

•She lauded Viel's postwar decision, not to reveal his *Waffen-SS* past, since it had become a custom in post-war Germany. But she submits that Adalbert Lallier's *curriculum vitae* had been "far less transparent" [*unübersichtlicher*], starting with my CLAIM to have been drafted against my will, that, not speaking German, I had been demoted to work with mules, and by asking how come that I, a mule-attendant, had suddenly been sent to officers' school ...insinuating that, even though only eighteen-years old, had become a stooge of my *Reichsdeutsch*-Nazi superiors-instead of recognizing that even in the *Waffen-SS*, high-school graduation for not only a requisite but also impossible to refuse (at the threat of instant execution).

• Friedrichsen demonstrates her neo-Nazi inspired report as journalist by insinuating that my willingness to assist the United States in its CICs effort to discover top-Nazis' escape routes through Switzerland constituted an act of betrayal... **a betrayal of what, if I may ask**?

• She then used the German "*er habe*" – the equivalent of the French *subjunctive* – thus expressing doubt about my university education, instead of fact-finding and asking howa firmer mule-attendant had been able to obtain graduate degrees from several of the world's ranking universities.

- She continues with her emphasis upon "doubting" the veracity of my testimony, again by using *"er habe"*, that I was claiming to have obtained an immigration visa to Canada because "Christian fighters against Bolshevism were preferred to Jews and communists"- a needless and vicious slander against the Government of Canada.

- Then Friedrichsen continues her dishonest tirade by using the defense-attorney's (Pfliegner) accusation that Lallier, afraid that his "past" might be discovered, had been enticed to go public AFTER the appearance of Nazi-hunter Steven Rambam in Montreal, in February 1997. As proof of neo-Nazi style falsification of the time sequence between February 1997 and November 1999 (when I went public), I will translate parts of seven paragraphs in her report to *DER SPIEGEL*:

•In 1997... flamed up in Canada the presence of numerous Nazi war criminals who had somehow managed to arrive there, following the news that an American Nazi-hunter, Steven Rambam, **not a man of Simon Wiesenthal's integrity,** *had discovered several of them, with the appropriate resonance by the press. Is it surprising that Lallier, specifically during those days turned to his lawyer Steven Korda in Montréal, who was a member of one of the ancient Jewish loges. Obviously Lallier's past must already have become known, since, as witness, he declared:* "Having been accused of being a war criminal, I had already suffered professional drawbacks, threatened with being removed from the university." My forced departure from Concordia was decided upon only two years later, in August 2000.

•After talking with his lawyer, Lallier was suddenly overcome by the urge to explain. He admitted his membership in the Waffen-SS always linked to Viel alleged war evil deed. The Jewish communities were deeply impressed. He meets Rambam: "For me it was the moment of waking up my conscience". *He lets himself being interviewed, describes in a* **kakanic outburst,** *his suffering from his, and half-century long nightmare, and how*

Viel's crime had caused him shame and pain and burdened his heart – real literary stuff.

•*As witness in Ravensburg, he reveals another reason for his strangely late revelation: He didn't know whether he was still subject to the Oath of Fealty of the Waffen-SS, quoting me as follows:* "I asked myself if I hadn't morally and philosophically prevailed over it ... whether to turn into a traitor or to remain quiet? Or whether, following the reasoning of Pufendorf, I should seek to liberate myself from the Oath and the command to remain silent?

•*No one confirmed Lallier's story about Viel's killing of the seven Jews in the anti-tank ditch.*

•*The defense discovered a whole set of serious contradictions in Lallier's testimony. Changing the days of the killing ... changing the distances ... naming witnesses who claim not even to have been there ... and so on. Lallier portrays Viel as the single, lone, perpetrator of the killing, while other witnesses describe the daily inferno of evil.*

•*Friedrichsen then asks why Kurt Schrimm, the Chief Prosecutor, had acted in Viel's case in such an irritable, aggressive, manner, why, in spite of the many contradictions and that none of the other witnesses had supported Lallier's claims, he had decided to view Lallier as trustworthy, since Lallier had absolutely no reason to concoct his story ... after all, Lallier was a professor, a scholar of the humanities.*

•*Friedrichsen's critique of Schrimm reaches a crescendo when, in her second last paragraph accuses him of the following: The other witnesses are unworthy. Lying, old men, while Lallier is viewed as 'peeled from an egg'* [meaning 'spick-and-span clean'], *the image of a trusted grandfather ... what insolence!*

Concluding, Friedrichsen accuses both Schrimm and Lallier for having manufacturedan accusation that relieved the accuser, thereby permitting that the "hero" be photographed with the "villain". All in all, Friedrichsen throughout the two years of the trial was siding more and more with the murdererwhile venting her wrath at my person, both of which by following the defense attorney's opening statement, and openly accusing me of creating a story that had never happened, with the intention that, by unfairly accusing Vielof murder, lallier would protect himself from being expelled from Canada.

Twenty years later, and with a remaining life expectancy of perhaps five more years, in my quest to prove worthy of Canada's trust when I was offered an immigration visa by the then Consular officer Mr. Classen, in Salzburg, I have no choice but to counter Gisela Friedrichsen's many neo-Nazi like misrepresentations and untruths, to start with, her untruths concerning the time frame between 1996 and 2002.

• It is totally untrue that my decision to "confess" followed Rambam's appearance in Canada, As a matter of true fact, in the summer of 1995 I had been sent by CESO to Prague, with the mandate to help the first democratic Czech government understand the working of Canada's capitalist system of banking and to use it in the attempt to restructure their previous, communist, financial system. During those eight weeks, my conscience compelled me to return – during three weekends – to the former concentration camp Therezin and the anti-tank ditch, to visit the site, and to beg for forgiveness for having been too afraid to prevent Viel's killing of those seven Jewish prisoners. On my flight back – August 1995 - I decided to find out if Viel was still living, by talking with Steven Kora; but was advised against it because it might endanger my academic post and my reputation as "excellent" professor.

During the summer 1996 I was sent by CESO to Thailand to study the feasibility of opening an English-language B.A. in International Business at Sripatum University, in Bangkok, whose Chairperson was the sister of the king. I gladly consented because it would enable me not only to demonstrate Canada's excellence in university education but also to establish direct linkages with Concordia University. With the mandate accomplished with a positive recommendation, I was promptly offered to create the proposed B. A. as well as to become its first Dean, a two-year contract, starting in June 1997.

It was only in April 1997when Korda finally informed me about Steven Rambam, but I had to wait until his arrival at Montreal airport and to give him the mandate to find Julius Viel. In the meantime, having decided to proceed I wrote a personal letter to my last Division Commander, Brigadier Kumm—still alive in Germany- asking if he had heard of the murder, as well as for his opinion on war crimes. Surprisingly, he answered that war crimes had to be punished, thus supporting my intention to proceed with Viel.

So, totally unlike Gisela Friedrichsen's dishonest claim, I had had absolutely no problems with my academic and social standing and with the Government of Canada, proud to serve Canada's interest inThailand, but also absolutely committed to bring Julius Viel to trial, not only in response to my conscience but also by serving the cause of natural justice. Actually, I am in possession of a statement by Canada's War Crimes Commission that my I had never had to be investigated by any of its agents.

My meeting with Rambam occurred in late May 1997, the day before my departure for Thailand, with my engaging him to find Julius Viel and to phone or Email me in Bangkok. He did late in August, confirming Viel's existence and planning to interview him. I immediately long-distance phone the Simon Wiesenthal

Centre in Vienna, fortunate to have him respond and listen, averring his instant intention to initiate his own search, and expressing his gratitude even though I had told him about my forced recruitment and my witnessing the murder. My official "confession" took place in Montreal in December 1997, arranged during my emergency return for a prostate operation. Rabbi Poupko, Steven Rambam, Steve Korda, a MOSSAD-agent, and a media person were present, each and every one convinced that I was speaking the truth, in spite of the fact that Julius Viel, during his first meeting with Rambam, had absolutely denied that he had even been at the officers' school in mid-March 1945.

Friedrichsen's claim that I had been "feted" by members of the Jewish community totally contradicts the events that followed immediately the newspapers' report about my "confession", that was immediately followed by groups of almost rioting HOLOCAUST survivors demanding the Federal government to explain the presence of Nazi war criminals, inducing my handful of Jewish-Canadian friend to advise me to hide for a while. I returned to Bangkok, completing my task by late August, and returned to Montreal, learning that the German War Crimes had commenced its investigation and that I would have my first interview at the German Consulate in Montreal. I find it very very strange that the only two persons who had officially accused me of "inventing the story in order to save myself from prosecution and certain expulsion from Canada", were Friedrichsen and the defense lawyer plus the several other neo-Nazis and old-Nazis who were present in court. Those angry Holocaust survivors needed to assign to me no motives because, understandably, since alone my service in the *Waffen-SS,* even though forced, made them view me as a criminal who had to be expelled.

• Friedrichsen's claim that I had problems relieving myself of the Oath of Fealty to Adolf Hitler constitutes another speculative lie: At oath-taking, in September 1942 I already in Serbia, during all that yelling I had managed to whisper my oath to the then in Hungary ruling Admiral Miklós Horthy, making Hitler totally irrelevant. What I had actually been concerned about was the order, after the killing, by the *Kommandant* of the officers' school to keep our silence to our deaths, an order that was annulled by Brigadier Kumm in response to my report of the killing. In her reporting upon the court proceedings, Friedrichsen's critique of my "having moral problems in dealing with the order to keep silence", clearly demonstrates her Neo-Nazi-linked impression that ALL SS-orders must be obeyed and that wishing to rid oneself of them does represent amoral problem: TREASON. But I'm willing to pardon her for this misrepresentation because, after all, as a German she could not help it feeling and acting like a neo-Nazi.

Finally, her statement that I had gone into rapture about officers of the *Waffen-SS* after I mentioned that during several lectures emphasis had been placed on "*Waffen-SS* officers, as officers, being obliged to respect the laws of war and to prevent war crimes". Mentioning was simply meant to be a fact, a fact that was the denied by Julius Viel's really pathetic, unprovoked, murder of the seven half-starved Jewish prisoners, by a *Reichsdeutsch*-officer. In short, instead of expressing horror and even disgust about the murder by one of her German blood-brothers, she accuses me of lauding the killer's wanton act – thus manifesting the viewpoint and behaviour of typical neo-Nazis: *We, the remaining Reichsdeutschen, are innocent because we were only following Hitler's orders.*

I shall not bother Frau Gisela Friedrichsen with a demand for a sincere apology for her misrepresentations and lies because, at her haughty *Herrenrassen-attitude*, she would lack the human moral perception as to why she ought to. Her disrespectful, vicious attack upon the Chief Judge Dr. Winkler and the Chief Prosecutor Dr. Schrimm, as well as her blatant, cruel attempt to destroy my integrity provide clear evidence that, unlike the millions of GOOD Germans, she has lost the human beings' most precious quality – CONSCIENCE.

Concluding statement: My accumulated vast knowledge, both theoretical and empirical, about events and happenings internationally and globally, has enabled me to provide interesting insights into and conclusions about the cause-effect linkage between determinants and outcomes. These reflections go well beyond the working of the world of economic activity and the material concern of national policy makers, as they also involve issues of national and international "morality": peace vs. war, disarmament vs. arms race, ecology vs. economic growth, and international human rights in a world with a surprisingly large number of despotic governments.

My direct involvement in the war crimes trial of Julius Viel originates with my forced induction, by the Nazi-occupying forces in southern-Hungary/ Northern Yugoslavia, during the years 1941-44, into the Waffen-SS, the so-called "Volunteer 7th Mountain Division "Prinz Eugen". Even though of a Hungarian mother and finishing my secondary-level education in a Hungarian-language high school, I was drafted along with thousands of Volksdeutschen, whose high-school students were attending school in the German language (following Hitler-Germany's curriculum). My brother was also drafted and eventually perished at the hands of Titoist partisans. To this personal misfortune was added the tragedy of the murder of seven Jewish KZ-inmates at the anti-tank ditch in the plain between Leitmeritz/ Litomerice and the KZ-Theresienstadt/Teresin, which I witnessed as an officer candidate who, with many other candidates, were ordered to stand guard duty during the days of completing the said anti-tank ditch. Instantly knowing that this, wanton, killing was wrong (but terrified to do anything for fear of being put up against the wall) and duly reporting it after the end of the war to responsible persons with the Allied occupation forces – without anything happening – I eventually landed a post with the International Refugee Organization, in Vienna, whose Director, the U.S. two-star General Wood, I informed about that war crime. He eventually hired me and put me in charge of the immigration desk for Canada, where I was able to help many refugees, with special attention to those of the Jewish faith, an expression of my lifelong commitment to help wherever I was able to, for Jewish persons to rebuild their lives and thereby diminish the extent of the catastrophe of the Holocaust. End-1951 I myself immigrated to Canada – having obtained full security clearance from the Canadian authorities upon my accounting, in full, for my wartime experience – and eventually settled down in Montreal. As a teacher and university administrator, I was then able to assist quite a handful of Jewish persons, in their quest to complete their university education (Messrs. Nachfolger and Hirshorn, both professors at Dawson College, and Maître Dr. Steven Korda, being particular examples of success and of deep friendship arising from it). However, the feeling of shame, impotence, and guilt continued deep within my conscience, and induced me – after hearing nothing about Julius Viel – to try to discover if he was still alive and then pursue the cause of justice. Steven Rambam was able to verify (May 1997) that Viel was indeed alive and living in Southern Germany. In November, while on my assignment in Thailand, I phone the Simon Wiesenthal office in Vienna and alerted

him to the whereabouts of Julius Viel, asking him to contact the Bundesrepublik office for war crimes (Ludwigsburg). Late in November 1997 I proceeded to "go public", in the presence of Steve Rambam, Rabbi Poupko, Steven Korda, and a couple of other persons. The rest is now matter of public knowledge. The only thing I wish to add is that the German *Bundesgerichtshof,* in reviewing the Viel case, found that the initial court process in Ravensburg was well conducted but that the sentence should have been "life". You may wish to know that Viel died towards the end of his first year of imprisonment. I would consider it an exceptional privilege to be allowed to address students in high schools and higher, about the tragedy —as viewed from the "other side"- of the Holocaust and the forever need to remind the world about those officially sanctioned and ordered acts of absolute injustice, the mass murder that quite a few persons in contemporary society seem ready to believe had never happened.

Dr. Adalbert G. Lallier, *Curriculum Vitae*

CURRICULUM VITAE

PERSONAL: Page
    General Background   218
    Social   218
    Hobbies   218
    References   218

EDUCATION: 219
    Lycée
    University: Undergraduate
    University: Graduate
    Academic   Honours
    Subject   Specialization
    Other   Studies

PROFESSIONAL CAREER   221

RESEARCH AND PUBLICATIONS: 227

POST SCRIPTUM and SPECIAL NOTE: 229

PERSONAL:

Austro-Hungarian born of French origin (Huguenot). Military service: June 1942 - May 45 (POW until August 1946). In Canada since 1951; Canadian citizen (1957).

Multilingual: Fluent in English, French, German, Hungarian, Serbo-Croatian. Working knowledge of Russian and Latin. Reading comprehension of Polish, Czech, Italian.

General Background: World-wide travels involving consulting and research assignments on issues and decisions concerning international law and human rights, international politics, internationalization of university education, international business, globalization and its effects on the populations of nation states, with particular emphasis on Europe, Africa, the Middle East, and South-East Asia.

Consulting affiliations with international organizations (UNRRA, UNCTAD, U.N.), government (Canada (CIDA), Québec (CESO); international banking and finance (RBC); international shipping (ALCAN), the import-export sector. Executive-level linkages in business and government.

Social: Member of various service clubs and organizations. Past President of the Austrian Society of Montreal. Chevalier of the Military and Hospitalier Order of St. Lazarus of Jerusalem (1976-86).

Hobbies: Chess, tennis, table tennis; mountain climbing, skiing; riding; farming.

REFERENCES: Dr. Steven Korda, Law Offices, Suite 1 500, 1 Westmount Square,
        Westmount, Que. (514) 935-6226. Fax: (514) 935-2314.
        Maître William W. McNamara, Torys Law Firm LLP, Montreal.
        514-868-5600.
        Maître Pierre Beaudry, Cowansville, QC, 450-266-4244.

EDUCATION:

1. Lycée: Senior Matriculation, May 1942

2. University: Undergraduate:

> (1) *Philosophisch-Theologische Hochschule* [Philosophy and Theology College], Bamberg, Bavaria, 1947-1948: law, politics and economics (*Staatswissenschaften*: [Sciences of the State]);
>
> (2) *Hochschule für Welthandel* [College for World Trade], Vienna, 1949-51: economics, commerce, commercial law; international trade and finance;
>
> (3) *McGill University,* Montreal, 1955-1958: Economics and political Science: B.A. (Honours): June 1958;

3. University: Graduate Schools:

> (1) Columbia University, New York City, 1958-1961: graduate studies in economics and international affairs and in international business: June 1960 : M.A. in Economics; June 1961: Graduate Diploma in International Affairs (Russian Institute and East European Institute); 1965-1966: Doctoral studies in economics.
>
> (2) *L'Université Paris II (ASSAS),* 1974-1975 and 1977-1978: Etudes doctorales (3e cycle) en sciences économiques, sciences politiques et droit. Thèse doctorale: *L'integration et la désintégration économique: l'histoire, la théorie, la politique* (711 pages). *Doctorat en sciences économiques (avec haute distinction),* conferred in June 1978.

(3) *The London School of Economics and Political Science,* 1981-82: Post-doctoral research: Marx, Capitalism, Globalization, and the international political economy.

4. Academic Honours: RAND Fellowship, Columbia University, 1958-1959.
Columbia University Fellowship, 1959-60, 1960-61.
Bourse du Gouvernement du Québec, 1965-66.
Sabbaticals: 1965-66; 1974-75; 1981-82.

5. Subject Specialization:

Economics: *History of Economic Thought. Economic History (Canada, Europe). International Trade Theory; International Finance. Political Economy and Policy; Micro and Macro Economics. Comparative Economic Systems; Socialist Economic Planning; Soviet Economics. Economics of Disintegration.*

Political Science: *International Politics; International Political Economy. Economics for Public Policy* (graduate level); *Marxism; Totalitarianism; Soviet Foreign Policy.*

6. Other Studies: Two years of intensive Russian at Columbia University.
Adult education courses in philosophy and sociology.
Audited graduate courses in law and international business.
Extensive research in archives and special collections on questions concerning globalization, war and peace; disintegration of empires.

PROFESSIONAL CAREER:

1. University Teaching – Full-time:

1960-1975: Loyola College, Montreal: economics; politics.
1975-1986: Concordia University, Montreal: economics; politics.
1986-1987: Bishop's University (Visiting Professor): economics
1988-1999: Concordia University: economics and international politics.
August 1999: I retired from my full-time university post.

2. Academic promotions:

August 1960: Lecturer
August 1962: Assistant Professor
August 1968: Associate Professor and Tenure
August 1985: Full Professor
August 1990: Adjunct Professor of Economics and International Politics, 1988.
June 1985: Recipient of the "John O'Brien Award for Teaching Excellence", May

3. University Teaching – Part-Time:

1959-61: Sessional courses at Brooklyn College and Columbia University
1962-99: Evening courses and summer courses at Loyola/Concordia.

4. Usual Annual Teaching Assignments:

Economics Department: Micro and Macro Theory: International Trade and Finance; History of Economic Thought; Marxist and Soviet economics;

Political Science Department: - International Politics (undergraduate); Economics for Public Policy (graduate).

Graduate School of Business (Thailand): -International Business; Globalization and Economic Policy;

5. University Administration:

<u>Dean of the Evening Division</u>, Loyola College, 1963-1965:

I was appointed to this post with the mandate to develop the already existing but loosely aligned evening courses for adults, into a complete undergraduate curriculum, with emphasis on integration and academic excellence, but also to provide this Division of Loyola College with a self-sustaining financial base. After designing an admissions policy specifically suited for the needs of mature students, I proceded with the alignment of the evening courses with the degree programmes of the Faculties of Arts and Science, and of Commerce. During my mandate, overall enrolment increased to about 3000 part-time degree students, with a total revenue in excess of two million dollars. For my efforts, I was elected to the National Executive of the Canadian Association of Deans and Directors of Evening Colleges and Universities. Upon fulfilling the terms of my mandate, I resumed full-time teaching (September 1965).

<u>Department Chairman</u>, Economics:

1. Loyola College, 1973-1975:

Mandate: Heading the operation of the Department, implementing College policy, setting up the structures and liaisons required for the merger with the economics department of Sir George Williams University, with a total of about 3000 students.

2. Concordia University: Merged Economics Department, 1975-1976:

Mandate: To render effective the process of integration and unification and ensuing economies of scale at both levels, undergraduate as well as graduate, with emphasis on budgetary efficiency and academic excellence.

3. Dean of International Studies, Spripatum Univerity, Bangkok, Thailand: June 1997 – July 1998:

Through my affiliation with CESO Canada (Canadian Senior Executives Organization), I was delegated to Sripatum University, in Bangkok, with the mandate to assess the feasibility of setting up an International B. A. in Business Communication (in the English language). After obtaining approval from the Thai Minister of University Education, the President of Sripatum University invited me to launch this programme, as its first Consulting Director.

6. Other School Administration:

During the years 1972-73 and 1973-74 I was invited by the Yeshiva Gedolah Merkaz Hatorah, in Montreal-Snowdon, to be the Consulting Director of its secular-education division, involving the first two years of the creation and initial operational stage of this

Orthodox Jewish school. My assigned mandate was to select and offer selection of courses and programmes as required by the Ministère de l'Education du Québec concerning private schools; the hiring of duly qualified teachers; the attainment of teaching and learning excellence; and, eventually, the preparation of graduating candidates for the official provincial matriculation examinations, all of which also concerned the teaching of the French language. After these two years, I was, understandably, replaced by a qualified person of the Jewish faith.

7.. Other Academic Activites and Affiliations:

My affiliation with Loyola College and Concordia University involved service on numerous Committees and several of the high-level administrative and executive-level decision-making bodies, including the Senate, Faculty Councils, Search Committees, Departmental Committees.

My activities have also involved memberships in the following professional associations:

Royal Economic Society.
American Economic Association.
Canadian Economics and Political Science Associatiion.
Canadian Association of Slavists.
l'Association des économistes du Québec.
Canadian International Affairs Association.
Canadian Association of University Teachers.

In addition, as an academic and consultant on problems of education, international trade and finance, and economic policy, I have been engaged in written and oral analyses of issues of concern to our institutions and to our public. The following are typical samples:

-luncheon and dinner addresses to Canadian service clubs or professional associations; -participation in conferences on globalization and its effects;
-seminar lectures on Soviet and East European economic conditions and indebtedness;
-seminar lectures (in Paris) on economic conditions in Canada and Québec, with emphasis upon the economics of federalism;
-seminar lectures (at the London School of Economics) on the Marxian concept of "international political economy";
-in Lagos, Nigeria, discussion of problems of university education in Canada;
- participation at the Conference on Ageing (March 1998, Vientiane, Laos).

7. Public Administration:

International Refugee Organization (I.R.O.), 10/1950-10/1951: Head, Canada Desk, Resettlement Section, Refugee Centre Vienna. During the course of this time, I was responsible for securing immigration visas for hundreds of refugees, mainly from Eastern Europe, many of whom were Jewish who had survived the Holocaust and/or were fleeing from communism.

United Nations, Secretariat, New York: Economics Affairs Officer at ECOSOC (short-term research appointment), 10/1960.

Canadian International Development Agency, 5/1968-12/1968:

During this period, I was engaged, at the level of Chief, Multilateral Organizations, to do research for the Agency and its then Director-General, Maurice Strong, on some of the major problems of foreign aid. In September 1968, I was appointed member of the Canadian delegation to the UNCTAD II Conference in Geneva. My other responsibilities included policy-level discussions of foreign aid, of aid disbursements, and of maintaining effective contact with other governments and organizations (DAG, IMF, ECOSOC, UNCTAD).

8..Consulting and Research, Government and Private Enterprise Sectors:

Government of Canada, summers 1961 and 1962: Department of Labour: Research on regional wage disparities.

Economic Council of Canada, 6/1974-11/1974: Senior economist and consultant for the Transport and Transport Equipment Committee of the Second National Economic Conference. Author of the *Report*.

United Nations Conference on Trade and Development, Geneva, Winter 1974: Chief economist and international-relations consultant on the task force on international shipping, with the mandate to study, on behalf of UNCTAD, the feasibility of setting up an international shipping line in the Arab Gulf area. After three weeks of on-the site fact-finding and discussions with the respective Ministers of the involved national governments (Bahrain, Qatar, United Arab Emirates, Saudi Arabia, Oman) a *Report* was submitted to UNCTAD, Invisibles Section, for approval and implementation. A shipping line was eventually set up in Doha (Qatar) in 1976, capitalized at U.S.$1.5 billion.

Gouvernement du Québec, winter 1980: Chief economist on the task force studying the future of the port of Montreal, 1980-2010. Undertaken by the prominent Québec consulting group, Beauchemin-Beaton-Lapointe, this report derived its economic significance from its emphasis on the "hinterland". growth factors, and its policy-significance from the desire to pool that required required federal and provincial resources and to arrive at an inter-governmental consensus concerning a "long-term development plan" for this port.

Alcan of Canada and Alcan Shipping Research of Canada, 1971-1973:

Economist and international-affairs consultant on transportation and shipping development, with particular emphasis on the evolution of world charter rates. Co-author of *The World Charter Market,* and author of several reports concerning particular development project.

S.E.R.V.O. France, 1972-1976: Various research and consulting assignments and studies concerning international investment, tourism, migration, and urban parking.

The Royal Bank of Canada, 1976-1981: Research and consulting on issues of international indebtedness and country risk, with particular emphasis on the U.S.S.R. and Eastern Europe, the Middle East, and the Caribbean. Policy-level discussions on these issues and on the economic consequences of debt rescheduling.

CESO Canada (Canadian Senior Executives Organization):

Aug.-Sept. 1995: **Senior adviser** on the working of capitalist financial markets and the transfer of economic and financial know-how from Canada to the post-communist Czech Republic;

August-September 1996 : Consultant to Sripatum University, Bangkok. Feasibility of setting up an International English-language B.A. in Business Communication.

June 1997-May 1998 : Consulting Director of Sripatum's B.   A   . International Business Communication (in the English language). Invited to teach a Seminar on International Business Finance, in Sripatum's Graduate School of Business.

9. Research and publications:

Unrestricted Circulation, published:

"The Behavior of the Japanese Economy", in *The World Charter Market.* Montreal: Alcan Shipping Services, 1971, 341 p.

"The General Cargo Trade." In *The World Charter Market,* rev. ed. 1972, 82 p. The revised edition also included an up-date of *"The Behavior of the Japanese Economy",* which study was of enormous significance to world shipping circles and shipping rates,

Review of *"Les entreprises internationales '*, in *Revue internatioinale,* automne 1972.

"Economic Conditions and Prospects in the Arab Gulf Countries." In *The Establishment of an International Shipping Enterprise in the Arab Gulf.* This report was written by the UNCTAD Task Force *(supra,* p. 7, 6. (3)), and was published both in Montreal and Geneva, in 1974, 360 p.

Book review of Maurice Dobb's *Theories of Distribution Since Adam Smith*, in *The Canadian Journal of Public and Cooperative Economy*, autumn 1975.

Peace Without Honour. A novel. Montreal: SERVO, 1975.

L'intégration et la désintégration économique: L'histoire, la théorie, la politique. 2 tomes, 711 pages. L'université Paris II (Droit, Economie, Politique), *1978*.

La souveraineté-association: Réalisme économique ou utopie? Montréal: Edition Le Cercle du livre francais, 1980. 47 p.

The Golden Triangle: Sexuality, Money, Power – Sexonomics, 1983. Available as E-book in www.adalbert lallier.com and www.sexoomics.com.

The Economics of Marx's "Grundrisse"' London: Macmillan. 1989.

Sovereignty-Association: Economic Realism or Utopia? Oakville and London:
The Golden Triangle: Sexuality, Money, Power – Sexonomics, 2nd ed. *ExLibris, 2013.*

A Peace Without Honour: Sin ad Retribution 1. 2nd ed, ExLibris, 2013.

I Swear to you, Adolf Hitler, Fealty and Obedience: Sin and Retribution 2. ExLibris, 2013.

This novel had been on my mind ever since the massive dislocation of displaced persons during and following the Second World War. It is about the killing of seven Jewish concentration camp prisoners (n March 1945) by a Waffen-SS officer, and the question of post war retribution. For this tragedy. The creates two fictitious families in Vienna, one Christian, the other Jewish, in a setting in which the son of the former becomes a war hero, but who then proceeds to kill the seven Jewish victims, one of whom was the only son of the Jewish family. The novel describes the Austrian experience of the Nazi-terror. It follows the conversion, in Germany, of the killer to fame and fortune. It describes the Viennese victim's daughter' long quest to find the killer, and to bring him top court, for genocide. But the German judge lets him go free, leaving the daughter with the terrible choice of letting him live ("retribution" in exchange for money payments) or of killing (following the Davidian "eye-for-an –eye" punishment. The killing had indeed taken place, the murderer was eventually caught and tried, and condemned to only twelve years in prison. Clearly, justice had not been served.

Ich schwöre Dir, Adolf Hitler, Treue und Gehorsam: Sünde und Vergeltung 2. ExLibris, 2013. This book is the German edition of the above.

Le Triangle d'Or: Sexualité, Argent, Pouvoir – Sexonomica. ExLibris, 2013.

Forever Guilty Unforgiven, Revised updated version of *I Swear to you Adolf Hitler,* XLibris, 2017.

Unrestricted Circulation, completed by not (yet) published

The Economics of Disintegration: A Model of Asymmetry in Economic Reasoning.

Lotus in the Sea of Fire. A novel, sequel to the Vietnam war.

3. Research and Publication, in progress:

The Last Great Migration:

A futuristic inquiry into the linkages between the world population explosion, particularly in the increasingly Malthusian setting in Asia and Africa, upon transcontinental migrations and the social structures, income and wealth redistribution effects, especially on the "rich and liberal West. I have already compiled the respective statistics on demographic trends and foodstuffs production forecasts (with particular reference to the time horizon of the United Nations population study). Empirical-scientific in its approach, this treatise derives its main concern from geo-strategic and power-political considerations.

Copyright: Adalbert Lallier, March 3, 2020.

Dr. Adalbert Lallier, professor emeritus of political economy and international politics, BA honors economics and political science, McGill University, Montreal; MA Economics, Graduate Diploma of the Russian Institute, Columbia University, New York City; *doctoraten sciences économiques,* Sorbonne-ASSAS, Paris; postdoctoral studies, London School of Economics and Political Science, London. www.adalbertlallier.comwww.sexonomics.comwww.symbolof universalhappiness.com facebook.com twitter.com Linkedin.com.

www.ingramcontent.com/pod-product-compliance
Lightning Source LLC
Chambersburg PA
CBHW021057080526
44587CB00010B/281